The Art of Sociological Argument

Also by Graham Crow

*Comparative Sociology and Social Theory**

Social Solidarities

Community Life (with Graham Allan)

*Families, Households and Society** (with Graham Allan)

The Sociology of Rural Communities (edited)

*Social Conceptions of Time** (edited with Sue Heath)

Lone Parenthood (edited with Michael Hardey)

*Home and Family** (edited with Graham Allan)

* Also published by Palgrave Macmillan

The Art of Sociological Argument

Graham Crow

University of Southampton

First published in 2005 by
PALGRAVE MACMILLAN
Houndmills, Basingstoke, Hampshire RG21 6XS and
175 Fifth Avenue, New York, N.Y. 10010
Companies and representatives throughout the world.

PALGRAVE MACMILLAN is the global academic imprint of the Palgrave
Macmillan division of St. Martin's Press, LLC and of Palgrave Macmillan Ltd.
Macmillan® is a registered trademark in the United States, United Kingdom
and other countries. Palgrave is a registered trademark in the European
Union and other countries.

ISBN-13: 978–0333–77844–9 hardback
ISBN-10: 0333–77844–8 hardback
ISBN-13: 978–0333–77845–6 paperback
ISBN-10: 0333–77845–6 paperback

This book is printed on paper suitable for recycling and made from fully
managed and sustained forest sources. Logging, pulping and manufacturing
processes are expected to conform to the environmental regulations of the
country of origin.

A catalogue record for this book is available from the British Library.

A catalog record for this book is available from the Library of Congress.

10 9 8 7 6 5 4 3 2 1
14 13 12 11 10 09 08 07 06 05

Contents

Acknowledgements

An author writing a book such as this incurs many debts. I have been extremely fortunate in being able to call on the professionalism and enthusiasm of Catherine Gray and her colleagues at Palgrave Macmillan, who have dealt with everything with customary efficiency and good humour. The anonymous reviewers of the book proposal and later of the draft manuscript made numerous helpful comments and suggestions that have undoubtedly improved the finished product. Thanks are due also to colleagues past and present in the Division of Sociology and Social Policy at the University of Southampton whose contributions have ranged from lending books, reading draft chapters and generally helping me to think things through. They deserve more than a collective acknowledgement, but it would be invidious to name only some and impossible to name them all. The same point applies to the several cohorts of students on whom prototype versions of the ideas contained in this book have been tried out. People at other institutions who must be thanked for allowing themselves to be diverted from their own work to discuss mine are Mary Boulton, Fiona Devine, Gayle Letherby, Larry Ray, Kate Reed and Jane Ribbens-McCarthy. Ann Oakley kindly provided me with unpublished lecture material. Rose Wiles has been a long-suffering sounding board for ideas, and has developed the skill of tactfully identifying as deliberate mistakes things that were nothing of the sort. And finally, I should mention Frank and Connie, who have unfailingly inquired into the progress of 'the book' over the several years of its gestation. I dedicate the book to them in recognition of their encouragement and support.

GRAHAM CROW

1

Introduction: the importance of sociological argument

According to Gans's 1999 survey, the best-selling monograph written by a living American sociologist since the 1940s was David Riesman's *The Lonely Crowd*. First published in 1950, it had sold one million copies by 1971 and a further 434,000 by the end of 1995 (Gans 1999: 283). It was, according to Riesman's obituarist, 'a surprise best seller' (Buhle 2002). At the time of its publication Riesman had 'thought it might sell a few thousand copies as reading in social science courses' (2001: li), and even after becoming famous 'he didn't quite believe his reviews' (Sennett 2003: 29). Riesman's rise to prominence as one of the most influential 'public intellectuals' (Kivisto 1998: 109) of post-war America was due in no small part to his book and its message, even if some of the complexity of that message was lost along the way (Bellah *et al.* 1996: 49). Its critique of consumerism caught the public mood, appealing to a broad 'audience of educated, paperback readers, who fretted about the widespread reports of alienation, juvenile delinquency and loss of religious faith' (Buhle 2002). *The Lonely Crowd* succeeded because it 'sympathetically exposed the anxieties of a middle class that was rising with the postwar boom' (Gitlin 2001: xiii). It echoed the concerns of the time that there was 'too much "community", not enough individualism, too much conformity to others' (Wrong 1999: 73). Its wide appeal is also attributable to the remarkable 'range of Riesman's sources, from psychoanalysis to economic history' (Lemert 1999: 321). The role played by the book's title deserves mention too, because it is so immediately engaging. Reference to *The Lonely Crowd* grabs our attention by presenting us with a paradox that requires explanation: how can one be lonely in a crowd? The same may be said of several other titles among the 56 books that Gans reports having sold in excess of 50,000 copies, including his own *The Urban Villagers* (Gans 1962), Sennett's (1970) *The Uses of Disorder* and Rubin's (1983) *Intimate Strangers*. The point also applies to other classic books (Atkinson 1990: 81) and articles (such as Granovetter 1973) and to the contemporary classic *Bowling Alone* (Putnam 2000).

It seems odd to highlight the use of paradox in the process of making sense of social phenomena, but it is one of a number of well-established techniques employed by sociologists as they engage with their audiences and seek to make them think differently. Numerous cases of sociological paradoxes are discussed in this book as examples of its central proposition that attention ought to be given both to what sociologists say and the way that they say it. Another technique of engaging an audience that will be considered alongside paradoxes is that of the use by sociologists of metaphors to help to get their messages across. Many sociologists' metaphors have entered popular culture. Metaphors matter in what Rigney (2001) has called *The Metaphorical Society* because they shape our conception of the social world as (for example) a theatre, a game or a war, all of which metaphors figure prominently in everyday expression. The ease with which we draw on the language of actors and audiences or winners and losers indicates their potential to become what Lakoff and Johnson (1980) call *Metaphors We Live By*, although we need to beware the common pitfall of treating metaphors as literal descriptions of reality (López 2003). Comparable studies of how arguments are developed have been undertaken in neighbouring disciplines, including psychology (Billig 1996), economics (McCloskey 1998) and anthropology (Geertz 1988) and the art of the use in sociology of rhetorical devices such as paradox and metaphor is equally deserving of attention. The rationale of this book is that the study of how sociologists develop their arguments offers valuable lessons to anyone seeking to persuade an audience of the merits of their case.

One of the things that sociologists' frequent use of paradoxical titles tells us is that audiences have to be attracted. Paradoxes are a particularly good way of getting people's attention. It is also possible to use ambiguity in a title in order to intrigue readers as to which of two or more meanings is intended, as, for example, Oakley (1980) does with *Women Confined*. Other authors are deliberately provocative, as Mills (1960) was in choosing the title *The Causes of World War Three*. Such titles are, of course, only the beginning of the process of persuading an audience of the merits of a case, but inattention to this aspect of developing an argument will decrease the chances of having an audience to persuade in the first place. Once attracted, the attention of an audience has to be kept. The level at which an argument is pitched involves a fine judgement, in which a balance has to be struck between intellectual rigour and intelligibility. Weber's view on this point was that one's terminology could be 'simplified as far as possible' but that there were limits to how far academic arguments could be 'popularized' (1978a: 3). Durkheim also cautioned against sociologists seeking 'to enlist a numerous clientèle', arguing that by seeking 'to take on the esoteric character which befits all science' the discipline 'will gain in dignity and authority what it will perhaps lose in popularity' (1982: 163). On the other hand, not all writers treat the idea of popular sociology as an oxymoron. Mills, for example, regarded sociologists as having a duty to realise their potential to reach a wide audience 'of intelligent people, academic and otherwise'. As he saw it, sociologists have an obligation to employ 'the simplicity of clear statement' and not lapse into the unintelligibility of 'socspeak' (2000: 218, 224, 220). Oakley's exhortation to use plain language 'to say what we think' (2002: 4) to a broad public audience of laywomen as well as laymen develops Mills's theme, and may be taken as an indication of sociology's democratisation in the century since Durkheim and Weber were writing.

There have been many notable figures in the development of the discipline of sociology whose contributions have helped to shape not only the content of sociological thinking but also the ways in which these ideas are expressed. The eight who have been selected for particular attention in this book are Karl Marx (1818–83), Emile Durkheim (1858–1917), Max Weber (1864–1920), Talcott Parsons (1902–79), Charles Wright Mills (1916–62), Erving Goffman (1922–82), Michel Foucault (1926–84) and Ann Oakley (1944–). They have been chosen for a number of reasons from a much larger pool of potential candidates who merit attention because of what is said in their work and how that message is conveyed. The first reason for their selection is that these are all thinkers who have wrestled with the problem of how best to present an argument that is both theoretically and empirically informed. Sociology does have a place for 'pure' theorists and for colleagues whose 'applied' work eschews extensive engagement with theoretical concerns, but it is in the work of authors that engage with both theory and evidence at the same time that some of the hardest problems are to be found, and some of the most useful lessons are to be learned. This theoretically and empirically informed approach characterises what Marx has to say about capitalism, Durkheim about social cohesion, Weber about religion and social change, Parsons about values and norms, Mills about power, Goffman about identity, Foucault about madness and deviance and Oakley about gender. Their arguments warrant especially serious attention because what they have to say about these topics cannot be dismissed simply as armchair speculation nor as hurried descriptive journalism. The rigour and commitment with which they have gone about their work places them among sociology's best representatives.

The second reason behind this book's selection of sociologists is their diversity of opinions and styles. The eight thinkers convey something of the heterogeneity of the discipline and raise the question of what it means to be a sociologist, particularly in the cases of Marx and Foucault as neither of them identified themselves as such and they might have disputed the way that their ideas have been claimed for sociology. The diversity of the eight thinkers' approaches extends to questions of what comprises appropriate sociological evidence, what constitutes convincing sociological reasoning and what the point of engaging in sociological argument is. Some place more emphasis than others on the idea of sociology as a science, some operate with the language of demonstrations and proofs that to others are highly problematic and some regard sociology as a means not only of understanding but also of changing the world in a way that others regard as illegitimate. Some, like Oakley, seek to draw conclusions from autobiographical material while others, like Goffman, draw a sharp distinction between their sociology and their private lives. The writers concerned have of course been mindful of these differences, and sought to use them to their advantage in the development of their arguments. Oakley's critique of postmodernists' language as 'dense, imprecise, long-winded, grammatically complex, hugely inaccessible and hence intrinsically undemocratic' carries the implication that the better arguments are those conveyed by 'plain speaking' (2002: 190, 3). This is a rerun of the argument that raged fifty years ago between Mills and Parsons over the most appropriate sociological style. The analysis of eight very different sociologists has not been undertaken for the purpose of identifying one best practice relative to which the other seven fall short; rather they are treated as proponents of diverse approaches that may be more or less useful, depending on the task in hand. Rodinson's metaphorical observation that 'no one has a key to fit all locks' (1977: viii) is apposite here.

The third reason for the selection of the eight thinkers whose work is concentrated upon in the pages which follow is that they all espouse the view that the development of an argument is a craft that needs to be worked at if that argument is to achieve its full potential. It is not too much of an exaggeration to suggest that this stands as central to their life's work. Mills's commitment to what he called 'intellectual craftsmanship' (2000: 195) spurred him to spend ten years working on *White Collar*, and this 'decade-long obsession' (Gillam 1981: 1) has parallels in the amount of time taken to prepare Marx's first volume of *Capital* (Rosdolsky 1980: 10), Durkheim's *Suicide* (Lukes 1975: 191), Parsons's *The Social System* (Wearne 1989: 85) and Oakley's *Social Support and Motherhood* (Oakley 1992: viii). Alongside these works that were subject to painstaking revision, these authors have also been able to produce publications in a matter of weeks, amongst which are numbered Marx's collaborative work with Engels, *The Communist Manifesto* (Taylor 1967: 7), Mills's *The New Men of Power* (Mills and Mills 2000: 107) and Oakley's *Sex, Gender and Society* (1985: 125). These latter were not written completely from scratch, in that they set down ideas that the authors had been mulling over for longer periods, but it is instructive that each of them sold well. They demonstrate that there is more than one way to achieve the objective of engaging with an audience, provided that the argument is tailored accordingly. The sociological careers of the eight writers focused on in this book also suggest that sociological argument is something that one learns by doing. Reflection on the reception of previous endeavours means that the adage 'practice makes perfect' is appropriate, or at least its modified version 'practice makes better'.

Fourth, the eight thinkers have been chosen because they lived in different places and at different times, and this allows consideration to be given to the question of whether sociology as a discipline has advanced in terms of the capacity of its practitioners to develop successful arguments. The eight are presented chronologically, and the century-long journey from Marx as one of the founding figures of the discipline to Oakley as a representative of contemporary sociology reveals that the subject is not cumulative in any simple sense. The chapters that follow will identify many ways in which the thinkers considered have sought to distance themselves from their predecessors and their agendas. It is evident, for example, that on the matter of the position of women 'Durkheim was writing in a bygone era' (Aron 1970: 43) and that in this respect it has been impossible for feminists to build on his writings. This case illustrates that as times change, so each generation of sociologists must take the discipline in new and unanticipated directions. Other aspects of the work of the founding figures of the discipline have proved more enduring, however, not least in terms of the types of questions that they sought to pose and the types of engagement with their audiences that they endeavoured to achieve. The writers considered here have many points of difference, but they share a common concern to engage interested others with their ideas. This common project reflects their shared belief that ideas matter, and more specifically that sociology has the potential, as Mills put it, 'to make a difference to the quality of human life in our time' (2000: 226). Engagement with sociological ideas requires preparedness on the part of an audience to be open to new ways of thinking, and to respond appropriately by suspending their existing world view for the sake of sociological argument.

None of the eight thinkers whose work is to be examined in the chapters that follow has claimed that sociology offers easy answers or timeless verities to which they have uniquely privileged access. The story of each of them is one of a personal journey of discovery in which they endeavour to move towards more precise formulation of the questions that they want to ask, gather more satisfactory answers to these questions and seek more effective means of communicating those answers. Very often literal journeys have been involved, supporting Mills's contention that it is 'helpful to try to get a *comparative* grip on the materials' (2000: 215, emphasis in original). Marx's exile from Germany forced him to think comparatively, just as visits to Germany stimulated Durkheim and Parsons to step outside their national contexts (albeit more briefly). Similar comments have been made about Weber's trip to the USA, Mills's visits to Latin America and Foucault's spells spent in various countries. The general point is summed up nicely in Oakley's remark about the capacity of 'travels abroad' to undermine 'parochial vision' (1986a: 7). It is intended that these accounts of personal change and discovery will encourage among readers the confidence to engage actively with the various points that are raised. Few sociological debates are finally settled, and the positions adopted by the eight sociologists on whose work attention is focused are not above criticism. Sociology teaches us to challenge what Bourdieu calls those 'internal censorships' by which we rein ourselves in, believing the voices that tell us ' "I'm not a theorist", "I can't write" ' and that adjectives like 'brilliant' (1993: 52–3) apply only to other people.

It is also to be hoped that the contemporary relevance of the historical material contained in this book will be appreciated. Stones provides a good example of how knowledge of the past can be useful in the present in his discussion of how 'the unsuspecting reader' may be persuaded by the well-worn technique of criticising an author previously introduced as 'an authoritative genius with the most marvellous of grasps' (1996: 220). The sleight of hand has a very respectable intellectual pedigree, as will be revealed in the discussion of Marx and others below, but even so it is a rhetorical device to beware. In a similar fashion it can be noted that although Miles's warning about the potential of sociological analysis to 'degenerate into meaningless rhetoric' (2001: 167) is made with contemporary writers in mind, such warnings have been given before. This is not the first generation of sociologists to be critical of the style of argument in which popular buzz-words and impressionistic analyses are substituted for hard thinking. We can also use knowledge of the past to reflect on current practice in other ways. Hochschild implies that her first drafts suffer from serious overuse of punctuation in the same way as Weber's did, the difference being that she is prepared to take on board the friendly reminder that quotation marks 'are a way of placing reservations on our use of a word, and we need to have a good reason for doing that' (2003: ix). It is instructive that one of her publications, *The Second Shift* (Hochschild 1989), is included in Gans's list of best-sellers that Riesman's *The Lonely Crowd* topped, despite having only six years before the census date for sales to exceed 100,000. Gans's comment that books would not have made it onto this list had they not been 'written in a language that at least educated general readers can understand' indicates that attention to style can pay off, in this instance quite literally. Gans's further suggestions about the desirability of greater knowledge of past research as an antidote to 'sociological amnesia' (1999: 285, ch. 14) can thus be complemented by a similar set of suggestions concerning the lessons that there are to be learned from the scholarly work of previous generations about what makes an effective argument. This is the reason why the final chapter of this book concludes with ten observations that are grounded in the analysis of the nature of sociological argument and reasoning that begins in Chapter 2 with Marx.

2

Karl Marx: sociology as radical criticism

Introduction and overview

Karl Marx was born in Germany on 5 May 1818 and died in London on 14 March 1883 aged 64, following several years of failing health. Many aspects of his family life were 'thoroughly bourgeois' (Blumenberg 1972: 126), but his lifetime's work was devoted to developing an unrelenting critique of capitalist society. It is for this critique that he is best remembered. His radical politics meant that he spent most of his life in exile, finding a haven in London where he oscillated between periodic involvement in political activism and long spells of solitary study in the Reading Room of the British Museum. He was an avid note-taker, and the published versions of his notebooks offer insights into the furious pace at which he worked, his zeal for questioning all aspects of conventional wisdom and his preparedness to 'turn everything upside down' (in Nicolaus 1973: 59) in his search for an analysis with which he could be satisfied. He was capable of being self-critical in his pursuit of a style of writing that achieved the exacting standards that he set, but he had the capacity to take his criticism of others much further, and few writers whose works he encountered escaped the uncomfortable experience of his waspishly critical attention. One of his opponents even characterised him as someone who had so much self-belief that he tended to 'divide mankind into two parties: Marx and the rest' (McLellan 1973: 247). He was aware that he had the physical appearance of a prophet (Wheen 2000: 379), and this befitted his role as an uncompromising critic of the social evils that he saw all around him.

Marx lived at a time when the transition to an industrial age was transforming all aspects of social and economic life and raising profound political and philosophical questions. The transition to an industrial order undermined previous certainties and represented to Marx a historically pivotal break with the past. The new economic order was open to criticism because of the alienating character of production governed by market forces, and because workers who produced commodities in the emerging

8

capitalist mode of production were vulnerable to exploitation. These evils were criticised so vehemently by Marx because they were in his view avoidable, at least once the transition had been achieved and the full potential of mechanised production realised. Marx was impressed by industrial society's potential to meet people's material needs in a way that no previous social order had been able to do, but was at the same time convinced that its organisation as a capitalist mode of production stood in the way of realising that potential. To Marx this was a political as well as an economic issue, since production takes place within particular forms of property relations in which typically those social classes that own the means of production dominate those who do not. Marx was thus led to an interest in the tendency of social classes to come into conflict, and also to a philosophical interest in how such conflicts unfold throughout history.

What Marx brought to the study of political economy, as these subjects were called at the time, was a preparedness to ask radical questions and a concern to follow through the logic of an argument to its conclusion, however contentious this may be. This took him beyond academic analysis into the realm of political interventions, and some of the writings for which he is best known are political tracts, such as *The Communist Manifesto* which he wrote in 1848 with his lifelong friend and collaborator Frederick Engels. This work caught the mood of the year of intense revolutionary activity in which it was published, and Marx continued to seek to make his writings relevant to the political agendas of his day. He was aware, however, that the 'popularization' of his ideas stood in conflict with his mission to be scientific in his analysis, and once remarked that '*Scientific* attempts to revolutionize a science can never be truly popular' (in Nicolaus 1973: 57, emphasis in original). He was torn between his aspiration to make the core of his approach 'accessible to the ordinary human intelligence, in two or three printer's sheets' (in Callinicos 1996: 77) and his consciousness of the dangers of oversimplification. It is instructive to note that *Capital*, his *magnum opus*, was a huge and complex work that was years in the making and ultimately left uncompleted. Only the first volume was published during his lifetime, in 1867, and many commentators have noted the commitment that is required of readers if they are to reach the end. It was typical of Marx that he could ask for such commitment, on the grounds that he regarded the topics with which he engaged as the most serious and challenging issues that we face.

The way in which Marx set about presenting his ideas was deliberately controversial. As befits someone whose favourite motto was '*De omnibus dubitandum*' (Blumenberg 1972: 175), that is, 'we ought to question everything' (Worsley 1982: 9), he set out to challenge conventional wisdom and its embodiment in everyday, taken-for-granted knowledge. This stance inevitably earned him notoriety in certain circles, among people who

possible unpleasant
dangerous
occurenc

regarded the communist ideas with which he was associated as a 'spectre'
(Marx and Engels 1968: 35). Marx defended himself against his critics by
casting doubt on their ideas and by claiming that his own point of view
could be demonstrated, scientifically, to be superior. In keeping with the
spirit of the times in which he lived, Marx positioned himself as someone
whose work was 'scientific', in contrast to the hidebound character of conventional thinking. Marx argued that his approach offered a radically different perspective on the world, one that people who benefited from
existing arrangements would be bound to seek to discredit. In the battle of
ideas in which he was engaged, Marx had no qualms about reinforcing his
scientific case with all manner of argumentational devices that advanced
his prospects of defeating his opponents. For example, early on in their
writing careers Marx and Engels had encountered the 'trick' of recasting an
abstract idea 'into a person' (1974: 67) with whom readers could more readily identify. The effectiveness of this ploy was not lost on Marx, in whose
later writings the 'whimsically nasty character' (Lemert 1995: 168) of
attach Imolycule
'Mr Moneybags' was created in order to pillory capitalism more effectively.

A great deal is required by Marx of his audiences. Marx's assumption of
'a reader who is willing to learn something new and therefore to think for
himself' (1976: 90) demands active engagement with ideas and preparedness to suspend disbelief in order that prevailing illusions might be challenged and secrets revealed. Engels took a different view of the needs of
prospective readers of *Capital*, and urged Marx 'to make it as easy for them
as one possibly can' (in Wheen 2000: 312), but Marx was not suited tem-
peramentally to writing in textbook fashion. Marx's *Capital* is written
instead in a style that revolves around, in Wheen's words, 'elaborate
metaphors … confusing digressions … philosophical orotundities … [and]
literary flourishes' (2000: 303). These devices may have been more or less
effective in helping to carry the argument along, but the underlying propositions that Marx sought to advance were necessarily hard to grasp because
they involved taking the world with which people were familiar and turning it upside down. Starting an analysis with things that we all know to be
'true' only to doubt how far these truths stand up to scrutiny reveals the
revolutionary potential of 'questioning everything'. Existing explanations
can be examined for inconsistencies and contradictions, and through a
process of dialectical reasoning more rigorous accounts can be derived, but
these may well appear strange at first sight. It is not surprising to learn that
ahead of the publication of the first volume of *Capital* in 1867 Marx spent 'a
nine-year period of experimentation and continual searching for a form of
presentation which would be adequate to the material' (Rosdolsky 1980:
10), material on which Marx had already by 1858 spent 'fifteen years of
research … the best period of my life' (in McLellan 1980: 122). Even if we
accept Harvey's claim that 'The exploration of contradictions always lies

at the heart of original thought' (1989: 345), it remains a formidable problem to demonstrate that they have been resolved satisfactorily.

Marx's efforts to establish the veracity of his ideas drew heavily on the development of a comparative perspective (Sayer 1979). Marx's writings are full of striking juxtapositions in which the implication is clear, that things do not have to be as they are. His message is that 'what was historically created can always be historically changed' (Eagleton 1999: 17). In 1856, for example, historical comparison led him to note that, 'In our days everything seems pregnant with its contrary. Machinery, gifted with the wonderful power of shortening and fructifying human labour, we behold starving and overworking it. The new-fangled sources of wealth, by some strange weird spell, are turned into sources of want' (1973b: 299). It was a recurrent theme of Marx that capitalism promised to liberate humanity from the constraints to which it had been subject under previous modes of production, but delivered only distorted versions of freedom. Building on the contrast between capitalism's boundless potential and its less impressive record in practice, Marx was able to pursue the idea that wage-labourers are 'free' in two senses, and that one of these, their freedom from property (i.e. their propertylessness) had far more impact on their lives than did their freedom to change employer. As a result, he concluded, 'the system of wage labour is ... a system of slavery' (1974: 352); the achievement of 'the true realm of freedom' (1981: 959) required in Marx's view the transcendence of capitalism. For Marx, the scientific analysis of the working of the capitalist mode of production pointed to this outcome as more or less inevitable.

The extent to which Marx resorted to the argument of historical inevitability is a matter of ongoing debate. There is much in Marx's writings that gives support to the view that he saw social change as a law-like process. Zeitlin has acknowledged that 'Marx and Engels must bear some responsibility for the widespread and persistent misapprehension of their theory' before going on to argue that it would be mistaken to treat 'their evolutionary metaphors as anything more than rhetoric' (1987: 107). Other commentators such as Cohen (1988: ch. 4) place greater emphasis on the role of inevitability in Marx's analysis, although even here care is taken to distinguish between this position and crude determinism. Ray's observation that Marx saw the resolution of the social crisis of his day coming about 'through a combination of scientific knowledge and social agency' (1999: 65) highlights that Marx was seeking to prompt people to act, rather than simply making his audience more aware of what was going on around them. Marx's critique of capitalism galvanised people to action because it had a moral dimension to it as well as a scientific one. According to Moore, 'For Marx there was no conflict between his position as a moralist and a scientist' (1962: 117), and so it is only to be expected that his writings are peppered with emotive and value-laden terms as well as more conventionally scientific language.

Marx's method of presentation

Over the course of his life Marx engaged with his audiences using a variety of different formats, including numerous speeches, letters, newspaper articles, pamphlets and books. The most ambitious of these was his study of *Capital*. The full six volumes that Marx planned to write were never completed, perhaps unsurprisingly, given the immensity of the task. In addition, Marx's mode of working did not lend itself to speedy and single-minded completion of projects (Pampel 2000: 16). Even so, the first volume of *Capital* is noteworthy both for its intellectual content and for its style of presentation. In the postface to the second edition of this work, Marx wrote with exasperation at how 'the method employed in *Capital* has been little understood', it being more obvious to him than it was to his reviewers that 'the method of presentation must differ in form from that of enquiry' (1976: 99, 102). A step-by-step chronological account of the process by which he reached his conclusions would not have kept the audience's attention, and instead Marx took advantage of the magical qualities of his subject matter. Woodiwiss has commented that *Capital's* 'first six chapters follow the narrative structure of a conjuring act: first we are reassured that everything is normal but suddenly a rabbit is produced' (2001: 36). Marx's surprise at the apparently supernatural appearance of surplus value in the process of production and exchange is of course feigned, but a necessary part of making his readers think in unaccustomed ways. To achieve this, Marx needed to locate his starting point as the position currently occupied by his audience, and then to proceed from there. It is no accident that 'Marx's writing is famous for its endings' (Berman 1983: 20), because he was mindful of the power of a dramatic denouement.

The common ground that Marx sought to establish with his readers at the start of *Capital* was a shared understanding of that central element of everyday life in capitalist societies, the commodity. Inclusion of a quotation from his earlier work in the opening sentence may have added to the authoritative character of his pronouncement, but this was not required to establish what Marx suggests is incontrovertible: that commodities are useful, and that they have prices. Everyone can agree that commodities need to be useful if people are going to want to acquire them, and everyone can also agree that commodities are acquired through being exchanged for money. In setting out these starting points, Marx did not make any claims to originality, and his text is replete with references to the work of forerunners in which the underpinnings of his argument had already been established. The years spent by Marx in the Reading Room of the British Museum where he 'read voraciously' and 'filled his notebooks' (McLellan 1973: 282–3) allowed him to draw on the ideas of great figures such as Adam Smith. Smith's *The Wealth of Nations* had pointed out that the value of goods 'has two different meanings. ... The one may be called "value in use"; the other, "value in exchange"' (1974: 131) nearly a century before Marx was writing, and this distinction played a key role in the development by Smith and later by Ricardo of the labour theory of value, according to which the prices of commodities reflect the amount and quality of the labour that making them requires (Meek 1973). Marx thus accepted much of what had already been written, but he then sought to take that analysis a crucial step further. In a letter to Engels in 1851 he expressed the view of the economics literature that he had read that 'Basically, this science has made no further progress since A. Smith and D. Ricardo' (in McLellan 1973: 283). The subsequent two decades only hardened Marx's opinion on this matter, for by 1873 he was characterising the successors to Smith and Ricardo as no more than 'hired prize-fighters' in whose writings disinterested inquiry and 'genuine scientific research' had been replaced by mere 'apologetics' (1976: 97) that dealt only in expressing expedient justifications for the status quo.

Marx referred approvingly to the reviewer of *Capital* who took it to be 'a necessary sequel to the teaching of Smith and Ricardo' (Marx 1976: 99). This supported Marx's designation of his endeavour as 'a critique of political economy', the subtitle that he gave to *Capital*. What has been called the 'paradox of value' (Meek 1973: 73), the situation whereby certain commodities (such as diamonds) are more expensive than others (such as water) despite being less useful, had led Smith and Ricardo to look elsewhere for the explanation of the price of a commodity, since it evidently could not lie in the commodity's usefulness. The conclusion that they reached was that commodities varied in price according to how much work was involved in their production, and it was this labour theory of value that Marx sought to develop. Marx could take it as given that Smith and Ricardo had already established that 'The value contained in a commodity is equal to the labour-time taken in making it' (1981: 133). He then proceeded to demonstrate that some startling consequences followed from this apparently innocuous premise when combined with the equally unremarkable premise that commodities are exchanged through the medium of money for things of equivalent value. For Marx the implications of these ideas had to be followed through, in order to reveal the 'secret' and 'mysterious' properties of commodities that remained hidden to the 'vulgar economists' (1976: 163, 175), his deliberately dismissive term for the blinkered thinkers of his day who were not prepared to venture beyond what seems obvious in the common sense view of the world.

Marx whetted his audience's appetite by indicating that things are not what they seem. As he later put it, scientific enquiry is justified on precisely these grounds: 'all science would be superfluous if the appearance of things directly coincided with their essence' (1981: 956). The observation that 'A commodity appears at first sight an extremely obvious, trivial thing' is followed by the intriguing claim that analysis reveals it to be, on the contrary, 'a very strange thing'. The commodity form that seems so unremarkable in the modern world would have appeared 'fantastic' to people in other eras, such as the inhabitants of medieval Europe. Only when money has become all-pervasive do 'labour and its products' come to assume the magical qualities of commodities. Only in the modern world have commodities become so familiar that they are routinely treated as 'natural'. When this happens commodities come to be 'endowed with a life of their own', and people lose sight of the historically distinctive circumstances that have led to this peculiar 'fetishism of the commodity'. Commodities come to dominate people's existence once sight is lost of the simple point that they are the products of labour, produced because they are useful and instead their exchange value, (that is, their price) becomes the exclusive measure of their worth. Marx spoke of this fetishism as 'peculiar to the capitalist mode of production', since it is only in this historical period that 'the process of production has mastery over man, instead of the opposite' (1976: 163, 170, 175, 165, 163, 1046, 175). By framing his argument in this way Marx was drawing a parallel with the critique of religious thinking that he had developed earlier in his career, and the term 'fetishism' was chosen deliberately to convey his comparable disdain for the worship of commodities.

Marx could have left his argument there, because already by the end of the first chapter of *Capital* he had developed a critique of the work of political economists, challenging their celebration of the bourgeois world view with his more hostile opinion that commodities have come to dominate people's existence. The alienating effects of commodification, making things (and also workers) into commodities that are judged according to the price for which they are bought and sold on markets, had been a key theme of Marx's early writings, but what he sought to do in *Capital* was to add a second and more deadly line of attack. In the interim the centrepiece of his argument had shifted from alienation to surplus value (Walton and Gamble 1976), and it was this latter concept that was presented as his key discovery. Marx argued that what political economy had left unresolved was how profit could arise in a system in which labour is the source of commodities' value, and markets involve the exchange of equivalents. How, as Engels later condensed Marx's question, 'is this then to be reconciled with the fact that the wage-worker does not receive the whole sum of value created by his labour but has to surrender a part of it to the capitalist?' (in Marx and

Engels 1968: 377). Marx anticipated the suggestion being advanced that surplus value might have its origins in commodities being sold above their value or bought below their value, but he rejected these ideas by arguing that 'In its pure form, the exchange of commodities is an exchange of equivalents, and thus it is not a method of increasing value' (1976: 261). It thus remains a puzzle how 'Mr Moneybags', Marx's illustrative capitalist figure, is routinely able to start out with £100 and then, by exchanging this for commodities and then converting these commodities back into money, is able to finish the process with £110, his original sum invested plus £10 profit. If labour is the source of value, and if commodities are necessarily exchanged for things of equivalent value, then the £10 profit which Mr Moneybags gains from the process of production appears to have materialised out of thin air.

Marx's use of 'Mr Moneybags' as a stereotypical capitalist helped to get across his more abstract ideas about capitalism. Mr Moneybags is 'one of the characters who appear on the economic stage', and this personification of the capitalist allowed Marx to arrive at the following statement of 'the problem' requiring explanation: 'Our friend, Moneybags ... must buy his commodities at their value, must sell them at their value, and yet at the end of the process must withdraw more value from circulation than he threw into it at starting.' This passage comes at the end of Chapter 5. The expectation that Chapter 6 will contain a crucial revelation is met, as here Marx's deductions led him to the conclusion that 'our friend, Moneybags, must be so lucky as to find within the sphere of circulation, in the market, a commodity, whose use value possesses the peculiar property of being a source of value'; that commodity is then revealed to be workers' 'capacity for labour or labour-power'. Of course, Marx's message was reinforced by his going on to show that luck has absolutely nothing to do with it, and that the availability for hire of free wage labourers requires historically specific conditions. The capitalist needs to employ workers who are 'free in the double sense' (1954: 89, 163, 164, 166) of being free to dispose of their labour power and free of any other options by virtue of being propertyless and therefore unable to sustain an independent existence.

Marx concluded from this that explanations framed in terms of the naturalness of capitalism are erroneous: 'Nature does not produce on the one side owners of money or commodities and on the other men possessing nothing but their own labour-power. This relation has no natural basis, neither is its social basis one that is common to all historical periods' (1954: 166). Only in capitalist societies can the Moneybags figure pay wages to workers equivalent to the value of their subsistence costs, how much it costs them to live, but sell the value embodied in the commodities that they have produced at a profit while all the time appearing to offer 'a fair day's wage for a fair day's work' (Marx, in Marx and Engels 1968: 229).

The appearance of fairness and naturalness arises because wage levels are determined by market forces that ensure the exchange of equivalents, and because workers are free and are not forced to sell their labour-power to any particular employer. But the quotation marks in his reference to 'the simple and "just" laws of equivalent exchange' (1973a: 504) imply that Marx regards the reality as anything but what it appears. The shocking argument to which Marx sought to lead his audience was that 'Capitalism is ... only another form of slavery' (in Padover 1978: 93). The change in the labourer's position in the transition from earlier modes of production to capitalism was for Marx *'purely one of form'* (1976: 1028, emphasis in original). This theme elaborated on the claim made by Marx 20 years before the publication of *Capital*, that 'Modern nations have been able only to disguise slavery in their own countries' (1975a: 104). By implication wage-labourers had not escaped being dominated, and their subordination, despite being less visible than the control exercised over other types of direct producers, was no less real in its consequences.

In developing his critique of thinkers who failed to penetrate beyond the realm of surface appearances, Marx was unable to resist a sideswipe at the influential utilitarian thinker Bentham for his assumption of the 'rational economic man' perspective. Marx took issue with the utilitarian doctrine that people are motivated by their narrow self-interest and that self-interested behaviour leads to 'mutual advantage, for the common weal and in the interest of all'. Marx implied that this perspective is nothing more than a convenient ideological belief on the part of those convinced of 'the pre-established harmony of things'. Were things really so, Marx suggested, Mr Moneybags and his worker would be equally keen to come together in the labour market. A more truthful account would portray a quite different 'physiognomy of our dramatis personae', as Marx described it: 'The one with an air of importance, smirking, intent on business; the other, timid and holding back, like one who is bringing his own hide to market and has nothing to expect but – a hiding.' For such reluctance on the part of the worker to make sense, Marx pointed to the need to explore in more depth 'the hidden abode of production', the labour process, in which 'the secret of profit making' is concealed. The self-interested account of the capitalist presents the status quo as 'the best of all possible worlds' (1954: 172, 85). Marx fundamentally disagreed with this optimistic view.

Scientific and historical comparisons

The contrast between surface appearance and underlying reality was at the heart of the way in which Marx presented his ideas. It followed that the results of scientific enquiry will frequently fly in the face of common sense and seem paradoxical; as Marx put it, 'Scientific truth is always paradox, if judged by everyday experience, which catches only the delusive appearance of things.' Marx presented himself as following in the footsteps of thinkers whose scientific endeavours exposed the shortcomings of widely held beliefs, as for example Ricardo had done in destroying 'the old, popular and worn-out fallacy that "wages determine prices" ' (in Marx and Engels 1968: 209, 202). Much of this activity is inherently abstract, and Marx appreciated that concepts such as 'commodity fetishism' and 'surplus value' were not easy to grasp. Abstract concepts are nevertheless a necessary part of developing an argument, and much of Marx's effort was devoted to demonstrating the superiority of his key ideas over those contained in rival perspectives. That said, Marx's analysis 'was not merely one of concepts' (McLellan 1980: 154) but was concerned to deploy these concepts to illuminate the history of social and economic relationships in all their diversity. In other words, Marx 'saw his critique as an empirically-grounded exercise' (Sayer 1979: 113) that needed to go beyond the universal categories with which the political economists of his day operated.

Marx argued that this could be done by highlighting the shortcomings of existing accounts, in terms of both their internal contradictions and their divergence from the growing body of knowledge about societies past and present. His demonstration that the political economists of his day were unable to explain satisfactorily the source of profit was complemented by his ability to marshal vast amounts of evidence from his extraordinarily wide reading about the realities of capitalism and (to a lesser extent) of pre-capitalist modes of production. *Capital* employed the method of critique to great effect by following ideas such as the labour theory of value through to their logical conclusions, but Marx's complaint was not only that the political economists of his day contradicted themselves; it was also that they were profoundly ignorant of the harsh realities of the world around them, and of the rich historical diversity of human society. As a result, Marx's *Capital* is not only a major work of social theory, 'it is also an enormously complicated work because of its immense historical coverage and theoretical scope' (Morrison 1995: 59). Marx set himself and his readers a highly ambitious target, since his point of reference was not only the logical consistency of his analytical framework but also the relationship that this framework bore to the historical record.

Marx was aware that he was adopting a style that involved, as he put it, 'very long and, I fear, tedious exposition' (in Marx and Engels 1968: 229). The method of analysis employed in *Capital* he described as one that made reading the early chapters 'rather arduous', but this was necessarily so because, to use a mountaineering metaphor, 'There is no royal road to science, and only those who do not dread the fatiguing climb of its steep paths have a chance of gaining its luminous summits' (in Althusser and Balibar 1975: 9). Marx's approach was to concentrate first of all on developing his arguments in their simplest form, and then elaborating upon them by relaxing some of the more unrealistic assumptions with which it had been necessary to start out. For example, the initial demonstration that workers produce a surplus over and above that required to pay for the cost of their subsistence did not need to question the assumption that all workers are equally productive. This was dealt with once Marx had established the basic principles of the labour theory of value and was seeking to acknowledge the greater complexity of the situation in reality. Marx recognised that a lazy or clumsy worker would take longer than others to perform any given task, but that this would not make the commodities produced by such a worker more valuable than ones produced more quickly by an average worker. Rather, Marx argued, the value of a commodity reflected 'the quantity of socially necessary labour' (in Marx and Engels 1968: 206) required for its production, and in this way he was able to work towards a better explanation of the prices of commodities.

A further example of Marx's method of 'rising from the abstract to the concrete' (1973a: 101) is provided by his discussion in volume 3 of *Capital* of 'the law of the tendency of the rate of profit to fall' (1959: pt III). The idea of a long-term tendency for profit rates to decline had been advanced by forerunners such as Smith and Ricardo, but Marx was able to take the analysis further by virtue of his development of the labour theory of value combined with observations drawn from the periodic economic crises in which large numbers of previously profitable firms went bankrupt. In its simplest form, Marx's argument was that the profits received by capitalists in return for their investment of capital would be bound to decline as the proportion of that investment spent on machinery and other elements of 'constant capital' rose and the proportion spent on wages (or 'variable capital') fell. If the only source of surplus value is wage labour and if a shrinking proportion of a capitalist's outlay is devoted to wages, then it follows (other things being equal) that profits will fall in a law-like fashion. Marx's formulation of this 'law' as a series of equations added to the scientific credentials of the argument, but Marx immediately identified six 'counteracting influences' that in practice modified the operation of the law. These were that declining profitability may be counteracted by increasing the intensity of the exploitation of workers, by depressing wages, by cheapening the elements of constant capital, by relative overpopulation, by foreign trade and by the increase of stock capital (1959: ch. XIV). These factors were not considered by Marx to have the capacity to prevent the rate of profit from falling in the long run, but their incorporation into his model made it more appropriate to treat the law as a 'tendency' rather than an inexorable process.

Marx was aware that this method of proceeding, with analysis conducted through abstract concepts, had the potential to appear 'an *a priori* construction', but he insisted that his analysis was in practice grounded in 'the material world'. Moreover, Marx regarded this world as being 'in a fluid state, in motion' (1976: 102, 103), as a result of which a dialectical method was required in order to make sense of it. Within this approach societies are conceived as dynamic and unstable entities in which distinct stages of development can be identified, with the process of change propelled by the working out of their contradictions. Marx claimed that the categories of political economy such as capital, profit and wages were by this method revealed to be anything but timeless and natural, because they required certain historical preconditions to be in place before they could emerge. He accepted that some features of production are present in all epochs, but argued that others are peculiar to specific modes of production, and that the former could be 'sifted out by comparison'. Thus instruments of production are found throughout human history, but only in the modern world have these taken the form of capital. By such comparison Marx was able to challenge the idea of 'the eternity and harmoniousness of the existing social relations' (1973a: 85). Sayer has noted how 'Marx went to considerable pains to collect such comparative data' (1979: 138) because he remained committed to the view that 'Empirical observation must in each separate instance bring out empirically, and without any mystification and speculation, the connection of social and political structure with production' (Marx and Engels 1974: 46). Marx's frequent reference to empirical evidence was undertaken for far more than 'purely illustrative purposes', since it was a crucial element in 'the dialectic of abstract and concrete' (Beamish 1992: 4) by which the dynamic and interconnected character of historical development was most effectively captured.

The inclusion in *Capital* of extensive and detailed discussions of evidence relating to the realities of capitalism's operation helped to make the first volume alone several hundred pages long. This allayed Marx's fears that 'too much conciseness will make the thing indigestible to the public' and also met his concern to avoid writing in a 'dull and wooden style' (in Beamish 1992: 58). Marx drew satisfaction from the fact that many of his sources were official reports, as is indicated by his reference to 'The odious acts of capitalist exploitation which the official surveys by the English government have revealed' (in Weiss 1973: 178). To take just one of literally dozens of examples of how Marx used such material to leaven his text, the Fifth Report of the Children's Employment Commission was drawn upon to establish that 'young persons have to do heavy work in rope-works, and night-work in salt mines, candle factories and chemical works; young people are worked to death at turning the looms in silk weaving, when it is not carried on by machinery' (1976: 592). This report was published only a year prior to *Capital*, showing that Marx continued to work on this side of his analysis, as well as on the more abstract conceptual side, in his search for the best way to present his writings which he regarded as 'an artistic whole' (in Kemple 1995: 78). These elaborations, together with the frequent literary references that Marx made, eventually produced a work that was anything but concise, and one that required a great deal of dedication on the part of any reader intending to go through it from cover to cover.

Concern to provide extensive supporting evidence for his case led Marx to make extensive use of footnotes. Korsch's reference to 'those profound and exquisite, though often seemingly digressive footnotes with which Marx almost overloads *Capital*' (1971: 41) hints at the potentially distracting effect that this style can have. The former British prime minister Harold Wilson reportedly gave this as his reason for not venturing beyond the second page of *Capital* (Wheen 2000: 299). Marx was quite capable of expressing his ideas more concisely, as his various pamphlets (such as the *Communist Manifesto*) attest. The most memorable brief statement of his thinking is the 1859 preface to *A Contribution to the Critique of Political Economy*, written as a deliberate 'popularization of his theory' (Mészáros 1987: 53). In this work Marx formulated what he referred to as the 'guiding thread' for his studies in one paragraph, which drew on his previous work in several ways to highlight the distinctiveness of his approach. His rejection of the practice derived from Hegel of focusing first on ideas was neatly captured in the inversion of that position: 'It is not the consciousness of men that determines their being, but, on the contrary, their social being that determines their consciousness.' Marx directed attention away from what people perceive on the grounds that this is not always reliable: 'our opinion of an individual is not based on what he thinks of himself' (in Marx and Engels 1968: 182–3). This echoed the observation made in *The German Ideology* that 'in ordinary life every shopkeeper is very well able to distinguish between what somebody professes to be and what he really is' (Marx and Engels 1974: 67). The 1859 preface stated succinctly the gist of Marx's alternative approach that focussed on material realities: 'In the social production of their life, men enter into definite relations that are indispensable and independent of their will, relations of production that correspond with a definite stage of development of their material productive forces' (in Marx and Engels 1968: 182). This sentence captures Marx's argument in a nutshell, insofar as any one sentence can.

Marx used the rest of this key paragraph in the 1859 preface to highlight two related points about his argument. The first was that 'the economic structure of society' should be regarded as 'the real foundation, on which rises a legal and political superstructure'. This structural metaphor, likening society to a building, has proved an enormously influential one, as has the second key point, that history is characterised by progress, driven forward by the working out of contradictions. The statement that 'In broad outlines Asiatic, ancient, feudal, and modern bourgeois modes of production can be designated as progressive epochs in the economic formation of society' conveys the same sense of historical movement on a global scale that Marx and Engels had conjured up with their declaration in the *Communist Manifesto* that 'The history of all hitherto existing society is the history of class struggles.' It is instructive that Engels subsequently qualified this latter statement by restricting it to 'all *written* history' (in Marx and Engels 1968: 182–3, 35, emphasis in original), just as he also noted after Marx's death that 'the production and reproduction of real life' should be thought of as 'the *ultimately* determining element in history'. Engels insisted that neither he nor Marx had ever asserted that 'the economic element is the *only* determining one', before conceding that they were 'partly to blame for the fact that the younger people sometimes lay more stress on the economic side than is due to it'. Engels explained interpretations of their work that exaggerated the role of economic factors by arguing that 'We had to emphasise the main principle *vis-à-vis* our adversaries, who denied it, and we had not always the time, the place or the opportunity to give their due to the other elements involved in the interaction' (Marx and Engels 1970: 487–8). In acknowledging that their summary positions ran the risk of oversimplification, Engels's elaboration introduced so much flexibility into the approach that its distinctiveness became 'hard to pin down' (Abrams 1982: 49).

The compression into a brief summary of a more complex argument about the relationship between base and superstructure goes some way to explaining the deterministic quality of the 1859 preface, but not all the way. Within the space of a few sentences, Marx wrote not only of the economic base being the 'real foundation' of the superstructure but also of how the former determines the latter, or conditions the latter and of how the latter corresponds to the former. As Williams noted, 'the shifting senses of "determine" ' (1977: 85) allow radically different interpretations to be made of Marx's message, with varying degrees of importance attached to the 'law-like' character of social development as opposed to the emphasis placed on the scope for human agency as people make history. This tension between structure and agency is present elsewhere in Marx's work, most famously in the passage in *The Eighteenth Brumaire of Louis Bonaparte* in which he declared 'Men make their own history, but they do not make it just as they please; they do not make it under circumstances chosen by themselves, but under circumstances directly encountered, given and transmitted from the past' (in Marx and Engels 1969: 398). In Craib's view, the presence of this tension in Marx's work is not necessarily problematic: 'rather it is a mark of Marx's greatness as a thinker that he was able to work with both sides of a dualism which ... inevitably must haunt social theory' (1997: 38). The process of showing how understanding people's actions is necessarily connected to structural explanations was one to which Marx's dialectical method was well suited. This was neatly complemented by his use of comparative material to highlight the scope that exists for diversity in the way in which structural forces work themselves out.

The moral critique of capitalism

The forcefulness with which Marx's ideas were expressed reflects his confidence that these arguments could be reinforced if necessary. Craib is right to say that 'Marx cannot be accused of being afraid of making rash statements' (1997: 102), but it does not follow that the statements regarded as his most controversial were penned rashly. One of the most shocking ideas associated with Marx is his likening of capitalism to slavery, but this was a theme to which Marx returned repeatedly and sought to elaborate. He undertook, for example, an extensive discussion of how the work of the free worker is 'more intensive, more continuous, more flexible and skilled than that of a slave' and of how 'the transformation from serf or slave into free worker ... appears to be an improvement'. That Marx thought these appearances deceptive is indicated by his reference to 'the veiled slavery of the wage-labourers in Europe' (1976: 1032–3, 925). Two decades prior to the publication of *Capital* Marx and Engels had advanced a similar argument: 'in imagination, individuals seem freer under the dominance of the bourgeoisie than before, because their conditions of life seem accidental; in reality, of course, they are less free, because they are more subjected to the violence of things' (1974: 84). Such statements are all the more shocking because they were written against the background of the worldwide movement for the emancipation of slaves and serfs, about which Marx also wrote, hailing them as progressive developments. Marx's reference to the prospect of a 'pro-slavery rebellion' (in Nicolaievsky and Maenchen-Helfen 1976: 405) by the English ruling classes in the event of the working class of their home country achieving a peaceful social revolution was a direct parallel with the actions of the slave-owning class in precipitating the American Civil War of 1861–65.

Marx's position regarding the slave-like character of the free wage labourer was only superficially contradictory. The argument that he sought to advance was not that moves towards freer forms of labour were unwelcome, but rather that they had not gone far enough. The capitalist system needed to be understood in terms of 'all the miseries it imposes' upon the working class, to whom Marx's advice was unequivocal: 'Instead of the *conservative* motto, *"a fair day's wage for a fair day's work!"* they ought to inscribe on their banner the *revolutionary* watchword, *"Abolition of the wages system!"*.' To focus on the level of wages was to be concerned only with 'effects' rather than 'causes' (in Marx and Engels 1968: 228–9, emphases in original). Marx returned to this theme in the *Critique of the Gotha Programme* where he argued that wage-labour's slave-like character can be seen to be 'increasing in severity commensurately with the development of the social productive forces of labour, irrespective of whether the worker is then better or worse paid' (1974: 352). The quantity/quality distinction, which Marx had borrowed from logic to use in his analysis of exchange value and use value (Carver 1982: 85), was in addition pressed into service in what Lockwood calls Marx's account of 'material and moral impoverishment' (1992: ch. 11). Marx acknowledged that capitalism did not operate universally to impoverish workers in an absolute sense, but argued that even where their living standards improved, workers would still be the victims of alienation, something that they would experience 'as a process of enslavement' (1976: 990). The agenda of 'the piecemeal reformers' (1975b: 289), whose attention was focused on raising wages, was for Marx insufficiently critical of the political economy perspective because of its failure to concern itself with the broader dimensions of human freedom.

The concept of alienation figured prominently in Marx's early writings and continued to perform an important function in his later work where it stood alongside the analysis of exploitation framed in terms of the extraction of surplus value from workers. Marx's early works conveyed a strong sense of moral outrage over the way in which 'the worker is degraded to the most miserable sort of commodity' (in McLellan 1980: 25). There is a degree of continuity between such youthful statements and the more mature reflections in *Capital*, where Marx wrote of how, as the process of capital accumulation proceeds, 'the mass of misery, oppression, slavery, degradation and exploitation grows' (1976: 929). The moral force of such statements is self-evident, but by the time Marx wrote *Capital* he had shifted 'from an anthropological to a historical conception of alienation' (Mandel 1977: ch. 10). As a result of this Marx no longer needed to contrast the present lot of workers with a metaphysical and backward-looking notion of labour in its unalienated form, but could instead point to the prospects for the realisation of higher levels of freedom that were unfolding through the development of the forces of production, albeit that the transcendence of capitalism was required for this to be achieved in practice. There is thus a qualitative sense of alienation as 'loss of labour's potential for creative activity' (Barbalet 1983: 100) as well as the quantitative one in which alienation refers to the appropriation of part of the worker's product by the employer, and it is for this reason that Marx regarded the redistribution of income in the form of raising wages as insufficient to resolve the problem of alienation. Marx thus used the term 'progressive' in two senses when discussing capitalism, regarding it as not only more productive than previous modes of production but also ushering in the possibility of a greater 'degree of freedom enjoyed by non-possessing groups' (Evans 1975: 73). Although Marx could rail against the 'frauds' (1976: 694) and 'trickery' (in Weiss 1973: 181) associated with the payment by capitalists of piece rates, the more incisive moral critique of capitalism was framed in terms of its waste of human potential.

The critique of capitalism that Marx advanced contained a strong moral element without being wholly reliant on this. He noted for example that the accumulation of capital may be propelled in part by 'avarice' (1954: 133). But for all the enjoyment that he gained from poking fun at the crassness of 'Mr Moneybags', his 'slightly dim embryonic capitalist' (Wheen 2000: 308), Marx's target was a more profound one than the moral shortcomings of individual money owners. Indeed, it was one of the central shortcomings of what Marx derided as 'utopian socialism' that they lacked his 'theoretical insight into the historical process' (Fernbach 1973: 32) and thus erroneously (in his and Engels's view) were wont to 'appeal to society at large, without distinction of class' (Marx and Engels 1968: 60). To Marx and Engels this overlooked how capitalism had atomised society by reducing relations between people to the cash nexus and thereby doomed to failure schemes that could only ever achieve an 'illusory community', as opposed to the 'real community' in which 'individuals obtain their freedom in and through their association' (1974: 83). The project of replacing 'the slavery of labour' by 'free and associated labour' could not in Marx's view emerge through the introduction of 'ready-made utopias', however well meaning their architects may have been, since it was a task for the working class themselves 'to work out their own emancipation, and along with it that higher form to which present society is irresistibly tending by its own economical agencies'. In relation to the 'benevolent patronizers' who sought to bring about utopia by 'genteel' means, Marx argued that their schemes were doomed to fail 'not because the working class had given up the end aimed at by these utopians, but because they had found the real means to realize them' (Marx 1974: 253, 213, 262). Socialism would not be advanced by appeals to the better nature of people whose interests lay in the preservation of the status quo.

Various commentators have noted that there is a rich seam of irony running through Marx's works (Ball 1991; Carver 1998: ch. 4; Wheen 2000: 308). According to Manuel, 'Marx's mode of expression is ironic, often cynical' (1995: 214), as it was for example in the account in the *Communist Manifesto* of how 'the bourgeoisie ... produces ... its own grave-diggers' (Marx and Engels 1968: 46). In *Capital* Marx returned to this theme of capitalism's contradictions ushering in its downfall, arguing for example that capitalists who introduce new methods of production do so with a view to increasing their rate of profit, but in the long run as such actions are copied by their competitors this has the effect of bringing about 'a fall in the rate of profit ... wholly independent of the will of the capitalist' (1959: 265). For Elster, the development of this type of argument about the unintended consequences of actions constitutes 'Marx's central contribution to the methodology of social science' (1985: 48). Marx's suggestion was that capitalists unwittingly bring about crises at the level of the economy as a whole by engaging in actions that at an individual level appear to be nothing more than the rational pursuit of their interests, and that they would be as bemused as anyone else by the resultant situation. For the capitalist, as much as for the alienated worker, the relations of production 'assume a material shape which is independent of their control and their conscious individual action' (1976: 187). This method of tracing the unforeseen effects of people's best laid plans applied as much to the 'greedy' capitalist as it did to the well-intentioned but naïve utopian socialist.

Marx's contribution to the practice of developing a sociological argument thus has several dimensions to it. His insistence that things should not be taken at face value, that social analysis should not begin with individuals, that social relations are not fixed and that phenomena needed to be understood in the context of a constantly changing mode of production were brought together to great effect in *Capital* which has been praised for its 'systematic, comprehensive, critical, historically sophisticated and empirically substantiated' (Shanin 1984: 4) mode of presentation. Others have also praised Marx for the efforts that he made 'to write clearly and stylishly' (Kitching 1988: 6), although what for Jessop is 'forceful elegance' (1998: 24) is to others 'assertive and self-confident' (Taylor 1967: 11) and 'brusquely scornful' (Eagleton 1999: 3). In relation to Marx's notoriously harsh dismissal of those who disagreed with him, questioning either their intelligence or their motives (Schurz in McLellan 1973: 453), Hook has suggested that 'These unlovely traits of character were undoubtedly exacerbated by a life of great hardship' (1955: 48). It is fitting that Engels not only ameliorated Marx's material condition but also made a significant contribution to the development and dissemination of his ideas, albeit on occasion at the cost of oversimplification (Pampel 2000: 16). The loss of some of the complexity of Marx's ideas might be expected in a body of work constituting potentially 50 volumes (Applebaum 1988: 19), even if his style had been more straightforward. Marx's academic thoroughness, his engagement with ideas drawn from a number of different disciplines and his tendency 'to forestall every possible objection' (Berlin 1978: 2) made for texts that were often overburdened with detail and digression, but he was also capable of turns of phrase that are so memorable that they have entered the language well beyond the confines of academia. That is also what he would have wished.

List of Marx's key sociological writings

Dates of original publication are given in ( ); English translations are given in [ ]

The German Ideology (1846) (written with F. Engels) [1968]

The Communist Manifesto (1848) (written with F. Engels) [1888]

The Eighteenth Brumaire of Louis Bonaparte (1852) [1967]

Grundrisse (1939) (written as notebooks 1857–58) [1964]

A Contribution to the Critique of Political Economy (1859) [1904]

Capital: a Critique of Political Economy (three volumes 1867, 1885, 1894) [1887, 1907, 1909]

3

Emile Durkheim: sociology as the identification of social facts

Introduction and overview

Emile Durkheim was born in France on 15 April 1858 and died 59 years later on 15 November 1917, following the death of his son André the previous year in the First World War. Durkheim lived through turbulent times in French history characterised by war and political upheaval, and his life-long engagement with the question of how social order comes about was an interest that he shared with many others of his generation. The sociological perspective that he developed on the so-called 'problem of order' [which might more accurately be called 'the problem of disorder' (Lockwood 1992)] was also influenced by his experience of discrimination against his Jewish background that prevented his full integration into French society. Anti-semitism in France he took to be 'the consequence and the superficial symptom of a state of social *malaise*' (in Lukes 1975: 345), an analysis that embodied his view of the need to look for deep-seated structural causes of social phenomena. It was his view that long-term processes of social change such as industrialisation, urbanisation and secularisation were profoundly unsettling in that they undermine the established traditions by which social life is ordered. Durkheim's understanding of such shifts was framed by the idea of 'declassification' (1970: 252), and it followed from his assessment that these processes of social change were irreversible that sociology's task is to help in the establishment of new classifications of people and things that are more fitting to the modern world.

Durkheim had to struggle to gain acceptance within mainstream French society, but his status as an outsider allowed him to develop those insights that come more readily to those with a degree of detachment from what they are studying. An outsider can more easily see 'how to go underneath the symbol to the reality which it represents and gives it its true meaning' (1976: 2), as he said in the introduction to his last great

27

work, *The Elementary Forms of the Religious Life*, published in 1912. This study of aboriginal religion grew out of Durkheim's conviction that there is much to be learned from the study of social arrangements different to those which our socialisation has made familiar to us, but its arguments are quite consistent with his earlier studies of the social organisation and disorganisation of late nineteenth-century Europe. These earlier works such as *The Division of Labour in Society* and *Suicide*, published when Durkheim was still only in his thirties, embody equally well his concern to explore what can be learned by applying scientific method to the study of what we tend to take for granted. Durkheim's challenge to common sense thinking had an 'unrelieved tone of high moral seriousness' (Bellah 1973: vii) that does not make for comfortable reading. He himself acknowledged that his thinking on the subject of moral education was likely to 'have the unfortunate effect of arousing passionate argument', but such controversy had to be faced 'resolutely' (1973: 3). This stance reflected his determination to deal in demonstrable social facts rather than ungrounded presuppositions, and sociologists in many different schools of thought besides the Durkheimian one have aspired to emulate the intellectual rigour with which he pursued this agenda, even if they deviate from the guidelines set out in Durkheim's prescriptively entitled methodological manifesto *The Rules of Sociological Method*. Durkheim's conception of sociology as 'objective, specific and methodical' (1982: 35) is a contentious one, but his status as a key sociological thinker is beyond question.

The consideration of Durkheim's sociological approach follows on neatly from that of Marx. Like Marx, Durkheim was keen to get across the point that the workings of society are not immediately perceptible, and he appreciated that, as Cuzzort and King put it, 'this constitutes a major methodological problem for the sociologist' (1989: 17). Also like Marx, Durkheim sought to present his work as scientific, although the way in which he went about doing this was quite different. This can be attributed in part to the divergent conclusions that they drew about how best to get their arguments across, even though these arguments had much in common, for example in terms of the critique of approaches that took individuals as their starting point. The 'sociological view of society' (Dumont 1977: 174) that led Marx to state that 'Society does not consist of individuals' (1973a: 265) is remarkably close to Durkheim's observation that 'it is not true that society is made up only of individuals' (1970: 313). Both recognised how individuals are constituted through their relationships of interdependence with others, although Durkheim disputed Marx's conclusion that economic linkages were crucial to that process of constitution. Durkheim would have agreed with Marx's sentiment that 'human beings become individuals only through the process of history' (1973a: 496) but not with his thesis that privileged class relations over moral ones as history's driving force (Giddens 1971b: 225). The targets of Durkheim's criticisms were broader than the ideas of the political economists on which Marx concentrated his attention, although there was inevitably some overlap, notably in their shared horror of the possible descent of society into Hobbes's 'Warre of every one against every one' (1968: 185) and Spencer's 'survival of the fittest' (1969: 95). But while Durkheim also saw the need to offer an alternative future to one in which Marx's 'individualized individual' (in Dumont 1977: 163) threatened to predominate, he could not agree with the socialist programme that appeared to him 'a cry of grief, sometimes of anger' (1962: 41) rather than the outcome of reasoned sociological analysis.

The strategy of critiquing existing analyses in order to advance his own sociological arguments led Durkheim to confront a wide range of ideas. Like Marx, Durkheim engaged early on in his career with the writings of the utopian socialist Saint-Simon, although he drew rather different conclusions about their merits and shortcomings as a practical basis for social reorganisation (Gouldner 1962, 1980; Zeitlin 1987: ch. 15). Durkheim went on to focus his critique on the widely held utilitarian view that material interests bring people together and provide a basis for social order. Any social solidarity founded on shared interests was, in Durkheim's view, at best transitory; as he put it, 'if mutual interest draws men closer, it is never more than for a few moments … Self-interest is, in fact, the least constant thing in the world' (1984: 152). Mutually beneficial economic transactions may appear to be the rationale for the development of the division of labour, but the case that Durkheim advanced was that the significance of the division of labour is more moral than economic. The adoption of a sociological approach allowed Durkheim 'to consider the division of labour in a new light', by which he could claim that 'the economic services that it can render are insignificant compared with the moral effect that it produces, and its true function is to create between two or more people a feeling of solidarity' (1984: 17). The function of a social arrangement such as the division of labour will not necessarily be immediately apparent; rather, the taken-for-granted character of the social world is most obvious when its normal functioning is interrupted. The essence of Durkheim's idea is captured by Collins saying that 'the forces that hold society together are invisible. One learns about them when they are broken, like walking into a plate-glass window' (1994: 185). Durkheim's approach led him directly to the study of social problems because of the potential that they have to reveal what is routinely hidden, such as the necessary presence of trust in everyday exchanges.

Durkheim attached great importance to proceeding in a methodologically rigorous fashion, and his style of argument frequently led him to emphasise the value of attending to 'the facts'. He was particularly critical of thinkers whose method of enquiry was speculative, and on this basis dismissed the idea of the social contract 'because it bears no relation to the facts' (1984: 151). His investigation into *Suicide* was designed to demonstrate the value of empirically grounded argument, and this study 'is commonly regarded as the first "scientific" work in sociology' (Nisbet 1970: 61). *Suicide* was the product of almost a decade of concentrated work, during which time Durkheim devoted his energies not only to amassing and analysing data but also to the deployment of this material to best effect in support of the general position that he held concerning the changing social order. Durkheim's account of contemporary society portrayed the emergence of individualism neither as an aberration (as it was for conservative critics of modernity) nor as the triumph of individuals asserting their independence (as it was for *laissez-faire* liberals). Instead, Durkheim treated individualism as an expected product of social evolution that nevertheless required certain controlling mechanisms to be in place if it were not to be accompanied by social problems such as the state of normlessness that he termed 'anomie'. Durkheim had argued in *The Division of Labour in Society* that 'liberty ... is the product of regulation' (1984: 320), and it followed that social forces could equally well be drawn upon to explain observable patterns in the suicide rate. To Durkheim it would have been no more than superficially paradoxical that 'what looks like a highly individual and personal phenomenon is explicable through the social structure' (Simpson 1970: 10), and it was his purpose to marshal the evidence necessary to demonstrate the veracity of this perspective.

Durkheim's practice of engaging with his audience by presenting them with paradoxes emerges at various points in his work. To state as he did that 'in a contract not everything is contractual' (1984: 158) requires the reader to work through the argument being made that contracts will be honoured only in a culture in which this behaviour is already the norm, backed up by legal and moral sanctions against people who transgress it. Elsewhere he opined that 'crime is normal' (1982: 99), and such statements have prompted Parkin to observe how Durkheim was fond of employing 'methodological shock-tactics of stating propositions designed to subvert everyday assumptions'. Parkin goes on to sound a note of caution about how 'Durkheim often seemed to operate under the conviction that any argument or thesis which flew in the face of common sense was thereby endowed with scientific status' (1992: 8), and it is certainly the case that the scientific credentials of Durkheim's approach have been subjected to intense scrutiny. To the extent that it failed to live up to the full rigours of the guidelines set out in *The Rules of Sociological Method*, Durkheim's *Suicide* can be considered a problematic study, but not all commentators regard its methodological shortcomings as fatally damaging to the case that it advances. According to Brown, Durkheim's argument remains 'true *because* it makes a good story' (1987: 95, emphasis in original), and in his view it is on these grounds that it should be assessed. By taking what 'everybody knows' (Durkheim 1984: 16) and showing it to be wanting, Durkheim succeeded in challenging set ways of thinking by contrasting them to new and counter-intuitive ones, even if his supporting evidence amounted to less than the compelling proof that his rhetoric suggested.

The distinctiveness of sociological explanations

When tracing the history of sociological thought it is useful to bear in mind that, as Turner puts it, 'Societies face two contradictory principles. They are organized around issues of scarcity, which result in exclusionary structures ... but they must also secure social solidarity' (1999a: 263). By the time Durkheim was writing, the question of 'who gets what?' had been the subject of extensive discussion by political economists and in the critique of their analyses produced by Marx and others. There was an even longer history to the debates about the bases of social order and cohesion that had been a fundamental concern of political philosophers from the ancient Greeks onwards. To make an impact on this intellectual terrain Durkheim needed to pursue a bold agenda. He did this by an 'imperialistic advocacy of sociology as the key social scientific discipline' (Giddens 1978: 15), arguing that the discussion of the central issues of scarcity and solidarity needed to be undertaken together, and that sociology provided the analytical framework within which this could be done. This stance inevitably brought him into conflict not only with contemporary thinkers in the political economy and philosophy traditions but also with prominent figures in psychology as well as representatives of other sociological perspectives than his own. His single-mindedness and dislike of intellectual 'showiness' (Pampel 2000: 47) contributed to the development of a style of argumentation that was 'highly polemical' (Lukes 1975: 34) in its treatment of rival positions. This, together with a personality described by some as 'austere' (Pickering 1984: 20) and 'rather difficult and humorless' (Madge 1970: 14), always made it likely that his ideas would be surrounded by controversy.

Durkheim's choice of subject for his first book was made deliberately in order to take his argument onto territory that appeared more favourable to his opponents than to him, as this would make a successful outcome all the more convincing. The division of labour had been written about extensively following the publication over a century earlier of Smith's *The Wealth of Nations*, but Durkheim stated that this literature was by and large inconsequential: 'since Adam Smith the theory of the division of labour has made very little progress'. This uncanny echo of Marx's judgement (discussed above in Chapter 2) might have been expected to lead Durkheim into a similar line of attack, but it was from quite a different angle that he developed his critique of attempts 'to justify, after the event, preconceived sentiments and personal impressions' (1984: 7, 6). Rather than follow through the labour theory of value to its logical conclusions and with mathematical precision as Marx had attempted to do, the approach that Durkheim preferred measured the value of things in terms of their usefulness to society: 'it is not the amount of labour put into a thing which makes its value; it is the way in which the value of this thing is assessed by the society' (1992: 216; see also 1984: 317). Durkheim thus differed from Marx by emphasising the moral dimension of his criticisms of class-based market relationships, in particular their 'instrumentalism, exploitative contracts and relationships, [their] system of degraded and desocialized labour, and denial ... of opportunity to develop and flourish' (Watts Miller 1996: 9). The declaration with which *The Division of Labour in Society* opened, that 'This book is above all an attempt to treat the facts of moral life according to the methods of the positive sciences' (1984: xxv), signalled this intention. Doing so would have been 'startling and even dramatic' (Bierstedt 1966: 33) to his audience, who were unaccustomed to this way of thinking.

The distinction between appearance and reality that Marx deployed to such effect at the beginning of *Capital* was also used by Durkheim at the start of *The Division of Labour in Society* in order to challenge his audience's presuppositions. His remark that 'At first sight nothing appears easier than to determine the role of the division of labour' worked as a prelude to raising questions about the conventional account in which increased productivity 'is the necessary condition for the intellectual and material development of societies'. Durkheim's mention of how 'The average number of suicides and crimes of every description ... seems to increase as the arts, science and industry progress' (1984: 12) served immediately to cast doubt on glib assertions relating to the benefits of civilisation and progress, and raised the prospect that the economic advantages afforded by the division of labour might have to be set against its morally damaging effects or, as Durkheim expressed it, 'the wounds that it inflicts' (1984: 15). Having voiced these concerns, Durkheim went on to argue that the construction of a balance sheet with economic advantages set against moral disadvantages would overlook the moral advantages that the division of labour brings by promoting a new form of social solidarity characterised by interdependence. Durkheim identified the role usually attached to the division of labour as 'to endow societies with luxury', but much more important than this, he suggested, was its pivotal contribution to 'the cohesion of societies'. The objective of the book was nothing less than to discover whether, contrary to appearances, 'the real function of the division of labour' (1984: 23, 24) was indeed the promotion of social solidarity.

Durkheim recognised that in order to make the case that the division of labour was fundamentally a moral phenomenon he would need to engage critically with several alternative perspectives. Economists were open to criticism because of their view that 'The whole of economic life' can be explained by 'the desire for wealth' (Durkheim 1982: 127), that is, their assumption of economic rationality whereby individuals were seen to be 'motivated solely by egoistic desires' (Thompson 1982: 51). Durkheim found this type of argument unsatisfactory because people have the capacity to behave according to the principles of justice rather than those of utility, and thus may act altruistically for the benefit of others rather than pursuing their narrow individual interests. In addition, Durkheim regarded it as inappropriate to start out analysis from the individual, since individuals are very much social products, and are shaped by the social structures into which they have been born. This point also informed Durkheim's critique of psychology, which he characterised as 'the science of the individual'. Sociology as Durkheim conceived it was concerned with society, which required a quite different approach because 'society is not the mere sum of individuals, but the system formed by their association represents a specific reality with its own characteristics'. If Durkheim was right that the whole of a social group such as a crowd is greater than the sum of the individuals that make it up then it could be said to follow that 'The group thinks, feels and acts wholly otherwise than its members would do if they were isolated. If therefore we begin by studying these members separately, we will understand nothing of what is taking place in the group.' The insistence that 'Sociology is not a corollary of psychology' (1982: 135, 129, 127) was, as Poggi (2000: 33) notes, a curt assertion of Durkheim's belief that his discipline merited attention in its own right and was not subordinate to its rivals.

There is a strong echo of Marx's ideas in the stance that Durkheim took in relation to consciousness. Durkheim's remark that 'social life must be explained not by the conception of it formed by those who participate in it, but by profound causes which escape their consciousness' (1982: 171) reflected his belief that sociologists needed to go beyond 'events that lie at the surface of social life' in order to study 'the less obvious points at the base of it – internal causes and impersonal, hidden forces that move individuals and collectivities'. Sociology practised in such a way promised to be 'a profound innovation' (1964a: 373), not least because it held out the prospect of revealing 'a reality different from the individual's reality'. For Durkheim the sociologist was akin to a detective: 'As the sociologist penetrates into the social world he should be conscious that he is penetrating into the unknown. ... He must hold himself ready to make discoveries which will surprise and disconcert him' (1982: 41, 37). Durkheim was aware that such a characterisation could also be made of the philosopher, but his project of establishing sociology as a distinctive academic discipline led him to claim that 'the sociological method ... is independent of all philosophy'. Unlike the philosopher, the sociologist 'must abandon generalities and enter into the detailed examination of facts' (1982: 159, 160). Durkheim's criticisms of philosophy were thus primarily of particular tendencies, notably those that had influenced earlier sociologists such as Comte and Spencer to deal in 'unsubstantiated generalization' (Thompson 1982: 31). As LaCapra notes, Durkheim's position was not 'antiphilosophical' (1985: 4), but he rejected the style of 'philosophical meditation' (in Alexander 1982: 212) that dealt in presuppositions and speculative hypotheses rather than facts. His warning about the danger of sociology 'degenerating into pure erudition' (1982: 35) echoed this sentiment.

The ambitiousness of Durkheim's claims regarding sociology's potential to inform debate about contemporary concerns, and the aggressiveness with which this case was advanced, drew extensive attention to his work. According to Alexander, 'When *The Division of Labour in Society* appeared in France in 1893 it was a major intellectual event' (1982: 211), and Durkheim himself noted about the *Rules* that 'When this book first appeared, it aroused some fairly lively controversy' (1982: 34). The same has been noted about the reception of *Suicide* (Giddens 1971a) and of Durkheim's last book, *The Elementary Forms of the Religious Life* (Nisbet 1976: xi). Durkheim's robust criticisms of other disciplines, including philosophy for its 'literary and unscientific character' (Lukes 1975: 106), obliged him to demonstrate the superiority of his approach, including its consistency with supporting evidence. Durkheim's family background would have made him familiar with 'the old Jewish proverb, "for example is no proof" ' (Bell and Newby 1971: 80) which appears in *Suicide* as 'an illustration is not a proof' (1970: 35), and yet the arguments that he advanced in support of his case for treating the division of labour as the basis of solidarity and cohesion in modern societies were presented as nothing less than 'proofs'. The boldness of this position was highlighted by Durkheim's acknowledgement that 'social solidarity is a wholly moral phenomenon which by itself is not amenable to exact observation and especially not to measurement'. His solution to this problem was to treat the law as a 'visible symbol' of social solidarity, 'a form that we can grasp'. The distinction that he then claimed to have discovered between the two types of law, 'repressive' and 'restitutive', provided the foundation for his identification of two types of solidarity, 'mechanical' and 'organic' (1984: 24, 27, 29, 31, 68), the former found where people are united by their similarities and the latter where their common bonds arise from the division of labour.

Several things can be noted about Durkheim's presentation of his case in *The Division of Labour in Society*. One is that his understanding of proof led him to seek evidence that was the product of systematic comparison. As he set out in *The Rules of Sociological Method*, rigour forbids researchers from simply citing cases that fit an argument: 'Nothing is proved when, as happens so often, one is content to demonstrate by a greater or lesser number of examples that in isolated cases the facts have varied according to the hypothesis. From these sporadic and fragmentary correlations no general conclusions can be drawn.' Since Durkheim held that 'To illustrate an idea is not to prove it', the demonstration of scientific laws required the collection and analysis of evidence covering 'an adequate range' (1982: 155), ideally relating to several societies and to different time periods. Second, it is apparent that Durkheim's search for the sorts of evidence best suited to revealing the 'underlying logic in the world' (Watts Miller 1996: 3) was still ongoing at this point. His preparedness in separate passages of the book to cite data relating to skull sizes in support of the argument that men and women and people of different 'races' necessarily have different relationships to the division of labour has rightly been questioned, not least because these data fit more comfortably into a biological analysis than a sociological one (Lehmann 1994; Sydie 1987). This relates to a third point, that in *The Division of Labour in Society* Durkheim was still constrained by the terminology of mechanical and organic solidarity which he had adopted as a deliberate inversion of Tönnies' characterisation of traditional societies as 'organic' and modern societies 'as a mechanical aggregate' (Durkheim 1972: 146). Over time, Durkheim came to be increasingly mindful of the limitations that he had already noted at the outset of his career of this organic analogy, likening society to a natural organism (Thompson 1982: 35). That said, his 'fascination with medical metaphors' (LaCapra 1985: 7) was still a prominent feature of the work generally regarded as the exemplar of his approach, *Suicide*.

Social facts and the power of logical argument

The sober tone of Durkheim's work matched his sense of the gravity of his subject matter. In a lecture series delivered in 1902–03 he declared that 'history records no crisis as serious as that in which European societies have been involved for more than a century' (1973: 101). Among the many social problems that accompanied the emergence of urban, industrial societies, the rising levels of suicide were a matter of particular concern to many commentators, and suicide thus provided a suitable focus for his close attention in relation to debates about 'social pathology' and the 'remedies' for these ills (Durkheim 1970: 361, 37). It offered to Durkheim the opportunity 'to demonstrate that the social sciences can examine an important social issue, on which other people have philosophized for a long time, and can show by the systematic presentation of existing facts that it is possible to arrive at useful conclusions which will help with practical proposals for future action' (Madge 1970: 16). Suicide understandably prompts strong emotions among people whose lives it touches, and Lukes notes that the suicide of one of Durkheim's close friends 'clearly affected him deeply' (1975: 191). Lukes then identifies a number of more dispassionate reasons that underpinned Durkheim's decision to focus on this subject. Extensive statistical data were available that could be deployed to illustrate the value of thinking in terms of the 'social facts' that Durkheim had pronounced needed to be treated as 'things' (1982: 60) if the distinctive contribution of sociology to the study of society were to be realised. *Suicide* promised to prove the existence of 'realities external to the individual' (1970: 37–8). In addition, the apparently individual character of suicide seemingly allocated the subject to the province of psychology, and therefore 'explaining differential suicide rates sociologically would be a singular triumph' (Lukes 1975: 194). The very implausibility in common sense terms of the argument that suicide rates have social causes made it an appropriate choice of topic for Durkheim's purposes.

The structure of the book has a compelling logic to it; it is 'a classical piece of sociological reasoning' (Ray 1999: 98). In the preface, Durkheim asserted that detailed investigations of problems that are 'clear-cut' are superior to the production of 'large and abrupt generalizations [that] are not capable of any sort of proof'. Such generalities might be 'brilliant', but they are also 'vague' and cannot lead to the discovery of 'real laws' of social organisation in the way that more empirically informed studies can. Referring to the 'maladjustment' of contemporary European societies, Durkheim cautioned against believing that 'a general condition can only be explained with the aid of generalities'; rather, he expressed confidence that the detailed analysis of suicide statistics would reinforce his own general argument that 'the individual is dominated by a moral reality greater than himself: namely, collective reality' (1970: 35, 38, 37, 38). These data included the analysis (delegated to Mauss, Durkheim's nephew and assistant) of 26,000 cases of suicide. Having used the preface to set out his ambition, Durkheim then set out to develop 'a logically consistent and complete theory of suicide' (Taylor 1982: 7). He adopted as his definition of suicide '*all cases of death resulting directly or indirectly from a positive or negative act of the victim himself, which he knows will produce this result*' (1970: 44, emphasis in original) partly for pragmatic reasons. This way of proceeding allowed him to use data already collected by others, for, as Madge observes, 'it was of no value for Durkheim to evolve a perfect definition that ruled out the use of existing statistics' (1970: 18), even if by following this route he inadvertently highlighted the difficulty of keeping the provinces of sociology and psychology entirely separate.

Durkheim was at pains to emphasise that his interest lay in the suicide rate for particular populations and not in the distinctive features of individual cases. When examined at the level of whole societies, suicide statistics revealed a remarkable constancy over time, and it was this phenomenon to which Durkheim wanted to draw attention as a social fact. The total number of suicides 'is not simply a sum of individual units, a collective total, but is itself a new fact *sui generis*'. Starting out by citing figures for six countries over a 30-year period, Durkheim concluded that year on year changes were remarkably small, even 'almost invariable'. When looked at as suicide rates, that is the numbers per million inhabitants taking their own lives in any one year, and averaging these out over different periods, to screen out 'temporary and accidental causes', what emerged from Durkheim's analysis was that within each of the 11 countries included in his third table of data, 'the variations observed ... become almost negligible'. Together with the related observations about the rates being markedly and consistently higher in some countries than in others, these findings are so remarkable as to demand explanation. If as the evidence indicated 'Each society is predisposed to contribute a definite quota of voluntary deaths' then logically, Durkheim reasoned, 'The phenomenon to be explained can depend only on extra-social causes of broad generality or on causes expressly social' (1970: 46, 51, 48). Having set out the problem to be investigated in this way, he then proceeded by the process of 'argument by elimination' (Lukes 1975: 32) to consider the various possibilities, beginning with the extra-social factors.

Durkheim drew on existing thinking to identify four different extra-social factors that might be hypothesised to cause the predictable patterns in suicide rates that he had shown were incontrovertibly present in the statistics. Devoting a chapter to the detailed investigation of each, on the grounds that it would be unscientific for them to be dismissed without due consideration, he focused in turn on mental illness, race and heredity, climate and imitation. In each case the evidence was examined and found wanting. Durkheim's judgement was unequivocal once the evidence had been considered, as for example was the situation in relation to the idea that a temperate climate promoted a high suicide rate, about which he commented 'One need dwell no further on an hypothesis proved by nothing and disproved by so many facts.' Likewise he dispatched the common sense suggestion that suicide rates might be explained by the harshness of the weather in winter months because 'statistics have definitely refuted it', adding laconically the observation that 'Man prefers to abandon life when it is least difficult.' About the proposition that suicide rates reflected the propensity of people to copy the behaviour of others Durkheim was scathing, because it had 'merely been stated as an aphorism, resting on vaguely metaphysical considerations' (1970: 106, 107, 142). Without empirical proof it and the other extra-social causes considered remained in Durkheim's view mere dogma, and unworthy of further attention.

Having considered and discounted these various extra-social causes of variations in suicide rates, the way was clear for Durkheim to make his case that the most convincing explanation is one framed in terms of social causes. Doubts might be expressed about this general mode of proceeding because it could be argued that 'the rejected explanations may not include all possible candidates' (Lukes 1975: 32) and that Durkheim had chosen for consideration only those that were most obviously flawed in order to enhance the impressiveness of his own position. In this instance, however, the extra-social factors considered by Durkheim did reflect the thinking prevalent at the time that he sought to challenge. Prior to Durkheim's work it was a basic assumption 'that reality is made up of particular phenomena like climates, racial groups, diets, poverty and wealth' which could each be correlated with suicide, and it was a radical departure from this perspective to propose that researchers should look beyond such individual influences, and also beyond people's states of mind, to 'some *third* entity called "society"; an entity that was in no way reducible to ... such "factors" ' (Johnson *et al.* 1984: 153, 154, emphasis in original). Durkheim's view that society exists over and above the individuals who make it up was the key presupposition embodied in his definition of social facts as things that are *'capable of exerting over the individual an external constraint'* (1982: 59, emphasis in original), and it was this case that the remaining parts of *Suicide* were devoted to establishing and elaborating.

The demonstration of Durkheim's argument is not as straightforward as might be expected; as Gane has noted, 'Durkheim prepared some surprises for his readers, especially sociologists trained on the *Rules*' (1988: 49–50). Chief among these surprises is Durkheim's admission that the limitations of the data that exist on suicide mean that the normal method of proceeding, from the study of the manifestation of a phenomenon to the identification of its cause, needs to be reversed. Because the suicide statistics with which he was working generally contained insufficient detail about the state of mind of those people who had taken their own lives, Durkheim argued that it was necessary 'to determine the social types of suicide by classifying them not directly by their preliminarily described characteristics, but by the causes which produce them'. The rationale that he offered for the adoption of this 'reverse method', that it was 'the only fitting one for the special problem that we have set ourselves' (1970: 146–7, 147), raises doubts about the wisdom of selecting the subject of suicide to demonstrate the power of the approach set out in *The Rules*. The fact that Madge describes the issue as 'a very familiar research problem' (1970: 31) does not provide a full defence of Durkheim's procedure, but merely suggests that the investigation of other topics would also have been hindered by the evidence not being available in the form most suited to Durkheim's purposes.

Durkheim's divergence from the methodological guidelines set out in the *Rules* in his study of suicide is not necessarily fatally damaging to the development of his case. As Lukes points out, it is possible to argue that 'What matters is not where the explanation comes from, but rather whether it is superior to all other available explanations.' Even so, the classification of types of suicide advanced by Durkheim was derived by his having '*identified* types of suicide by means of their alleged causes' (Lukes 1975: 202, emphasis in original); that is, it started off by assuming to be true propositions that he was seeking to demonstrate, that suicide rates reflected states of anomie, egoism, altruism and fatalism within populations. However 'ingenious and brilliant' (Zeitlin 1987: 260) Durkheim's case was, it was not 'scientific' in the way that his readers had been led to believe it would be, although it is easy to be carried along by the sheer force of the way in which the ideas are presented. The 'remarkable capacity for sophisticated, persuasive argument' (Poggi 2000: 5) for which Durkheim is famous is readily apparent in his account of how societies constrain individuals. This constraint was argued to operate in two ways, by integrating them into a common set of purposes and ideals that generates in them a sense of belonging to the collectivity, and by keeping in check their desires and aspirations which require regulation because of their potentially limitless character. Durkheim claimed that when societies are functioning normally integration and regulation are appropriately balanced, but that this 'state of balance' (Lee and Newby 1983: 223) can be upset in any one of four directions: too little or too much integration, and too little or too much regulation. In the extreme the loss of balance in society can result in an increase in suicide rates, suicides termed egoistic where there is too little integration and altruistic where there is too much, anomic where there is too little regulation and fatalistic where there is too much.

Durkheim was particularly concerned with the two types of suicide reflecting the lack of constraint in modern societies, egoistic and anomic. Altruistic suicide did have a separate chapter devoted to it, but a person giving up their life for the good of the group was treated by Durkheim as typically a phenomenon of pre-modern societies in which this expression of duty was more common, while fatalistic suicide was regarded as even rarer in modern societies and mentioned simply in a footnote, considered only 'for completeness' sake'. Durkheim treated egoistic suicide as the outcome of 'excessive individuation' leading to a person becoming 'detached from society'. He reasoned that religion might be expected to protect people from vulnerability to suicide by providing a strong sense of collective identity, but showed that even cursory inspection of the evidence revealed a striking picture: 'in purely Catholic countries like Spain, Portugal, Italy, suicide is very little developed, while it is at its maximum in Protestant countries, in Prussia, Saxony, Denmark'. These data Durkheim interpreted as indicators not of differences in religious ideas but of variation between countries in the number and strength of the ties binding an individual into the wider society, these being fewer and weaker in Protestant lands. In general, 'religion has a prophylactic effect upon suicide', but this is more marked in Catholicism and Judaism than in Protestantism. Durkheim then proceeded to make parallel cases about the greater protection from suicide found among populations who are better integrated into what he termed 'domestic society' and 'political society' (1970: 276, 217, 152, 169, 208), for example people sharing a household with several others and members of societies undergoing challenges such as wars that engender a strong sense of collective purpose.

In relation to anomic suicide there is an apparent continuity between the discussion and his earlier analysis of the anomic division of labour in *The Division of Labour in Society*, but Durkheim's understanding of the concept of anomie had evolved in the interim (Parsons 1968: 334). In *Suicide*, Durkheim used anomie to expose the tendency for unlimited aspirations to produce unhappiness. What he referred to as a 'fever' (1970: 256) of the imagination, and elsewhere called 'the malady of infiniteness' (1973: 43), was explored in detail to advance the case that suicide resulted where people's expectations exceeded their ability to fulfil them. He supported this argument by pointing out that, contrary to what might be expected, suicide rates increased during periods of booming prosperity as well as during times of economic downturn, that is, whenever there are 'disturbances of the collective order'. The corollary of the finding that suicide rates increase with prosperity and are highest among the better off ('the possessors of most comfort suffer most') was the equally unexpected situation whereby people who are accustomed to being poor have low rates of suicide. Because people are unsettled by sudden changes, those who are used to having little money show that 'Poverty protects against suicide'. The same theme of the desirability of 'established classification' (1970: 246, 257, 254, 253) emerged from Durkheim's analysis of family relationships, where he argued that widowhood and divorce deprive individuals of familiar arrangements and make them statistically more vulnerable to suicide than are their married counterparts.

Durkheim concluded *Suicide* by discussing at some length the practical consequences of his analysis. It followed from the language of social pathology that permeates Durkheim's work that he saw himself as 'the doctor who lucidly diagnosed the ills of society and prescribed rational remedies' (LaCapra 1985: 7). The re-establishment of balance to social relationships by a return to past social arrangements he regarded as impractical as well as undesirable. Traditional religious, family, community and state forms had been irreversibly eroded with the coming of modern society, Durkheim argued, so the solution was not to try to restore them but rather to foster new social arrangements that had the potential to 'have the same effect' of providing people with the constraint that they needed. In Durkheim's view neither economic relations nor the state were sufficient to unite people in the positive way required by modern conditions in which the division of labour had developed to such prominence. In the light of this, Durkheim reasoned that 'the occupational group or corporation' was the only realistic candidate 'to give the individual a setting, to draw him out of his state of moral isolation' and to place social solidarity on a sound foundation through the generation of 'a new sort of moral discipline' (1970: 378, 379, 383). What was required, in the language of *The Division of Labour in Society*, was something that would replace the 'common consciousness' (1984: 121) or collective conscience of shared beliefs that religion and other traditional institutions had provided as the foundation of mechanical solidarity. He was careful to note that he had not sought 'to draw up in advance a plan anticipating everything' (1970: 392), but was rather attempting the more modest objective of sketching the outlines of what logically needed to be done and encouraging action in that direction. It was not the task of sociologists to be politicians, in Durkheim's view; rather, they 'must be *advisers, educators*' (in Bellah 1973: 59, emphasis in original), affecting the policy process at one remove through their publications and lectures.

Sociological paradoxes

Almost a century after his death, Durkheim's work continues to generate fierce debate. The frequency with which this work has been summarily dismissed led Stedman Jones to lament 'The gap between Durkheim's thought and what has been made of him subsequently in the social sciences' (2001: vii). Several scholars have sought to identify 'the other Durkheim' (Jones 1997), and to rescue 'the radical Durkheim' (Gane 1992; Pearce 1989) from those commentators who have presented him as a conservative. The conventional treatment of Durkheim as a positivist has also been widely questioned. Given the position attributed to him by critics of his reliance on statistical data, it is surprising to find Durkheim's acknowledgement in *Suicide* of the limitations of 'what are called statistics of the motives of suicides' because they 'are actually statistics of the opinions concerning such motives of officials, often of lower officials' (1970: 148).

As Craib (1997: 32) has pointed out, the suspicion is that such critics have misunderstood what Durkheim was trying to do, in particular in relation to his argument that everyone within society (including officials) is more or less subject to the norms embodied in its 'collective conscience'. This idea of 'shared thinking' (Stedman Jones 2001: 86) had been adopted and developed in *The Division of Labour in Society*, but it continued to be a crucial part of Durkheim's analytical framework which formed a complex totality that requires dedicated reading to grasp (Gane 1988: 3–5). Given such observations, LaCapra's claim that 'Durkheim is one of the best known and one of the least understood major social thinkers' (1985: 5) can be endorsed.

Various reasons might be advanced to explain this paradoxical situation. One is that Durkheim was fond of employing paradoxes in his writing, even though his reading of the American pragmatist James led him to conclude that the use of paradox did not necessarily help to clarify arguments: 'He expresses ideas which would be more easily acceptable if they were expressed in a different way. ... and one ends up wondering whether one perhaps agrees with him' (1983: 10). It is instructive that Durkheim commented in the preface to the *Rules* that 'If the search for paradox is the mark of the sophist, to flee from it when the facts demand it is that of a mind that possesses neither courage nor faith in science' (1982: 31). In other words, reality often appears contradictory, and the application of 'logical understanding' in this situation Durkheim acknowledged to be 'disconcerting for us' (1976: 237). The paradoxical argument developed in *Suicide* about the dangers of unlimited aspirations makes sense when it is recalled that Durkheim had argued in *The Division of Labour in Society* that 'liberty ... is the product of regulation' (1984: 320). Other examples exist in Durkheim's work of what appears to be a 'topsy-turvy vision of the relationship between the individual and society', at least when considered 'from the individualistic point of view' (Campbell 1981: 148). His first book also highlighted the non-contractual elements of contracts and the roots of modern solidarity in individualism and social differences, and Durkheim retained the use of paradox in his armoury of presentational devices throughout his career. The very idea of 'mythological truths' appears to be a contradiction in terms, but Durkheim's later work revealed not only their possibility but their necessity. Mythological truths Durkheim contrasted with scientific truths, but he argued against treating them as 'mere illusions' because they 'have some connection with reality'. Indeed, he suggested, 'Mythological truths have been, for those societies that have believed in them, the conditions necessary for their existence. Communal life in fact presupposes common ideas and intellectual unanimity' (1983: 86–7). To have any chance of living together successfully, we need to speak the same language both literally and metaphorically.

Durkheim's use of paradox may have contributed to his work being hard to understand, at least on first acquaintance, but a related reason that made it 'hard to follow' (Bryant 1976: 71) is that for many people his arguments were hard to accept because of their underlying moral position. Durkheim's logic led him to the conclusion that secularisation required the replacement of traditional religious beliefs by a modern equivalent that would perform the function of binding people together, but his identification of 'the worship of the dignity of the human person' whereby 'the individual becomes the object of a sort of religion' was to some people sacrilegious. This 'cult of the person and individual dignity' or 'cult of the individual' was central to Durkheim's key question, 'How does it come about that the individual, whilst becoming more autonomous, depends ever more closely on society?' (1984: 122, 333, 338, xxx), because without it there would be only the shallow individualism associated with the utilitarian ideas of 'Spencer and the economists'. Durkheim insisted that a society in which individual differences were able to flourish needed more than 'that egoistic cult of the self for which utilitarian individualism has been rightly criticized'; it required that the individual be 'placed in the ranks of sacrosanct objects'. The moral order of modern societies necessarily generated the 'cult of man', the 'religion of the individual', because respect for the individual was at the heart of the collective conscience among people who otherwise would have 'nothing in common' and thus be vulnerable to social disorganisation as 'everyone tends to go off in his own direction' (in Bellah 1973: 44, 45, 46, 49, 53, 51). Durkheim's quest to promote scientific understanding of the god-like character ascribed to the individual in the modern moral order appeared not only paradoxical (Watts Miller 1996: 247) but also offensive to the representatives of traditional religious morality (Aron 1970: 106). To many of his critics Durkheim resembled a 'secular pope' (Jones 1986: 20).

Durkheim's very public intervention in the debate over the Dreyfus Affair in which the anti-Semitism of the French establishment had been exposed was interesting for the way that he went about advancing his argument by 'providing not simply an account of modern individualism but rather a defense of it' (Kivisto 1998: 104). The opportunity to advance public debate about racism was not taken up (Lehmann 1994: 99), nor did Durkheim see any point in further 'discussion of facts' because what was needed to rescue the debate from being 'bogged down in repetitiveness' was discussion at 'the level of principles'. For Durkheim, reasoning had the potential to win the argument against opponents whose convictions were merely 'improvised'. His statement that 'our adversaries are strong only because of our own weakness' (in Bellah 1973: 43, 57) revealed a cast of mind confident that the dedicated assertion of reasoned arguments would prevail. The method of proceeding by what Durkheim termed a 'thought-experiment' (in Stedman Jones 2001: 219) was employed at various times in his work, as for example when he invited the readers of the *Rules* to 'Imagine a community of saints in an exemplary and perfect monastery.' The purpose of doing so was to reinforce the point about the normality of crime, 'a conclusion which is apparently somewhat paradoxical' but which can be shown to make sense by pointing out that deviance would be present even in such a community of saints: 'crime as such will be unknown, but faults that appear venial to the ordinary person will arouse the same scandal as does normal crime in ordinary consciences' (1982: 100, 98, 100). The search for timeless moral absolutes was shown to be doomed to failure by this simple exercise.

The normality of deviance was not a message likely to endear Durkheim to an audience unaccustomed to thinking in this way, and Durkheim himself admitted being 'disconcerted' by the idea 'for a long time' (1982: 98–9). Durkheim's way of distinguishing between 'normal' and 'abnormal' or 'pathological' forms of the division of labour and of other social phenomena has rightly been questioned, not least because it 'assumed an identity between the "normal", the ideal and the about to happen'. Durkheim was led to use the distinction partly by his 'fundamentally dichotomizing temperament', but also by his 'evolutionary optimism' (Lukes 1975: 177, 30, 174). As Aron has noted, the normal/pathological distinction 'is related to Durkheim's projects for reform' because it was a device whereby science's contribution to social improvement could be highlighted. The organic analogy allows 'pathological' phenomena to be designated as in need of attention, while 'If a phenomenon is normal, we have no grounds for seeking to eliminate it, even if it shocks us morally.' Provocative arguments such as this allow Durkheim's style of presentation to be characterised as 'calculated to cause an uproar', which they did. This and the 'difficulty of entering into Durkheim's way of thinking' (1970: 76, 106, 66) that Aron and others have reported encountering go at least some way towards explaining why there is no consensus about his ideas.

Durkheim's work presents us with several paradoxes besides those that he deliberately advanced. One is that, according to Pampel (2000: 46), Durkheim's preference was for co-operation in academic endeavour, but he was no stranger to expounding and defending his views through forcefully expressed criticisms of others, and even if as Lukes notes 'He did not ... enjoy these polemics' (1975: 303), they were on occasion characterised by 'intolerance and unfairness toward his rivals and opponents' (Poggi 2000: 5). A second paradox is that he was concerned about 'the danger of "eloquence" replacing "vigour and method" ' (Stedman Jones 2001: 220) but that his own writings have often been commended for their eloquence; Runciman, for example, applauds Durkheim's 'elegance and cogency of argument' (1969: 36). That said, not everyone is engaged by his style of presentation. Jones has complained that Durkheim is 'utterly humorless' (1999: 308) and devoid of irony, while LaCapra has compared his work unfavourably to that of Marx on the grounds that 'Durkheim rarely displayed a telling sense of the concrete with which to bring to life … his analytical models and statistical surveys' (1985: 23). To illustrate the point, it can be noted how Durkheim's figure referred to simply as 'an industrialist' has much less rhetorical impact than Marx's 'Mr Moneybags' (Lemert 1995: 24). A final paradox is that the logic of Durkheim's position on the division of labour led him to anticipate the development of a degree of academic specialisation that he was not himself constrained by in a career that was remarkably broad in terms of the topics with which he engaged. His advice to 'would-be disciples to choose a circumscribed area of enquiry' (LaCapra 1985: 2) may well have envisaged these specialist parts being brought together as part of 'a totalising sociology' (Gane 1988: 108), but even without these other contributions Durkheim's work amply demonstrates how the whole is greater than the sum of the individual parts.

List of Durkheim's key sociological writings
Dates of original publication are given in ( ); English translations are given in [ ]

The Division of Labour in Society (1893) [1933]

The Rules of Sociological Method (1895) [1938]

Suicide (1897) [1951]

Moral Education (1925) (given as lectures 1902–03) [1961]

The Elementary Forms of the Religious Life (1912) [1915]

Professional Ethics and Civic Morals (1950) (given as lectures 1890–1912) [1957]

4

Max Weber: sociology as the science of interpretive understanding

Introduction and overview

Max Weber was a contemporary of Durkheim. He was born on 21 April 1864 and died aged 56, of pneumonia, on 14 June 1920. He lived in Germany and was fervently nationalistic, but was at the same time fascinated by social arrangements in other countries and studied them extensively in order to produce writings in comparative sociology that have never been matched in terms of scope or complexity. He was particularly struck by what he learned from his visit to the USA in 1904 that followed a prolonged period of mental illness that had prevented him from working for several years. The breadth of his intellectual interests is indicated by the range of issues that captured his attention during his 3-month spell in America; according to Gerth and Mills, these included 'labor problems, the immigrant question, problems of political management – especially of municipal government – all expressions of the "capitalist spirit", the Indian question and its administration, the plight of the South, and the Negro problem' (1970: 16). Aspects of these experiences were fed into his (and, arguably, sociology's) most famous work, *The Protestant Ethic and the Spirit of Capitalism* (1905), in which he developed a characteristically controversial line of argument about the contribution of religion in the making of the modern economic order. His training as a historian gave him a profound sense of the distinctiveness of the modern world and of the seemingly irresistible force with which it was developing. His key concept of 'rationalization' captured his ambiguous feelings about this process which simultaneously impressed him by its power to transform social and economic relations yet troubled him because of the threat that it posed to the values that he held dear.

The visit to America provided Weber with a stark sense of the direction that modern societies were taking. His impression of Chicago was that 'this is what modern reality is like'; here the emergent social world was laid bare 'like a man whose skin has been peeled off and whose intestines are seen at work' (in Weber 1988: 286–7). It was a trait of Weber's to use such imagery, since his assessments were typically frank. He was not impressed by analyses that shied away from uncomfortable truths, but sought rather to promote an understanding of the realities of life in all their harshness. Weber could be scathing about romantic adherence to 'the dream of peace and human happiness' (in Weber 1988: 217), as he put it in his inaugural lecture. Yet at the same time Weber used sociology to champion the need to understand the plurality of people's motives and the diversity of their interpretations of the world. The passage in his first book, published in 1889, in which he described 'the familiar reluctance to live under another person's roof for rent' (2003: 85) because of how this made an individual appear dependent shows that from the outset of his career he was sensitive to the importance of people's understandings of their situations. His awareness of people's capacity to attach a variety of meanings to any given situation led him to question the automatic imputation of rationality. It was his view that non-rational bases of social action did not deserve to be ruled out as readily as some of his Marxist adversaries were wont to do, and this standpoint allowed him to develop a distinctive agenda in relation to the study of religion and of politics as well as of economic life.

The comparison of Weber's approach to sociological analysis to Durkheim's is revealing at several levels. Despite the fact that they were contemporaries, there was almost no mutual recognition in their writings (Giddens 1987a). The differences between the German and French traditions of thought from which, respectively, they came may be part of the explanation (Hughes 1974: 287–8); certainly Durkheim was 'deeply offended' (Jones 1999: 172) at the suggestion by one of his critics that his sociological ideas were German in origin, although Meštrović (1991: ch. 6) has argued that some such influence can be detected. Weber would have agreed with Durkheim's (1982: 157) pronouncement that sociology is an inherently comparative discipline, but he put this perspective into practice in a quite distinct way. Durkheim did not have Weber's training as a historian that allowed him to write works such as *Economy and Society* in which, as Collins put it, 'The sheer knowledge of history that is summed up in sentences (or even parts of sentences) is usually intellectually overwhelming.' Collins's further comment that 'the sensation of dealing with the Weberian style of comparison is dizzying' (1986a: 130) is not one that would be made of Durkheim's more tightly focused approach; Durkheim was not the 'encyclopaedic thinker' (Giddens 1978: 9) that Weber was. A further difference lies in the tone of the two thinkers' work, about which Aron has used the adjectives 'dogmatic' for Durkheim and 'pathetic' (1970: 259) for Weber. The latter reflects the sense of fatefulness and pessimism that runs through Weber's work (Turner 1981). But Durkheim and Weber did engage with related problems; notably they shared a 'distrust of the status of economic theories' (Eldridge 1971: 18) and both were 'preoccupied by religion and its role in society' (Nisbet 1976: v). Bryant's remark that both thinkers had about them the air of 'an old testament prophet' (1976: 122) is apposite. The firmness of their convictions led them both to return repeatedly to debates generated by their work (Chalcraft 2001; Gane 1988: 161), even though the persistence with which critics misunderstood their positions seemed at times wilful.

Weber's mode of presenting his ideas invited controversy. This was literally true, as when he solicited a response by requesting, 'Please polemicise as sharply as possible against those of my views from which you differ' (in Marshall 1982: 11), and it was, he said, 'not agreement, but opposition' (in Scaff 1989: 40) that prompted him to publish. In addition to his 'love of argument' (Käsler 1988: 17), controversy was also the result of his method of developing ideal types of phenomena under investigation. The ideal type was for Weber an '*analytical* construct' that in its pure form 'cannot be found empirically anywhere in reality', since it emerged from the deliberate 'one-sided *accentuation* of one or more points of view' (1949: 90, emphases in original). Weber's works contain ideal-typical analyses of many phenomena such as bureaucracy, about which there has been extensive discussion (Albrow 1970: ch. 3), but the one that generated most debate is the ideal type of the spirit of modern capitalism that he developed in *The Protestant Ethic and the Spirit of Capitalism* (Weber 1976a, 2002). This has been described as 'one of the great works of the social thought of our time' (Hughes 1974: 319), even 'the single most significant text of sociology' (Barbalet 1998: 34), and its publication 'caused a great sensation' (Käsler 1988: 75). This debate remains unresolved, not least because of the problems to which analysis using ideal types tends to give rise (Cohen 2002: 266; Runciman 1972: ch. 3). Weber's (1978b) hopes of having the 'last word' on the matter proved vain, and he continued to be drawn back to the subject (Poggi 1983: 5). The 'polemical intent' (Giddens 1976: 8) with which *The Protestant Ethic* was written reflected Weber's concern to engage with fundamental questions such as the relative importance of material and ideal factors in explaining the course of historical development, although the characterisation of his work as a 'debate with Marx's ghost' (Zeitlin 1987: pt. IV) captures only part of his much broader purpose.

Weber was sceptical of the simple certainties with which many of his contemporaries claimed to be able to speak about social issues. His early research into the agrarian question in the Prussian heartland of eastern Germany challenged the widespread assumption that labourers were migrating in order to achieve a higher standard of living. Prefacing his analysis with the remark that it 'might appear surprising', Weber argued that 'it is the urge for personal freedom that drives the worker to employment away from his home'. What was required in Weber's view was an explanation that combined 'economic and psychological factors', since material interests alone could not account for the motivation of individuals seeking 'personal emancipation' (1989: 173, 175, 172). Weber's use of quotation marks in his reference to 'the tremendous and purely psychological magic of "freedom" ' flagged up the problematic nature of the liberation achieved by workers as market forces eroded traditional social bonds to employers, but his acknowledgement that this 'freedom' may be 'a grand illusion' did not lead to acceptance of the Marxist idea of wage slavery. His citation of the maxim that people do not live 'by bread alone' (in Bendix 1966: 22–3) disputed the Marxist analyses of the time in which there was no place for the aspirations to individualism that Weber saw as central to 'the worker's point of view' (1989: 174). This approach highlighted the importance of the subjective meanings attached by people to their actions, and provided a framework for Weber's subsequent work. For Kalberg, 'His entire sociology is driven by a wish to understand how social action, often viewed by observers as irrational, foolish and strange, becomes plausible and altogether "rational" once its subjective meaningfulness is comprehended' (2002: xlvii–xlviii). In this context it is relevant to note that Weber began *Economy and Society*, the major (if unfinished) work on which he was engaged for over a decade, with a discussion of the different types of social action. This produced a typology in which people's behaviour may be accounted for by habit or by emotion as well as by rationality as it is more usually understood (1978a: 24–6).

Weber's early work revealed his penchant for the development of typologies in other ways besides the distinction between traditional and rational action. As Callinicos has noted, 'Weber's researches into ancient economic history, which immediately preceded his study of Prussian agriculture, already showed an analytical interest in distinguishing between types of economic structure' (1999: 149). Weber recognised that modern capitalism's reliance on free wage-labour distinguished it from feudalism and from slavery, but unlike Marx he did not restrict the use of the term 'capitalism' to the modern period. In Weber's view, the rational capitalism that dominated the modern Western world was merely one of nine different types of capitalism that had existed down the ages (Gerth and Mills 1970: 66–7; Parkin 1982: 41), albeit that it was the one among these that had had the most far-reaching effects. The process of rationalisation that the development of modern rational capitalism had helped to usher in was deeply troubling for Weber, because it created a world that increasingly constrained individuals. Weber's anticipation of 'a polar night of icy darkness and hardness' (1970a: 128) conveys the pessimism that pervades his work. Such evocative language may seem at odds with Weber's (1949) commitment to objectivity and value-freedom in academic analysis, but anyone seeking to expose inconsistencies and contradictions in his work must first acknowledge its 'complexity of argument and illustration' (Turner 1974: 8). We are also confronted by the fact that for Weber, science was a 'vocation' (1970b) that required a 'sturdy and robust mode of expression' (Hennis 2000: 42) that made few concessions to his audience's sensitivities and none to courting popularity by playing to the crowd. As befitted someone who felt himself to be 'swimming "against the stream" of material developments' (1978c: 282), Weber recognised that his bleak outlook did not present people with messages that they were particularly likely to welcome.

Ideal types and one-sided accentuation

The debate prompted by Weber's publication of *The Protestant Ethic* is one of sociology's classic disputes, and it helped enormously to make Weber famous (Ray 1987). The argument that Weber advanced is considerably more complex than it appears at first sight, and there is an irony in the extent to which an author who sought analytical clarity has been misunderstood. Part of the reason for these difficulties is that *The Protestant Ethic* explored the relationship between Protestantism and the spirit of modern rational capitalism by developing 'not one argument, but several' (Liebersohn 1988: 95), and the tension between these different theses was further complicated by Weber's other writings on the matter (Cohen 2002; Marshall 1982: 58ff; Turner 1974: 8ff). Also relevant to the confusion surrounding the debate is Weber's style of presenting his ideas. According to Bendix, 'Weber's work is difficult to understand' because of its tendency 'to bury the main points of the argument in a jungle of statements that require detailed analysis' (1966: xvii). Other commentators have likewise pointed out the difficulties of following Weber's train of thought when he expressed himself in long and complicated sentences and relied on extensive use of emphases, exclamation and quotation marks and footnotes (Andreski 1983: 2; Antoni 1962: 121; Harrington 2001; Löwith 1982: 21; Oakes 1977: 7; Pampel 2000: 103). Marianne Weber wrote that her husband 'did not care about the systematic presentation of his thinking.... And he attached no importance whatever to the form in which he presented his wealth of ideas.' This reflected his need to set down quickly the great number of ideas that came to him at speed, and his belief that the reader could be expected to work at understanding them and to 'take as much trouble as he himself did' (Weber 1988: 309). That said, *The Protestant Ethic* also contains some extremely compelling expressions of sociological ideas, such as his usage of the image of the 'iron cage' (1976a: 181) to capture the constraining character of the modern world. Such ideas repay the dedicated reader, not least for what they reveal about the workings of a scholar whose commitment to hard work meant that he had much in common with the subjects of his study.

The original version of *The Protestant Ethic*, to which the 'Author's Introduction' was a later addition, began with the specification of 'The problem' (1976a: 33). Just as Durkheim had noted in *Suicide* that a correlation existed between Protestantism and suicide rates, Weber began *The Protestant Ethic* 'almost casually' (Liebersohn 1988: 98) by pointing out that a correlation between Protestantism and business activity could be observed in countries such as Germany whose populations adhered to more than one faith. He presented as an acknowledged 'fact that business leaders and owners of capital, as well as the higher grades of skilled labour, and even more the higher technically and commercially trained personnel of modern enterprises, are overwhelmingly Protestant'. He noted that this situation was not new, but could be traced back to the Reformation of the sixteenth century when Protestantism took root most firmly in areas that were most economically developed. Why this should have been the case constituted a puzzle to which the answer was 'by no means so simple as one might think'. The intuitive suggestion that Protestantism freed believers from traditional economic as well as religious practices did not stand up to scrutiny because, Weber argued, Protestants became more rather than less regulated in their everyday lives. Calvinists in particular were subject to what would seem to modern day observers 'the most absolutely unbearable form of ecclesiastical control of the individual which could possibly exist'. The reasons why such 'tyranny' was not resisted but actively embraced needed to be sought by dispensing with 'vague and general concepts' (1976a: 35, 36, 37, 45) and replacing them by a more rigorous analytical framework.

Before undertaking the detailed analysis of the historically unique Protestant religious outlook, Weber first needed to set out what he understood by 'the spirit of capitalism'. Quoting extensively from the writings of the eighteenth-century American figure Benjamin Franklin, Weber identified the peculiar character of the ethic which combined 'the earning of more and more money ... with the strict avoidance of all spontaneous enjoyment of life'. Weber observed that there is nothing 'natural' in such thinking; rather it appears 'irrational from a naive point of view', and it represented a radical departure from the traditionalism according to which a man's goal is simply 'to live as he is accustomed to live and to earn as much as is necessary for that purpose'. Economic traditionalism required people to work only as much as they had to, and led them to respond to increases in wage rates by working fewer hours. In such circumstances economic innovation is confronted by what Weber called 'the stone wall of habit'. Weber then noted that 'the conception of money-making as an end in itself to which people were bound, as a calling, was contrary to the ethical feelings of whole epochs' (1976a: 53, 60, 62, 73). As a result, he argued, it was necessary to trace the genesis of the idea of hard work undertaken as a duty and without material gratification as a reward, since it was not clear to modern minds why anyone would choose to follow such a calling. From a utilitarian point of view it makes no sense, as is indicated by Parsons (the translator into English of *The Protestant Ethic*) noting that Weber's reference in this context to 'worldly asceticism' is a 'seemingly paradoxical term' (in Weber 1976a: 193), given that the discipline and self-denial of the ascetic is normally associated with withdrawal from the world into an environment such as a monastery.

The crux of Weber's thesis was that the development of the spirit of modern rational capitalism whereby people strive to work hard in order to acquire ever-greater levels of material goods is (in part at least) an unintended consequence of Protestantism. By developing the argument that people's actions may have outcomes other than those that they envisage, he sought to show that there existed a logic to the 'seemingly paradoxical relationships' (1976a: 175) between Protestantism and capitalism. There were, Weber claimed, 'elective affinities' between Protestant religious beliefs and the vocational ethic that stressed the importance of hard work, rational organisation of business matters and thrift. The 'virtues cultivated by Calvinism' were singled out for comment by Weber because of the extent of their 'elective affinity to the restrained, strict and active posture of capitalist employers of the middle class' (2002: 49, 89). The Calvinist teaching that everyone was predestined to be either saved or damned in the afterlife led believers to experience profound uncertainty about their position, and this 'feeling of unprecedented inner loneliness' prompted individuals to search for signs that they were among those for whom a place in heaven had been reserved. In Weber's words, 'The question, Am I one of the elect? must sooner or later have arisen for every believer and have forced all other interests into the background.' The worldly activity into which they were thus impelled through the belief that 'God helps those who help themselves' was characterised by a sober, frugal, industrious and methodical approach that unwittingly 'favoured the development of a rational bourgeois economic life'. Indeed, so powerful was the impetus given to the process of economic rationalisation that within a relatively brief historical period this theological underpinning of the economic order was no longer needed as the new structures of rational capitalism quickly became 'an immense cosmos into which the individual is born, and which presents itself to him, at least as an individual, as an unalterable order of things in which he must live'. There was deep irony in Weber's observation that 'The Puritan wanted to work in a calling; we are forced to do so', since the materialistic culture of the 'iron cage' (1976a: 104, 110, 115, 174, 54, 181) that the Puritans had helped to usher in would have been an anathema to them.

The concept of 'elective affinities' played an important role in Weber's sociology (Howe 1978). Parsons's rendition of this term as 'correlations' and 'relationships' captures Weber's meaning 'rather inadequately' (Marshall 1980: 364), although the difficulty is not merely one of translation but is connected to the ambiguity surrounding Weber's aims in writing *The Protestant Ethic*. Marshall notes that 'Weber's "Protestant ethic thesis" is clearly two theses', one concerned with 'specifying the origins of a partic- ular orientation to economic activities' and the other seeking to identify 'one of a number of factors that were causally effective in the development of modern western capitalism' (1982: 58). Liebersohn has also noted that *The Protestant Ethic* 'contains not one argument but several' (1988: 95), while Parkin makes the point more bluntly by distinguishing between the 'weak thesis' and the 'strong thesis' in *The Protestant Ethic*. According to Parkin, the former identified Protestantism and the spirit of modern capi- talism as 'two outlooks ... in close harmony with each other', in contrast to the latter which proposed 'that the distinctive ethic of early Protestantism was not merely historically prior to the capitalist spirit but that it was the decisive force in shaping this spirit'. Parkin is aware of the 'customary qualifications and caveats' (1982: 43, 44) that Weber inserted at various points in *The Protestant Ethic*, such as his concluding remark that he did not seek 'to substitute for a one-sided materialistic an equally one- sided spiritualistic causal interpretation of culture and of history'. The dif- ficulty is that elsewhere in *The Protestant Ethic* Weber made statements that many of his critics have read as very close to just such an argument. One such occurred when he pronounced that 'the Puritan outlook ... favoured the development of a rational bourgeois economic life; it was the most important, and above all the only consistent influence in the development of that life. It stood at the cradle of the modern economic man.' Another is the declaration that 'The question of the motive forces in the expansion of modern capitalism is not in the first instance a question of the origin of the capital sums which were available for capitalistic uses, but, above all, of the development of the spirit of capitalism' (Weber 1976a: 183, 174, 68). These remarks appear to go beyond cautious hypothesising about the correspondence between sets of ideas that is conveyed by the term affinity.

Weber was certainly not the first person to observe a connection between Protestant thinking and the new business mentality of the early modern period (Giddens 1971b: 125; Käsler 1988: 75). There are, for example, scat- tered passages in Marx's *Capital* that refer to 'the "spirit" of Protestantism' and to the religious underpinnings of the drive to accumulate capital in the context of his discussion of the irrationality of 'Accumulation for the sake of accumulation' (Marx 1976: 882, 742). More directly, Weber was prompted to develop the 'pointed and controversial argument' (Poggi 1983: 13) of *The Protestant Ethic* as a means of contesting the view being advanced by his contemporaries that Protestantism was a direct product of modern capitalism. Sombart had claimed that 'the Protestant religion was not the cause but the result of modern capitalist thinking' and challenged his readers to provide 'empirical proof of *concrete-historical contexts* to the contrary' (in Kalberg 2002: xxvii, emphasis in original). Weber took up this challenge, not least because it seemed to him implausible that the relationship between people's material interests and their ideas could ever be reduced to such a crude and deterministic formulation. In doing so, Weber in places overstated his case, as he did elsewhere when arguing against positions that he regarded as flawed. Runciman has observed of Weber that 'in controverting a view which he holds to be incorrect he sometimes implies a more exaggerated counter-claim than would be consistent with what he says elsewhere' (1972: 3). This goes some of the way to accounting for the difficulties surrounding *The Protestant Ethic* although it cannot be more than a subsidiary part of the explanation.

Highlighting the role played by Protestantism in the emergence of modern rational capitalism was the deliberate outcome of Weber's adoption of the methodology of developing ideal types. Weber believed that the complexity of the social world meant that a degree of theoretical simplification was necessary in order for its workings to be understood. Ideal types had 'artificial simplicity' (1976a: 98), and were generated by focusing on particular aspects of a situation to produce '*partial* explanations' (Hughes 1974: 306, emphasis in original). They thus played a 'tactical role in an analytical strategy' (Ringer 2000: 113) by providing a yardstick against which empirical reality could be compared and measured. This was on the understanding that they described 'a utopia' (Weber 1949: 90) and were deliberately one-sided, presenting an exaggerated picture that would nowhere be found in its pure form; in this sense they did 'violence to historical reality' (Weber 1976a: 233). Weber regarded Marx's model of capitalism as an example of ideal-typical analysis, since it directed attention to particular features of that system and its logical organisation, although he rejected the view that such models were 'capable of penetrating to the essence of things' (Freund 1972: 60) and generating law-like certainties. For Weber, the subject matter of the social scientist necessitated proceeding with greater caution than this, as the concluding sentence of *The Protestant Ethic* conveyed when he observed of materialistic and spiritualistic interpretations of history that 'Each is equally possible, but each, if it does not serve as the preparation, but as the conclusion of an investigation, accomplishes equally little in the interest of historical truth' (1976a: 183). The function of an ideal type was 'comparison with empirical reality in order to establish its divergences or similarities' (1949: 43), and Weber's argument was that since there were potentially an infinite number of ideal-types that could be constructed, judgements about their respective merits needed to be made in the light of how successfully they aided the interpretation of the available evidence.

Weber's decision to focus on the ideal type of the spirit of capitalism and its relationship to Protestantism was not a random one; as Kalberg notes, 'In searching for the sources of the spirit of capitalism, Weber never pursued a trial-and-error pathway' (2002: xxvi). Weber felt that the argument that he advanced was in principle at least as plausible as 'the antiquated notion that all cultural phenomena can be *deduced* as a product or function of the constellation of "material" interests' (Weber 1949: 68, emphasis in original). *The Protestant Ethic* offered the opportunity to demonstrate empirically that 'religious ideas themselves simply cannot be deduced from economic circumstances' (1976a: 277) by showing that under certain conditions the causal relationship might reasonably be expected to flow in the opposite direction. *The Protestant Ethic* thus set out to establish that behaviour arising from religious motivations had played a part in the development of modern business practice. In order to show this Weber's ideal-typical methodology required him to work 'on the basis of the assumption that only one or a few motives which are compatible with each other are operative in an actor' (Burger 1987: 127), even though in reality the situation would have been more complicated. Weber's separate essay on 'The Protestant Sects and the Spirit of Capitalism' (1970c), which was published a short time after *The Protestant Ethic*, developed the complementary argument that people's religious behaviour might have economic motivations, the reverse of the situation described in *The Protestant Ethic* whereby people's religious motivations have consequences for their economic behaviour. Much of Weber's subsequent engagement in the debate about *The Protestant Ethic* involved him in restating his position that Protestant beliefs had been one factor among many that had contributed to the rise of modern capitalism. That the subtleties of this position were missed by many of his critics rests to a significant degree on Weber's ideal types being deliberate exaggerations developed for this particular style of sociological argument in which the complexity of real situations is bracketed out in order to achieve analytical clarity.

Multi-causality, methodological individualism and typologies

The logic of Weber's approach meant that *The Protestant Ethic* study served as a preliminary (or as he expressed it 'preparatory' (in Hawthorn 1976: 157)) piece of work anticipating further research rather than being self-contained. According to Poggi, Weber's 'lifelong intellectual pursuit' revolved around 'the genesis, nature and destiny of modern capitalism'. In particular, he interprets Weber as being centrally concerned with 'the social history of the Western bourgeoisie' and he posits that '*The Protestant Ethic* contains a "story" which can in turn be treated as one chapter (and an extremely important chapter) within that social history' (1983: 13, 92–3). In the series of lectures delivered at the end of his life and published posthumously as the *General Economic History*, Weber set out six presuppositions of modern rational capitalism: rational capital accounting, freedom of the market, rational technology, calculable law, free labour and the commercialisation of economic life. His discussion also considered 'the evolution of the capitalist spirit', and in his reprise of the themes first developed in *The Protestant Ethic* he remarked of 'the Protestant ascetic communities' that 'Such a powerful, unconsciously refined organization for the production of capitalistic individuals has never existed in any other church or religion.' Weber's final account of 'the religious root of modern economic humanity' (1981: 276–7, 368) is, as Collins (1986b: ch. 2) has shown, far more explicit than the account in *The Protestant Ethic* about the institutional factors that also needed to be present before modern capitalism could appear. In *The Protestant Ethic* their significance was left implicit by the way in which Weber constructed his argument. By concentrating attention on one aspect he neglected to make it sufficiently clear that, as Marshall puts it, 'this changed capitalist mentality was a necessary though not sufficient condition for the emergence of modern capitalism itself' (1982: 59). In other words, by the time of writing the *General Economic History* Weber had been made all too painfully aware by the critical responses to *The Protestant Ethic* of the potential for misinterpretation that one-sided exaggerations have.

Weber reacted to the charge that *The Protestant Ethic* presented an idealist account of the development of modern capitalism by writing numerous restatements of his position that were more carefully worded, but as Marshall (1982: 59) notes it proved difficult to undo the damage caused by the lack of clarity in the original articles. In his various pieces of substantive research Weber endeavoured to show that he was 'attuned to the interrelationships among the economy, society, polity, organization, social stratification, religion, and so forth' (Ritzer 1992: 220). This commitment to multi-causal explanations is nicely captured in the passage in the *General Economic History* in which Weber brought together the various factors identified as influences on the development of modern capitalism in Western Europe: 'In the last resort the factor which produced capitalism is the rational permanent enterprise, rational accounting, rational technology and rational law, but again not these alone. Necessary complementary factors were the rational spirit, the rationalization of the conduct of life in general, and a rationalistic economic ethic' (1981: 354). This is an extensive list, but it reflects Weber's view that the social scientist was confronted by complex realities in which 'The number and types of causes which have influenced any given event are always infinite' (1949: 78). For Weber any sociological explanation was therefore tentative, sensitive to the uniqueness of every context and 'necessarily limited in scope' (Eldridge 1971: 11) since an exhaustive account of social phenomena would be a practical impossibility unless it were framed in terms of the sort of vague generalities that Weber regarded as trite and meaningless.

Although Weber rejected the notion that a single, all-encompassing set of guidelines for sociological research could be set down, he remained committed to the view that accounts that omitted the dimension of subjective understanding were seriously flawed. His definition of sociology identified it as 'a science concerning itself with the interpretive understanding of social action and thereby with a causal explanation of its course and consequences' (1978a: 4). Weber's emphasis on the importance of *verstehen* or understanding treated people's motives as 'the meaningful causes of action' (Albrow 1990: 201), and thus any account of social phenomena needed to include an analysis of how individuals made sense of the world and acted upon these understandings. Parkin observes that 'no one is more insistent than Weber that the fundamental unit of investigation must always be the individual' (1982: 17), although Weber argued that this methodological individualism was distinct from psychological reductionism in which attention is restricted to people's mental states (Eldridge 1971: 18). Understanding people's motives also involves the analysis of the institutions within which actors operate, and on this basis Weber was able to develop his focus on people's motives as an integral part of his broad-ranging comparative historical sociology within which he dealt with 'the actions and beliefs of social *groups* and even of whole *cultures*' (Ringer 2000: 158, emphases in original). The same method employed by Weber in *The Protestant Ethic* to highlight the motivations of the business entrepreneur of early modern capitalism was employed in later studies such as those of ancient China and India, and on this basis Weber could reveal that 'the way that traditional China's civilization gave a pivotal role to the administrator, the Mandarin, contrasts with the way the Indian caste system was centred upon the priest/teacher' (Hughes *et al.* 1995: 140). In Weber's view the spirit of capitalism originated 'not in isolated individuals alone, but as a way of life common to whole groups of men', who individually acted as 'bearers' (1976a: 55, 65) of the emergent culture.

Weber's approach enabled him to illustrate the more general points that he sought to make by referring to particular examples. As Wrong has noted, there is 'a tendency in Weber's thought to see a system of cultural values or an institutional structure as embodied in a concrete human type. Thus Weber stresses the Calvinist rather than Calvinism'. In *The Protestant Ethic*, 'Weber selected Benjamin Franklin as the very prototype of the secularized Protestant impelled by inner-worldly asceticism to devote himself heart and soul to commerce' (1970: 23). This is, Lemert comments, a 'simple literary gesture' (1995: 106), but it is also a problematic one, since Franklin did not live up to the high standards of conduct that he set out in the writings from which Weber quoted. There was, Wrong says, 'nothing ascetic about Franklin's personal life' (1970: 23), and this necessarily calls into question the practice of imputing motives on the basis what Franklin wrote. The same problem arises in relation to the interpretation of the motives behind people's actions where no written record akin to that of Franklin exists, since it is equally problematic to deduce outlook from behaviour (Marshall 1982: 66). The more general point is that Weber did not always provide an explicit justification for his choice of illustrations when developing an argument. Chalcraft has noted that the debate prompted by *The Protestant Ethic* was dogged by difficulties around 'the status of anecdotal and personal evidence' (2001: 14). Weber's *Protestant Ethic* drew on recent family history in its account of the spread of modernising business practices (Poggi 1983: 109). It also drew on his travels in the United States (Weber 1976a: 283), as did his essay on the Protestant sects which discussed at length various 'personal observations' that he intended to 'serve as illustrations' (1970c: 303) of his argument. Similarly, in his second reply to Rachfahl's criticisms of *The Protestant Ethic* Weber returned to the example of the young man 'entering a Baptist congregation in North Carolina' (2001b: 111) who was motivated to do so by his desire to open a bank, reckoning that admission to the local congregation offered him an excellent way to establish his trustworthiness.

Weber's rationale for using individual examples derived from conversations while travelling could not be framed in terms of their representativeness in the statistical sense. Rather, the justification for observations 'made from a "worm's eye view"' was that they provided a better understanding of the way in which the ordinary people spoken to saw the world than 'learned intellectuals' (1971b: 191, 215), hampered by romanticised preconceptions, were able to provide. The 'consistently "empirical" research' (Hennis 2000: 143) which Weber sought to promote required social scientists to leave to one side any preconceived ideas about what people's understandings of the world ought to be like. In the study of industrial workers with which he was associated, Weber emphasised the importance of presenting 'the unbiased, objective statement of facts and the ascertainment of their causes' since it is the task of the researcher 'objectively to *explain*' but '*not* ... to pronounce judgement' or allocate blame. It was the role of the researcher to specify 'what *kind* of workers' (1971a: 104, 105, 108, emphases in original) was being shaped by modern industrial conditions, but not to praise or condemn these outcomes. Research such as this Weber described as quite different from writing in the light journalistic style of 'an entertaining *Feuilleton*' since 'it is unbelievably difficult to compose a scientific presentation' (in Hennis 2000: 46). Weber's sociological approach required sensitive analysis of carefully collected evidence; it was, as Kalberg describes it, '*both* empirically based *and* vigorously theoretical' (1997: 213, emphases in original).

Particularly prominent among Weber's theoretical concerns was the question of the extent to which individuals' actions could be construed as 'rational'. Weber's key distinction between traditional and modern, market-based economic orientations was already present in his early analysis of the 'proletarianization' of rural labourers, where the problematic nature of rationality was apparent in the actions of the labourer who 'seeks money wages which free him from the dependence and good will of the landlord despite the economic decline that is a result' (1989: 168, 172). The agrarian question continued to engage Weber's attention (Scaff 1989: ch. 2), and featured in *The Protestant Ethic* where he discussed the 'peculiar difficulty' of increasing rural productivity in the context of the traditionalism that led the worker to respond to increased rates of pay 'not by increasing but by decreasing the amount of his work' (1976a: 59). A similar story featured in the *General Economic History* (1981: 355), but Weber argued that the 'power of tradition' was being eroded by the spread of capitalism: 'The old economic order asked: How can I give, on this piece of land, work and sustenance to the greatest number of men? Capitalism asks: From this given piece of land how can I produce as many crops as possible for the market with as few men as possible?' (1970d: 364, 367). Weber remarked in *The Protestant Ethic* that the pursuit of money as an end in itself appeared from some points of view 'absolutely irrational', and the footnote to this comment concluded by suggesting that bringing out 'the complexity of the only superficially simple concept of the rational' (1976a: 54, 194) was the most important insight contained in the study.

It has been suggested that Western rationality constituted Weber's 'overriding problem' (Hughes 1974: 292) or 'driving force' (Albrow 1990: xi), and that Weber's writing came to be 'saturated with the notions of rationality and irrationality' (Sica 1988: 113). It is certainly the case that the issue featured prominently in his work, although as Brubaker notes 'he frequently uses the term "rational" without qualification or explanation'. Brubaker identifies 'No fewer than sixteen apparent meanings of "rational"' in *The Protestant Ethic* alone, which he lists as 'deliberate, systematic, calculable, impersonal, instrumental, exact, quantitative, rule-governed, predictable, methodical, purposeful, sober, scrupulous, efficacious, intelligible and consistent' (1984: 1, 2). Weber had already expressed his disagreement with abstract economic theory because its imputation of 'economic rationality' to agents meant that it proceeded 'on the basis of *unrealistic* men, analogous to a mathematical ideal', and in doing so it '*ignores*, treats as if *not present* all those motives which have an influence on real men which are specifically *non-economic*' (in Tribe 1989: 6, emphases in original). The logic of his position propelled him towards the development of a typology of social action that went beyond such narrow confines. Weber's immense historical knowledge had led him to the unexpected conclusion that 'religiously or magically motivated behaviour is relatively rational behaviour … . It follows rules of experience, though it is not necessarily action in accordance with a means-end schema'. In order to incorporate this point into his typology he needed to distinguish between actions that were 'instrumentally rational' and those that were 'value-rational', so that rationality was not restricted to describing actions that were calculated according to means and ends but could also be applied to action 'determined by a conscious belief in the value for its own sake of some ethical, aesthetic, religious, or other form of behaviour, independently of its prospects of success'. Alongside these two types of rational action, Weber identified two types of non-rational action, 'affectual' in which emotions and other 'feeling states' explained the actor's orientation, and 'traditional' in which habit was the crucial characteristic (1978a: 400, 24–5).

Weber made a number of qualifying comments about his typology of social action, including the point that concrete cases of action were unlikely to reflect these types in their pure form. In addition, he left open the possibility of the extension of the typology to include further types beyond the four that he outlined, remarking that 'The usefulness of the classification … can only be judged in terms of its results' (1978a: 26). Clarke (1982: 206–7) has argued that the application of Weber's typology is problematic and that in practice Weber himself was primarily concerned with the contrast between rational and traditional action. This is consistent with Roth's observation that 'Weber's comparative strategy was directed toward establishing, with the aid of his typologies, (1) the *differences* between modern and older conditions, and (2) the *causes* of the differences' (1978: xxxix, emphases in original). Among the many typologies that Weber developed one of the most important was that which identified 'three possible types of legitimation' of authority, which Weber drew on particularly to contrast the rational and traditional types, with charismatic authority treated as a more extraordinary phenomenon. His discussion of this typology commenced with an account of the rational form of authority, 'modern bureaucratic administration', on the grounds that it makes sense to 'proceed from the type that is the most rational and the one most familiar to us'. Weber's preceding discussion had already established that he was treating bureaucratic administration as 'the most rational type from a technical point of view' (1978a: 954, 223). From a personal point of view Weber was greatly troubled by the process of bureaucratisation, mindful as he was of the lessons of ancient Egypt and Rome where it had led to 'the total subordination of the population in a highly bureaucratised state' (Giddens 1971b: 181). Weber's designation of a phenomenon as rational in no way implied his approval of it, as is readily apparent in his association of the process of rationalisation with Schiller's phrase 'the disenchantment of the world' (Weber 1970b: 155).

Values and vocations

Weber's comparative historical approach rejected the notion of progress as it was used by many of his contemporaries. It was a logical outcome of his insistence on multi-causality that he should be sceptical of simple typologies in which societies moved from one stage to the next in an orderly, law-like fashion; such accounts of 'unilinear development' (Weber, in Gerth and Mills 1970: 51) tended to rely on a single causal factor that was endowed with undue capacity to determine the flow of events. They also were too abstract and generalised and had no place for phenomena such as the 'refeudalization' (Liebersohn 1988: 94) of the countryside that his own research had highlighted. A further objection that Weber raised to theories of progress was that by claiming that social changes constituted an improvement over time they illegitimately imported value judgements into scientific analysis (Hennis 2000: 182–5; Ringer 2000: 137). For Weber, value judgements were to be kept separate from 'detached analysis' (1952: 425), since it was not the job of scientists to impose their opinions of the phenomena under discussion onto their audience. He saw it as an 'intrinsically simple demand that the investigator and teacher should keep unconditionally separate the establishment of empirical facts ... and ... his evaluation of these facts as satisfactory or unsatisfactory' (1949: 11). Weber acknowledged that complete objectivity in the study of social phenomena was impossible to achieve because the researcher's viewpoint was bound to enter into how issues were 'selected, analysed and organized for expository purposes' (1949: 72). Weber regarded what the researcher decided to focus their attention on as a matter of judgement, but beyond this point the highest scholarly virtue was for Weber 'simple intellectual honesty' (in Lukács 1980: 618).

Weber felt that many of his contemporaries fell short of his exacting standards of value freedom. He was, for example, a 'resolute opponent ... of nostalgia for earlier forms of *Gemeinschaft*' (Liebersohn 1988: 79), but he was equally scathing about the 'Vulgar opinion ... that political science is capable of supplying formulae for the happiness of the world' (in Antoni 1962: 135). He was also critical of those who advanced arguments without supplying supporting evidence, as in his dismissal of racial theories on the grounds that such ideas required demonstration that race could be isolated as an analytical variable that could be shown to be causally effective. His assessment that 'Not a single fact of this kind has yet been found' (in Liebersohn 1988: 119) suggests a parallel with the technique of judging rival theories that Durkheim employed in *Suicide*. A further parallel with Durkheim lies in Weber's attempt to establish sociology as a reputable discipline. As Tribe (drawing on Käsler) notes, Weber's 'demand for "value freedom" was in this context not merely a methodological principle, but also a strategy for the creation of academic "respect"' (1988: 4). Weber's view was that social scientists could not tell people what they ought to do because 'the various value spheres of the world stand in irreconcilable conflict with each other', and science cannot arbitrate between these different values. He held that personal political views have no place in the academic environment; rather, 'The primary task of a useful teacher is to teach his students to recognize "inconvenient" facts' (1970b: 147), and thereby to educate their judgement by challenging their preconceptions.

Roth has suggested that *Economy and Society* reveals Weber's 'love of paradox' (1978: xxxiv), and it is not only there that Weber employed this device for engaging with his audience. Early in his career he had commented that 'homelessness and freedom are one and the same' (in Scaff 1989: 60) in his account of how agricultural labourers were prepared to pursue freedom even at the expense of their material security and wellbeing. Weber's 'keen feeling for historical paradox' (Poggi 1983: 52) is also evident in *The Protestant Ethic* where he explored various aspects of what he later called 'Protestant asceticism's (apparently!) paradoxical attitude to wealth' (2001a: 68–9), that is, the combination of devotion to production with abstinence from consumption that is paradoxical to the utilitarian mindset (Liebersohn 1988: 100). Weber's study of Confucianism provided a contrasting example of 'the paradox of rationality' (Bendix 1966: 139). The study of politics also threw up material for Weber to use in this way, as it did in his discussion of the 'ethical paradoxes' whereby high-minded leaders, in order to achieve positions of power from which they can effect change, may come to rely on the 'predominantly base' (1970a: 125) motives of their followers. Likewise it could be considered paradoxical that 'the despotism of Frederick the Great was a force for healthy growth' (1976b: 390). More broadly, it is possible to interpret Weber's work as a wide-ranging engagement with 'the paradox of rationalization' (Schluchter 1979), of which there are several dimensions. Rationalisation can be seen to have emerged out of 'certain irrational forces' (Holton and Turner 1990: 73) such as the Calvinists' quest for salvation, and to have spread into allegedly irrational areas of life such as music (Käsler 1988: 169). Furthermore, Hughes has pointed out Weber's ambiguity concerning reason and his 'distress at the paradox that made it both the highest achievement of the West and the source of the "soullessness" of contemporary life' (1974: 323). Marianne Weber described her husband as committed to study 'without any illusions' (1988: 679), but this pursuit of 'the demystification of the world' (Eldridge 1971: 10) at times pushed him to the limits of what he could stand.

The ultimate irrationality of the rationalisation process was one of the discomfiting lessons that Weber sought to draw to the attention of his audience. In the conclusion to *The Protestant Ethic* Weber was clearly troubled by how 'the modern economic order ... is now bound to the technical and economic conditions of machine production which determine the lives of all the individuals who are born into this mechanism ... with irresistible force' (1976a: 181). This 'devastating indictment of modern industrial civilization' (Wrong 1970: 28) was combined with scepticism about the prospects for escape from what Weber referred elsewhere to as the 'monstrous cage' (in Hennis 2000: 44) of modern large-scale industry, either through some future socialist transformation of that system or through a return to the way of life of so-called 'golden ages' (1976b: 51). In relation to the former, Weber spoke of Marx and Engels' *Communist Manifesto* as 'a work of scholarship of the highest order' (1971b: 204) but argued that its central premises had subsequently been empirically refuted. Nor did the past offer any more hope in Weber's view. Concluding his study of ancient civilisations, Weber remarked that 'A storyteller can always count on heightened interest if his listeners believe that the story applies to their own lives too. Then he can end with a moral exhortation.' Having raised his audience's hopes in this way he then dashed them: 'My story, however, is not of that sort. There is little or nothing that ancient history can teach us about our own social problems. ... Our problems and those of Antiquity are entirely different' (1976b: 390–1). Scaff argues that this is also a conscious rebuttal of Marx, since Weber reproduced the same epigram Marx had used in volume I of *Capital*, ' "this story is about you (*de te narratur fabula*)" – in an identical context but with a precisely opposed meaning. For Weber, history issues a harder lesson: It is never simply a story about ourselves, but rather a record of differences, contingencies, unanticipated consequences, and paradoxical meanings' (1989: 63). To the extent that history did provide a parallel to the present, the scenario to which Weber referred was not a utopia but the ossified 'bureaucratic "order" ' (1976b: 365) of ancient Egypt.

Power and domination are central themes in Weber's sociology (Hennis 2000: 194; Käsler 1988: 161ff; Wrong 1970: 54) but, as Kalberg (2002: xv) argues, his pessimism about the prospects for individualism should not be mistaken as fatalism. Weber had been emphatic that his methodology had no connection to 'An *attitude of moral indifference*' (1949: 60, emphasis in original), and it is well known that his own political activism was informed by his academic conclusions. Thus while *The Protestant Ethic* is a story about how the West came to be 'apprenticed to a machine it could not control' (Lemert 1999: 27), its message is not necessarily one of despair. Ray has written that 'it is possible to read Weber in a way that suggests a more open and nuanced conception of modernity than simply an iron cage' (1999: 187). Weber did employ the metaphor of the development of an 'inanimate machine' in relation to bureaucratisation, but he presented this outcome as a possible future '*if* a technically superior administration *were to be the ultimate and sole value*' (1978a: 1402, emphases in original) within the bureaucracy. To Weber this was a big 'if'. His studies of history suggested that we should cultivate 'the capacity to be astonished about the course of events' (1952: 207). Ideas had a part to play in this challenge to deterministic thinking, since 'very frequently the "world images" which have been created by "ideas" have, like switchmen, determined the tracks along which action has been pushed by the dynamic of interests' (in Gerth and Mills 1970: 63–4). As Gerth and Mills note, 'Mechanical imagery of this sort seems to stand opposite the organic metaphors of growth and development favoured by more conservative writers' (1970: 64), and in the process opens up scope for the individual freedom that Weber prized above the system of ' "organic" social stratification' (1978a: 1402) that in his view threatened to snuff out individualism. On this point Weber would have found very little common ground with Durkheim.

Weber's combative debating style, which he himself likened to participation in a duel (Chalcraft 2001: 16), reflected his understanding of the role of the scholar. Weber's polemics were deliberately 'committed', to the point of being 'caustic' and 'brutal', because this was in his view necessary to expose what he regarded as 'sophistry and intellectual dishonesty' (Oakes 1977: 8, 36, 37). The intolerance shown by Weber towards many of his intellectual opponents may, along with the more general difficulties of his style of argument, be attributed to the fact that he 'could not bear to reread … his manuscripts' (Frank 1976: 28), to his troubled personality and the prolonged psychological illness from which he suffered (Oakes 1977: 8) and to his 'masculine thinking' (Bologh 1990). In addition to these points, Poggi has suggested that Weber's approach is understandable in terms of 'the intensity with which he felt the urge of contradictory passions' (1983: 2), and this interpretation is consistent with Green's argument that his sensitivity to ambiguity and to conflicting values 'makes Weber's style an intrinsic, indispensable feature of his mode of theorizing' (1988: 182). It is also worth noting that Weber's sociological project was one of 'theoretical synthesis' (Alexander 1983). There are, as Wrong has pointed out, several ways in which Weber attempted 'to bridge the chasm between two extreme viewpoints representing rival intellectual traditions' (1970: 8). Thus he 'considered himself to occupy a kind of middle position between materialists and idealists' (Albrow 1990: 107), from which he was subsequently to be 'attacked from both sides' (Rex 1971: 23). Weber was engaged in adding 'his own interpretations to existing theories or perspectives, trying to reconcile competing ideas' (Pampel 2000: 116). This form of 'mediation' (Käsler 1988: 214), which involved following a viewpoint through to its logical conclusion, led Weber to attempt to build bridges between sociology and its neighbouring disciplines, including history, economics, psychology, political science and law. Weber's familiarity with all of these disciplines meant that he stood 'at more decisive meeting points than any other thinker' (Hughes 1974: 288). Weber's mode of argument is not exclusively sociological, reflecting the store that he set by 'a thinker's "multidimensional" capacity to unify and integrate diverse ideas and concepts' (Kalberg, in Weber 2002: 246). Weber sought to address a very wide audience indeed.

List of Weber's key sociological writings
Dates of original publication are given in ( ); English translations are given in [ ]

The Protestant Ethic and the Spirit of Capitalism (1904/5, 1920) [1930]

The Methodology of the Social Sciences (1904, 1906, 1917–18) [1949]

Ancient Judaism (1917–19) [1952]

'Science as a vocation' and 'Politics as a vocation' (in H. Gerth and C. W. Mills *From Max Weber* (given as lectures 1918) [1948])

Economy and Society (1922) (written 1910–20) [1968]

General Economic History (1923) (given as lectures 1919–20) [1927]

5

Talcott Parsons: sociology as systematic reflection

Introduction and overview

Talcott Parsons was born in America on 13 December 1902 and died of heart failure while revisiting Germany having just given a lecture on 8 May 1979. The fact that he continued to be engaged in academic activity right up to his death and well past normal retirement age is symptomatic of his prodigious energy that resulted in an astonishing intellectual output over the half century that followed his first scholarly publication. In a touching dedication to his wife Helen of his book *The Social System* Parsons described himself as 'an incurable theorist' (1951: v), and Rocher has remarked that 'It would be difficult to find two words which better defined this man's career and the role he has played in American sociology' (1974: 1). Parsons's influence reflects the enormous respect that many in his audiences have for his determination to engage with academic problems with an unusual degree of persistence and rigour. This approach led him to look for solutions in unexpected places. His final visit to Germany was planned to mark the fiftieth anniversary of the award of his doctoral degree from Heidelberg (Hamilton 1983: 52), and it is instructive that Parsons had looked to Germany for an alternative source of ideas to the 'Anglo-American economic thought' (1991: 3) which he came to consider 'way off the main track' (in Camic 1991: xxii). A crash course in German allowed him to read Weber's *The Protestant Ethic and the Spirit of Capitalism*, the subject matter of which resonated with his upbringing in a staunchly Protestant household headed by his father, a Congregationalist minister (Wearne 1989: 11). It was typical of Parsons to look beyond conventional disciplinary boundaries in the development of his thinking, and he went on to draw on Freudian psychoanalysis and then on cybernetics in his restless search for intellectual satisfaction.

Parsons's modest and self-critical character did not spare him from some extremely hostile reactions. The position that he held at Harvard, following his return from Germany, until his death contributed to some people's identification of him with the establishment, and in certain circles his works came increasingly to be read as an exercise in apologetics for the status quo, identifying reasons why things have to be the way that they are. Gouldner, for example, attacked what he called 'the moralistics of Talcott Parsons' (1971: ch. 7) because of the emphasis that he placed on religion, morality and shared values in securing social order and his concomitant neglect of more controversial factors such as the use of force. In a similar vein, Buxton portrayed Parsons as someone engaged in 'preserving capitalist social relations' (1985: 4). In addition, Parsons's style of writing attracted many brickbats from commentators who found his mode of expression verbose and convoluted. Yet the answer to Bryant's question 'Who now reads Parsons?' (1983) is not the same as Parsons's answer to the same question when it was asked about Spencer, for while the latter's writings can rightly be considered to have become a spent force after his death (if not before), Parsons's legacy is proving far more enduring (Turner 1999b). In one sense Parsons's death did mark 'the end of an era in sociology' (Merton, in Ritzer 1992: 343), but his influence endures in a variety of ways.

One reason why Parsons's works continue to attract interest is that they occupy a pivotal position in the history of sociology and of how sociologists present their arguments. As a translator of *The Protestant Ethic* and of part of *Economy and Society* [published as *The Theory of Social and Economic Organization* (Weber 1964)], Parsons played an important role in bringing Weber's ideas to the attention of the English-speaking world. He used his knowledge of the works of Weber and other European social scientists to develop an ambitious synthesis of their ideas into his 'theory of social action' (Parsons 1968). On the basis of the development of this argument he became pre-eminent during what has been called 'the golden moment' (Lemert 1999: pt 3) or 'the golden age' (Callinicos 1999: ch. 10) of social theory in the years following the Second World War, when his optimistic perspective 'resonated with the times' (Kivisto 1998: 65). Subsequently the hegemony of Parsons's functionalist mode of argument came under increasing attack, both for the content of his ideas and for the way in which he expressed himself. Lemert's assessment is that 'Parsons's writings are nearly impossible even for the trained eye to read' (1995: 22), while for Runciman, Parsons is a 'platitude-merchant' whose works are full of 'empty verbiage and unnecessary jargon' (1998: 57, 59). Ritzer has even suggested that 'it is hard to imagine his lengthy, convoluted prose being published today' (1998: 46). Parsons himself acknowledged other people's concerns over 'the difficulty of simply reading my work intelligibly' (qtd in Menzies 1977: 2) and he referred self-mockingly to his first book's 'seductive and charming literary style' (1968: v), but although his ideas were undeniably complex, they could not easily be ignored. Consequently, as Layder notes, 'when the popularity of Parsons's ideas declined, the theories that replaced them were often of the form of a critical dialogue with them' (1994: 5). Thus it is a 'paradox of the Parsonian legacy' that although it is 'conventional for sociologists to reject the work of Parsons', his ideas have nevertheless been 'extremely influential' (Robertson and Turner 1991: 1). This is because Parsons posed challenging and important questions in new ways. Even the celebrated critique by Mills of what he dubbed Parsons's 'grand theory' conceded that 'Something is there, buried deep to be sure, but still something is being said.' By 'translating ... into English' (Mills 2000: 27) Parsons's major work *The Social System*, Mills enjoyed a joke but also made the serious point that its ideas were worth expressing in a more accessible form in order to promote discussion.

Weber has been called Parsons's 'intellectual mentor' (Hamilton 1985: 15) and there are several parallels between the two. Like Weber, Parsons wrote prodigiously. His work spanned a wide range of issues and academic disciplines including economics and psychology as well as sociology, and his output totalled over 280 items (Parsons 1999e). He shared Weber's impulse to build on the work of other scholars by combining insights from their writings into a conceptually rigorous synthesis, and although he was partly responsible for the fact that he is known primarily as a theorist he was committed to the empirical application of his analytical framework. His empirical essays were intended to be 'an integral part of Parsons's work' (Rocher 1974: 124). A further similarity is that both Weber and Parsons 'have often been interpreted in the most one-sided and superficial manner' (Holton and Turner 1988: 5–6). This can in part be attributed to the acknowledged difficulty of their writing styles, which contrasted with their other modes of engagement, since Weber's lectures have been described as 'rhetorical masterpieces' (Roth 1978: xxxiv) while it has been said of Parsons that he 'was clearly an exciting and inspirational teacher' (Hamilton 1985: 10). Among the most misleading interpretations of Parsons is the suggestion that he was a conservative; in fact, like Weber, he was a liberal, and his criticisms of McCarthyism even led to his being 'placed under surveillance by the FBI' (Kivisto 1998: 66). Neither Weber nor Parsons was convinced by explanations of social organisation and change framed in terms of Spencer's expression 'the survival of the fittest' (Eldridge 1971: 56; Parsons 1968: 113–14), a philosophy Parsons had the misfortune to experience first-hand during his austere schooling (Wearne 1989: 19). Parsons's declaration that 'Spencer is dead' was a prelude to his argument that a better solution to 'the problem of order' (1968: 3, 89) was required, and in the search for this, Parsons drew on several other thinkers besides Weber, the most prominent of whom was Durkheim.

It was noted in Chapter 4 that Weber and Durkheim worked almost entirely independently of each other, and that their perspectives were not obvious candidates for being brought together. Parsons's synthesis of Durkheim's interest in social order and Weber's analysis of the meaningfulness of social action led to his development of a theory of the social system that was 'an attempt to understand sociology in relation to the issues of integration and motivation of social actors' (Turner 1999b: 5). Parsons saw his project as 'furthering the development of scientific theory in the field of human behavior' (1976: 311). To his mind the development of sociology as a science involved tracing the path towards greater sophistication and explanatory power that had been followed by longer-established disciplines such as biology, one of the subjects that he had studied as an undergraduate (Camic 1991: xiv). As he put it, 'When scientific observation begins to transcend common sense and becomes to a degree methodologically sophisticated, there emerge explicit schemata which may be called descriptive frames of reference' (1968: 28). One of the key concepts developed by Parsons in order to describe, understand and explain the social world better than common sense approaches are able to is that of differentiation. According to Parsons, 'Differentiation refers to the process by which simple structures are divided into functionally differing components, these components becoming relatively independent of one another, and then recombined into more complex structures in which the functions of the differentiated units are complementary' (1999e: 275). The influence of both Durkheim's analysis of the progressive development of the division of labour and Weber's theory of rationalization can be detected in Parsons's account of how the social system tends towards ever-greater specialisation of roles. Parsons later came to be more aware of the drawbacks of overspecialisation and in his final writings paid greater attention than he had previously to the reverse process of 'de-differentiation' (Bourricaud 1981: 293), but this was more an elaboration than a rejection of his earlier insights.

Parsons regarded the individual as an agent who has choices to make, but not completely free ones. As a result of the differentiation of the social system, he argued, people face 'a strictly limited and defined set of ... alternatives'. These 'pattern variables', when expressed 'in their simplest form, can be defined as polar alternatives of possible orientation-selection' (1951: 59). Parsons's early interest in the professions prompted his recognition that professional traditions and ideals such as commitment to disinterestedness and high ethical standards 'provided a bulwark against the wholesale commercialization of modern social life' (Wearne 1989: 123). Parsons's analysis of the reasons why professionals are bound by codes of ethics that discourage the pursuit of narrowly self-interested behaviour led him to formulate a more general list of dilemmas that people confront in everyday life, such as whether to treat everyone the same or to treat people differently according to their particular characteristics. At work a professional would be expected to treat all clients with equal respect, but if in their domestic life they treated members of their family as no different to the rest of the population it would be regarded as inappropriate. The distinction between what Parsons called 'particularism' and 'universalism' can be illustrated by Craib's reference to 'the difference between the way I treat my children and my students' (1984: 45). The analysis of this and other constrained choices was for Parsons a key element in his account of the systematic character of social relationships, developed at length in *The Social System*. By likening the functioning of society to that of a biological organism Parsons was adopting a theme that Durkheim (amongst others) had developed, but his abstract and logical approach was for many commentators too neat and tidy to capture the inherent messiness and unpredictability of the real world. In particular its treatment of the individual as 'the bearer of socially predetermined roles' (Dahrendorf 1973: 7) was challenged on the grounds that it represented people as 'oversocialized' (Wrong 1999: ch. 2), that is, so well groomed for the positions that they occupied that they performed their roles with no more difficulty than a robot. The more general lesson of Parsons's likening of society to a biological organism was that 'it is always dangerous to push an analogy too far' (Craib 1984: 39). Parsons responded to his critics without the invective that characterised many of their attacks, but although he modified and extended his analysis in important respects the central problem that he addressed remained that with which his career began, the problem of order.

Standing on the shoulders of giants

The idea that knowledge is advanced by building on the work of previous generations was famously captured in Newton's remark, 'If I have seen farther it is by standing on the shoulders of giants.' Parsons's student Merton (1965: 1) drew upon this idea in his analysis of the history of science, the serious point of which was 'to indicate metaphorically that any one of us scholars or scientists are merely dwarfs as we draw upon the gigantic intellectual legacy which provides our points of departure' (Merton, qtd in Sztompka 1986: 22). Parsons was suitably modest in acknowledging his intellectual debts to the generation of European social scientists whose ideas excited his interest. He did this by devoting his first major study, *The Structure of Social Action*, to the exposition of the common analytical framework towards which they were gravitating, albeit from what he acknowledged to be 'diverse points of view' (1968: xxii). Parsons argued that Weber and Durkheim, together with the Italian economist and sociologist Pareto and the English marginalist economist Marshall, were all in their different ways confronted by the inadequacy of the explanation of social order proffered by utilitarian thinkers. At the same time that Durkheim was exposing the shortcomings of Spencer's view that people pursuing their individual self-interest with minimum regulation by the state would result in an orderly world, Weber was emphasising that individuals do not always behave as rationally as the utilitarian model suggested. Pareto and Marshall were also writing on the theme that the interface between economics and sociology required a more nuanced account of people's motivations than that provided by a narrow focus on rationality and the satisfaction of wants. For all that they were 'elegantly analytical and systematic', economic theories fell short for Parsons because they 'do not apply very precisely to the empirical world of on-going economic activities' (Devereux 1976: 8, 9). Parsons argued that it was possible to synthesise elements from all four writers' ideas into a rigorous analytical framework that could account more convincingly for the orderliness of social relationships. Parsons's logic was that it could be demonstrated that 'A purely utilitarian society is chaotic and unstable' (1968: 93–4), and that therefore there existed a need to develop a better way of understanding the social order.

Parsons has been described as 'a charming man' (Hamilton 1983: 8) and he was famously modest about his achievements (Treviño 2001: xviii), but this in no way compromised his commitment to intellectual rigour; as Wearne has noted, 'Parsons aimed for a high quality in his work' (1989: 38). The authors on whose writings he focused in *The Structure of Social Action* were selected on the grounds that 'the best place to go to find the starting points of the breakdown of a system is to the work of the ablest proponents of the system itself', just as Marx had done in devoting so much of his critical attention on the writings of Smith and Ricardo, which he held in great esteem. The 'ablest and most clear-headed' thinkers were, Parsons recognised, 'difficult' but ultimately more rewarding than engagement with 'mediocre proponents of a theoretical system' because 'lesser lights' were less mindful of the limitations of that system and of the 'residual categories' (1968: 18) that are revealed when a theory is tested to the point of destruction. For all his respect for their achievements, Parsons wanted to take things further than his chosen authors had done by concentrating on the problems contained in what they had written. Alexander's description of Durkheim and Weber as 'Parsons' primary and direct theoretical adversaries' (1984: 14) conveys this sense of critical engagement.

Together with Pareto and Marshall, Durkheim and Weber had each by a different route arrived at the conclusion that economic theories framed in terms of the rational individual neglected the important dimension of non-rational action, but none of them had resolved the problem of how to incorporate this into a satisfactory account of how society worked.

Familiarity with Weber's critique of Marxist ideas led Parsons to doubt the proposition that material factors determined the goals that people pursued, but he was equally unconvinced by the view that people's ends are selected randomly. Parsons insisted that the study of action necessarily involved a consideration of means as well as ends, and the 'logical framework' that he sought to develop was centrally concerned with the systematic relations between means and ends. As he saw it, 'it is impossible even to talk about action in terms that do not involve a means – end relationship'. Thus although he was critical of the assumption of rationality that economists typically made, economics had provided a crucial element of Parsons's 'frame of reference' (1968: 733) for analysing social action. It was quite consistent for him to hold that economics was 'the theoretically most advanced of all the social sciences' (Rocher 1974: 16) while at the same time recognising that no account of economic phenomena could be complete without a sociological dimension to it.

Parsons's project was ambitious not only in terms of the intellectual traditions that he sought to develop but also in relation to those that he sidelined. His decision to engage with the work of European rather than American writers reflected his view that the predominant strain of American sociology at the time was flawed. Mills was later to criticise not only Parsons's 'grand theory' but also the longer-established tradition of 'abstracted empiricism' that constituted the opposite pole of American sociology and produced an excessive concern with 'empirical studies of contemporary social facts and problems' (2000: 23). This latter approach was the dominant one among American sociologists of the inter-war years, but it offered little of interest to Parsons who duly sought to draw inspiration from elsewhere. It is, as Rocher has noted, 'something of a paradox that out of the prevailing empiricism of American sociology should have sprung the most abstract theorist' (1974: 1). One of Parsons's objections to the work of his contemporary sociologists in the USA at the point when he transferred to the discipline from economics was that it was atheoretical (Baert 1998: 48), and he later referred to the obstacle presented to the acceptance of his work by 'the general American scepticism about high levels of generalization' (1976: 315). Parsons was equally unattracted by the ideas of those American sociologists who had a greater predisposition to employ theoretical arguments, since they tended to treat behaviour as nothing more than an unthinking response to a stimulus (Adriaansens 1980: 32; Hamilton 1983: 17). Such behaviourism was rejected by Parsons because, following Weber's lead, he 'explicitly and emphatically stresses that social behaviour is intentional' (Smith 1979: 50). Parsons's deliberate 'failure to build on the work of other pioneers in American sociology' (Devereux 1976: 4) meant that the initial impact of *The Structure of Social Action* was limited. In the period immediately following its publication it was,

Hamilton has suggested, 'probably little read except by those at Harvard' (1983: 38), Parsons's own institution. Wrong (1995: 31–2) has even specu-lated on the possibility that its central message about the resolution of the problem of order through adherence to shared norms reached the public domain more effectively through the work of the popular novelist of the time Schulberg, who may have heard indirectly about Parsons's ideas.

Parsons was quite prepared for a controversial reception to his ideas. He later remarked that 'It is almost a commonplace that ideas which entail a major reorganization of patterns of thinking in their field are very likely to encounter severe opposition' (1976: 312). The 'devious route' by which Parsons became a sociologist explains part of how he came to privilege European over American traditions of thought, but it is worth noting that he was also 'something of a maverick' (Devereux 1976: 4) in the sense that his style of working was less concerned than many writers are to gain the approbation of other academics. Camic has described Parsons's theoris-ing as having 'a self-referential orientation', and notes that this character-istic was already apparent in his early works, such as when he reviewed a book and took the opportunity to elaborate on his own position but said 'virtually nothing' (1991: lxvii, xxvii) about the main argument of the author under consideration. Gouldner's criticism of Parsons that he 'does not have a strong impulse to be understood by others' drew from Parsons's style the implication that he neglected not only lay audiences but also fellow sociologists: 'he has not been terribly concerned about communi-cating effectively with his peers, or even about being understood by them' (1971: 200). Black, for example, has referred to some of the words coined by Parsons in his effort to develop a more precise sociological vocabulary as 'barbarous neologisms' (1976: 286), and while it is possible to argue that new terms need to be invented where the existing language proves inade-quate (Hamilton 1983: 14), those developed by Parsons have tended not to be widely adopted, in contrast to those developed by Merton (such as 'the self-fulfilling prophecy', 'disciplined eclecticism', and 'manifest and latent functions') (Sztompka 1986: 31).

This apparent disdain for his readers can be regarded as a by-product of Parsons's practice of writing in which he sought to set down his 'thinking in progress', as a result of which 'the problem becomes clearer as we go along' (qtd in Wearne 1989: 27). Parsons had adopted this method of working as a student, and it makes sense of his comment that *The Structure of Social Action* was 'a clarification and development of my own thought' (qtd in Hamilton 1983: 38), as well as of Wearne's observation that he worked on *The Social System* primarily 'to satisfy *himself* that all the effort was worth it' (1989: 155, emphasis in original). An obvious danger of focussing on one's own understanding of a problem is that others may not be carried along by the argument, and Craib has likened Parsons to 'a filing clerk who is too intelligent for his work. ... [and who] develops a new and complicated system ... . The problem is that he is the only person who can work it, and without him, nothing can be found' (1984: 37–8). This difficulty is heightened if Savage is correct in his characterisation of Parsons as a thinker who 'sought to answer questions where others have not even seen the possibility of a question' (1981: 235). This is not to say that Parsons worked entirely independently while writing. Engagement with students provided a testing audience, and one of the students whom he impressed was Merton, who later reported that 'his first course in theory ... would provide him with the core of his masterwork, *The Structure of Social Action* which ... did not appear in print until five years after its first oral publication' (qtd in Ritzer 2000: 235), that is, its airing in the classroom.

Even though *The Structure of Social Action* had a long gestation period, it was still only preparatory for what was to follow. It provided, as Parsons later expressed it, 'the basic reference point of all my subsequent theoretical work' (1976: 316). Parsons ended his first book with the remark, 'We have sound theoretical foundations on which to build' (1968: 775), and his justification for devoting so much effort to laying these foundations was that misunderstandings about the legacy of ideas of previous sociologists had to be cleared up before any further progress could be made. Parsons found that much of what he had been taught was incorrect, and in particular noted that 'much unlearning of what was not true about Durkheim became necessary' (qtd in Rocher 1974: 7). Durkheim's influence on Parsons's thinking was especially evident in his conclusion that 'In order that there may be a stable system of action involving a plurality of individuals there must be normative regulation of the power aspect of the relations of individuals within the system.' The argument, in short, was that 'integration of individuals' requires 'a common value system' (1968: 768). From this position Parsons now felt able to explore the implications of the 'major breakthrough' (1976: 313) that Durkheim and Weber had facilitated.

As this investigation proceeded he found it increasingly useful to draw on the works of Freud (Rocher 1974: 10), the 'neglect' (1968: xvi) of whose ideas in *The Structure of Social Action* Parsons, therefore, sought to redress. This took Parsons on to what he described as the first of three distinct phases of his work following *The Structure of Social Action*, what he called 'the phase of "structural-functional" theory' (1968: x), in which the conceptualisation of the social system owed less to the models of economics and physics and more to biology and anthropology. It is in this period that Parsons published *The Social System*, widely regarded as his *magnum opus* (Adriaansens 1980: 164). This may have been a 'major exposition' (Wearne 1989: 155) of his thinking, but his position continued to evolve as he worked on further 'refinement' (Hamilton 1983: 19) of his ideas, partly in response to criticism and partly as a result of his pattern of pursuing the *'personal* discovery of the analytical elements implicit in his earlier formulations' (Wearne 1989: 156, emphasis in original). Treviño has described Parsons's theorising during this period as developing 'at break-neck speed' (2001: xviii). Parsons was mindful that the speed with which thinking changed involved not only substantial departures from what he had said in earlier publications but also that it posed a risk to the 'internal consistency' (1951: x) of *The Social System*, publication of which he justified on the grounds that it would in any event need to be revised within a few years (although this projected revision never materialised).

Parsons's work does not form a single coherent, consistent whole because, as Wearne has pointed out, '[h]is theory was always subject to rapid development, with unevenness of progress on its various fronts'. Since publication was merely 'a convenient sign-post' (1989: 5) as this process unfolded, he was constantly moving on, even though this presented his audience with the difficulty of keeping abreast of his latest thinking. Adriaansens has defended Parsons against critics such as Mills for their 'one-sided concentration on *The Social System*' and their corresponding neglect of 'the conceptual changes which Parsons introduced into his schema after 1953' (1980: 164), and it is true that Parsons 'added important new items to his conceptual armoury' (Rocher 1974: 10) at each stage of his career. The rationale for doing so was, he claimed, 'pragmatic', governed by the specific problems that he sought to address as his research agenda unfolded, rather than by the search for 'a logically tight theoretical system' (1976: 317). Harris has suggested that Parsons came to recognise quite early on that, because of its complexity, operationalising the theoretical frame-work contained in *The Structure of Social Action* would have been 'so "awk-ward" as to be impossible' (1980: 226). The decision to approach things from the different angle employed in *The Social System* thus has a pragmatic aspect to it, but it should be remembered that Parsons 'set himself very high standards' (Wearne 1989: 38) and did not change his perspective without the prospect of a better theoretical account emerging. One of the new ideas that Parsons found himself ' "playing" with' was the scheme of 'pattern variables' that emerged after consideration for 'some years' (1964: 359) and that constituted an important part of the argument contained in *The Social System*. The fact that Parsons identified different numbers of pattern vari-ables before settling on four (Rocher 1974: 37, 52) makes it a good example of how his 'thinking in progress' operated as he reworked and developed the ideas bequeathed by the classical figures of social science.

The systematic differentiation of social roles

Parsons's concept of '*institutionalized* individualism' (1999a: 95, emphasis in original) was central to the understanding of modern societies that he derived from Durkheim. For Parsons, as for Durkheim, the other side of utilitarian individualism's overemphasis on the importance of self-interest was its neglect of the conditions that needed to be in place before orderly and predictable interactions could occur, not least of which was the requirement that people share a common set of values that set limits to self-interested behaviour. Without such a normative framework the problem of order would remain unsolved, as the exercise of power over people by the state cannot generate the type of social solidarity required for the operation of a society based on the social differences that result from a specialised division of labour. It was noted in Chapter 3 that one of Durkheim's points of reference in the development of his thinking on this matter was Tönnies, whose concepts of *gemeinschaft* and *gesellschaft* he rejected for their implication that relationships became progressively more instrumental and less 'organic' as modernity developed. Parsons had included some discussion of Tönnies at the end of *The Structure of Social Action* (1968: 686–94), and he returned to the theme in his analysis of the role of the doctor, which led him to the recognition that people do not always act as they would be expected to had the world become as impersonal as Tönnies anticipated. In his discussion of the process whereby people select their doctor, Parsons observed that 'the judgement of his technical competence on which the choice of a physician is supposed to rest is a universalistic criterion. Deviantly from the ideal pattern, however, some people choose a physician because he is Mary Smith's brother-in-law' (1964: 360). This illustrates the more general point that kinship and friendship are not completely displaced by universalistic criteria with the advent of modern society. The fact that much of people's behaviour continues to be influenced by the sorts of considerations that Tönnies in his *gemeinschaft/gesellschaft* dichotomy portrayed as being in decline meant for Parsons that the simple generalisation of a shift from personal to impersonal relationships needed to be re-cast with greater subtlety and analytical precision.

First, the choice between a doctor who is best qualified to do the job and a doctor who is known through a kinship network provides an example of how we may act in what Parsons calls a universalistic or a particularistic way. A second pattern variable is that of 'affectivity' and 'affective neutrality', and an example of the latter orientation is provided by Parsons in terms of doctors treating all patients the same, leaving their emotions to one side: 'The physician is expected to treat an objective problem in objective, scientifically justifiable terms. For example whether he likes or dislikes the particular patient as a person is supposed to be irrelevant' (1951: 435). Third, relationships can be characterised by functional 'specificity' or 'diffuseness', that is, by one connection or several, and the doctor–patient relationship will generally be functionally specific rather than bundled up with other ties such as those between family, friends and neighbours.

Fourth, people face a choice between what Parsons called 'ascription' and 'achievement', or a concern with the characteristics that people have ascribed to them (such as those associated with their race or ethnicity) as opposed to their achievements in performing a particular role. In addition to these four pattern variables on which Parsons finally settled he also referred to 'self-orientation' and 'collectivity-orientation' (Parsons and Shils 1951: 77) which relate to an actor's opportunities to pursue private interests as opposed to responsibility to the collectivity of which the actor is a part. On the basis of these five binary oppositions Parsons suggested that the doctor's role could be 'characterised by universalism, achievement, functional specificity, affective neutrality and collectivity orientation' (Gerhardt 1989: 17), and that this pattern could be applied to professionals more generally. This is the pattern of behaviour that professionals are 'supposed to' follow if they are to act in accordance with the appropriate norms.

Parsons presented the pattern variables as 'a series of major dilemmas of orientation, a series of choices that the actor must make before the situation has a determinate meaning for him' (Parsons and Shils 1951: 76). Parsons regarded the principles underlying the pattern variables as ones that require choices to be made, because one or other has to be selected; in any situation an actor can choose to behave according to universalistic or particularistic criteria, but not both. Likewise an actor can be affective or affectively neutral, but not both at the same time, and so on with all of the pattern variables. In other words, each pair is made up of 'mutually exclusive alternatives' (Black 1976: 284). In relation to the choice between 'self-orientation' and 'collectivity-orientation', Parsons acknowledged that every role must 'both provide for pursuit of private interests and ensure the interests of the collectivity', but argued that '[t]his circumstance is not a paradox' because 'these alternatives apply to specifically relevant selection-contexts, not necessarily to every specific act within the role'. Parsons's point was clarified by the provision of an illustration: 'the public official has an interest in his own financial well-being, which for example he may take into account in deciding between jobs, but he is expected not to take this into consideration in his specific decisions respecting public policy where the two potentially conflict' (1951: 60-1). The pursuit of self-interest is necessarily limited for precisely the same reason that Durkheim advanced when arguing that freedom is the product of regulation: restraint of self-interest is necessary to prevent Hobbes's war of all against all from breaking out.

Parsons developed the pattern variables approach initially in order to challenge the widely held belief that the actions of professionals stood in sharp contrast to those found in business transactions. The view that he sought to contest was that in which 'the business man has been thought of as egoistically pursuing his own self-interest regardless of the interests of others, while the professional man was altruistically serving the interests of others regardless of his own'. He argued that it was wrong to charac- terise business activity solely in terms of self-interest and the professions in terms of altruism and disinterestedness since it was not clear whether the most important difference between the two was one of motivation. Furthermore, he argued, the business world and the professions have much in common. Parsons saw both as characterised by rationality in that both involve the efficient pursuit of an end, whether this is profit-making or treating illness. Echoing Weber, he noted that there is nothing 'natural' about behaving rationally, but that it must be seen in the wider institu- tional and social context that establishes rational behaviour as a norm. Business executives and professionals both employ universalistic criteria and behave in an affectively neutral way, and such similarities might be expected of those located in the same social system. Parsons's view was that 'the occupational structure of any social system does not stand alone, but is involved in complex interrelationships, structural and functional, with other parts of the same social system' (1964: 36, 37, 46). It is an impor- tant part of his message that people's behaviour is oriented to securing recognition and approval from those around them (Menzies 1977: 49), as this ties them to society and acts as a sanction against acting in ways that work against the smooth functioning of the system.

Parsons's analysis of the pattern variables represented an advance on Tönnies's account. Although *gemeinschaft* could be said to be characterised by particularism, affectivity, diffuseness and ascription, and *gesellschaft* by universalism, affective neutrality, specificity and achievement, Parsons did not hold that modern society had moved straightforwardly from the former to the latter (Rocher 1974: 39). He thus rejected the simplicity of 'the older evolutionary sociology' because while some social structures might combine universalism and achievement or particularism and ascrip- tion, the combination of universalism and ascription or particularism and achievement were also identified as possible 'principal types of social structure'. The discussion of these abstract types Parsons justified on the grounds that 'they stimulate many insights and seem to make otherwise baffling features of certain societies understandable'. They can be used, for example, to reveal the operation of hidden structures within social sys- tems. He saw himself as developing 'a highly useful set of tools of com- parative empirical analysis' which would require 'careful checking of empirical evidence' (1951: 182, 180, 200). He had already observed that particularistic and diffuse relationships continued to exist in several areas of modern social systems, 'notably ... family and kinship, friend- ship, class loyalties and identifications so far as they are bound up with birth and the diffuse "community" common styles of life, and loyalty to particular leaders and organizations as such, independently of what they "stand for" ' (1964: 46). It therefore made perfect sense for him to go on to explore in greater detail the American family and its connections to the wider social system.

Parsons claimed that the process whereby a social institution such as the family becomes increasingly differentiated into specialised roles 'can be formulated in pattern variable terms' (Parsons and Bales 1956: 134). The 'deductive rigour' (Wearne 1989: 172) of his approach led him to recognise that tensions would be generated wherever people attempted to combine the two elements of any one pattern variable, and this provided the basis of his answer to the question 'Why are kinship units not patterned like industrial organizations?' In Parsons's view, families cannot be run like businesses because roles within kinship units 'are always functionally diffuse and collectivity-oriented. Their constitution on the basis of biological relatedness precludes the primacy of universalistic orientations, and narrowly limits the relevance of achievement patterns, at least as criteria of membership, to the marriage selection process' (1951: 154–5). In other words, members of families are interconnected in a variety of ways, they are expected to put the good of the family before their individual interests, and they relate to each other as a distinct group deserving of a special status that sets them apart from the rest of the population, because of which they are judged by who they are rather than what they have achieved. Parsons sought to make the further point that comparative analysis showed family structures to be far from static, and claimed that the changes with which his audience would have been familiar could be explained in terms of the shifting functions performed by the family within the developing social system.

Parsons's ability to present this analytical framework in a more accessible fashion in his empirical studies is nicely demonstrated by his chapter on the American family of the 1950s. He commenced this with the observation that 'The American family has, in the past generation or more, been undergoing a profound process of change', and observed that this had been the subject of competing interpretations among social scientists. He noted in particular that the rise in divorce rates had been identified by some writers as evidence of growing social disorganisation, a thesis on which he sought to cast doubt by the presentation of 'certain facts'. He pointed out that divorce rates had oscillated between a low of 1.3 per 1000 of the population at the depth of the inter-war depression to a peak of 4.3 in 1946, the year following the end of the Second World War, but that they had dropped consistently since. This fact, along with the concentration of divorces among recently married and childless couples and with the high rates of remarriage were to Parsons 'suggestive of a process of readjustment rather than of a continuous trend of disorganization'. Furthermore, the recovery of birth rates following their decline in the 1930s meant that

'the recent facts have shifted the burden of proof to him who argues that
the disorganization of the family is bringing imminent race suicide in its
wake' (Parsons and Bales 1956: 3, 4, 5, 6–7). This style of presenting ideas
is reminiscent of Durkheim's *Suicide*, and demonstrates that Parsons's
approach was quite capable of incorporating statistical and other empirical evidence and of engagement with important issues in current affairs.

Having established that the changes underway in the American family
patterns of his day were not as wholesale as the more extreme interpretations had suggested, Parsons went on to argue that the changes reflected
the process of 'structural differentiation in societies'. During the course of
social development a variety of functions had been transferred from the
family to other institutions, most obviously in relation to the separation of
families and work organisations. Parsons argued that the decline of family businesses was not evidence of 'a "decline of the family" ' but simply
of the concentration of the family on the performance of more specialised
tasks to which it was best suited. According to Parsons, there are two of
these: 'first, the primary socialization of children so that they can truly
become members of the society into which they have been born; second,
the stabilization of the adult personalities of the population'. Children
need to be socialised into the culture of the society and to learn its norms,
while adults derive from their marriage partners emotional as well
as practical support. Families can thus be considered to be ' "factories"
which produce human personalities'. The process of differentiation is
taken further by the specialisation of roles within the family, whereby
husbands become breadwinners and wives homemakers, so that men
have 'the instrumental responsibility for a family' while women 'take the
primary responsibility for the children' and are 'expressive' rather than
'instrumental'. The argument that these roles are characterised by 'com-
plementarity' (Parsons and Bales 1956: 9, 16, 23, 51, 24) was asserted rather
than demonstrated, but it arose out of the logic of Parsons's position that
specialisation is more efficient than diversity of function because it allows
better adaptation to the environment. From the perspective of there being
a long-term tendency towards 'increased adaptive capacity' (Parsons
1977: 230) of social institutions such as the family, the specialisation of
roles between the sexes and the move away from the extended family to
the independent nuclear family can both be considered to be 'normal'
(Parsons and Bales 1956: 10, 12) developments.

Functionalist explanations

Parsons's sociological writings reveal a great deal not only about the
particular subjects that he discussed but also about the ambitiousness of

his project. He attempted nothing less than 'to outline in an unambiguous manner a map of the "social" ' (Holton and Turner 1988: 3). His work was both theoretical and empirical, and it was also multidisciplinary; there is an irony in the fact that a writer who wrote so much about differentiation should himself 'reject the excessive development of intellectual specialisation' (Holton 1998: 96). He adopted, developed and synthesised ideas drawn from various classical social scientists in a way that others did not always endorse (Cohen *et al.* 1975; Giddens 1996: 128–31), being concerned more with the analytical rigour of his approach than with faithfulness to any particular canon. He also immersed himself in some extremely abstract academic debates but at the same time engaged in critical discussion of a wide range of contemporary social issues. Runciman's opinion that Parsons frequently advanced arguments that 'are little more than common sense observations about the institutions of American society' (1998: 58) is at odds with the view that Parsons's conclusions often went against common sense, as they did for example when he pointed out that 'higher divorce rates do not necessarily indicate a flight from the institution of marriage but may, paradoxically, reflect the high expectations that individuals have of marital relations' (Morgan 1975: 27). Similarly, Parsons's analysis of illness revealed that it relieves a person from their usual obligations but, contrary to popular opinion, it does not free them from social control, since there are norms governing the behaviour of anyone adopting the 'sick role'. As Parsons observed, 'exemption from obligations and from a certain kind of responsibility … is given at a price' (1999b: 104), notably the requirement that an ill person strives to become well again as soon as possible. Douglas's comment that 'Parsons founded medical sociology when he identified and named the "sick role" ' (1996: 34) gives some indication of the path-breaking significance of this analysis. More generally, Holmwood has argued that '[t]here is something "counter-intuitive" and, therefore, interesting about the way in which Parsons "re-interprets" circumstances which others have claimed are contradictory'. For Holmwood, this 'is what sociological argument should be about – claim and counter-claim, giving rise to further theoretical elaboration and research' (1996: 128). It makes sense to interpret Parsons's relationship with the writings of the sociological classics in this light.

There is an optimistic character to the account of social life that Parsons presented that stands in sharp contrast to the pessimism of writers such as Weber. As Layder has noted, 'Parsons was keen to emphasise the potential for individuals to benefit from the system and to control their own future' (1994: 14). The assumption that the different elements of a society together constitute an integrated system in the same way that a living organism is made up of various parts underpinned Parsons's analysis of the interconnectedness of modern social life, and he anticipated the further development of interdependence, since '[d]ifferentiation inevitably entails mutual dependence: the more differentiation, the more dependence' (1999e: 287). Parsons's view that specialisation of roles had the potential to work to everyone's advantage reflected his acceptance of Durkheim's point about society that the whole is greater than the sum of the individual parts. From this point of view Parsons developed a measured critique of Mills's *The Power Elite* on the grounds that it operated with what Parsons called a 'zero-sum' concept of power in which one person or group can have more power only at the expense of another having correspondingly less. Parsons's preference was for an approach to power that recognised the necessity for specialised institutional leadership, reflecting 'the deeper and longer-run dependence of the goals and capacities of individuals themselves on social organization' (1999d: 232, 233). Parsons had come to this position by the analytically useful device of exploring the implications of the assumption that social arrangements were functional and had emerged for a purpose, even if that purpose was not readily apparent. By the time of his response to Mills it appeared to his critics that it had become an article of faith to Parsons that 'the development of the United States was one of rational progression' (Buxton 1985: 151). So great was Parsons's concern 'to emphasize that power does not necessarily entail the coercive imposition of one individual or group over another' (Giddens 1977: 341) that his portrayal of the world presented social change as a process of 'adaptive upgrading' (Parsons 1966: 22) that had the potential to benefit all members of a society.

Kivisto has rightly pointed out that 'Parsons was never a conservative apologist for the status quo' (1998: 66), but his theory of social change was like his theory of social order in its reliance on the assumption (imported from other disciplines such as economics and biology) that systems tend to gravitate towards equilibrium. Thus in his account of the modern American family Parsons acknowledged that there had been 'swings of great amplitude' in birth rates but that these were returning to levels that were compatible with 'longer-run stability'. Similarly, although the proportion of married women in paid employment in the USA had grown by over 50 per cent during the 1940s, he argued that there was 'no serious tendency' (Parsons and Bales 1956: 6, 14) in the direction of symmetry between the sexes in the labour market. Parsons was by no means alone in his failure to predict the extent to which women's position in the labour market and the wider society would change in the second half of the twentieth century (Bell and Graubard 1997: xvii–xviii), but the reasons for this failure are instructive. Parsons's explanations of the social arrangements that he described took the form of arguing that social systems have certain prerequisites, 'the conditions which must be met by any social system of a stable and durable character ... the minimum structural features of all societies'. Parsons argued, for example, that societies all have some form of kinship system and that while it was conceivable that other social institutions might perform the same functions, 'in the case of kinship this is highly unlikely' (1951: 167, 169, 172). The difficulty that this presented to many of Parsons's critics was that the identification of a need of the system was not always experienced in positive terms by actors performing their allotted roles. A notably eloquent expression of this point was made in Friedan's discussion of the dissatisfaction with the femininity allotted to suburban American housewives of the 1950s. She termed this 'the problem that has no name' because in the Parsonian scheme of things no recognition was given to 'that voice within women that says "I want something more than my husband and my children and my home"' (1999: 359). The social system may have functioned more smoothly than it would otherwise have done had women not concentrated on the socialisation of children and supporting their husbands, but their feelings and behaviour were not adequately explained by reference to the requirements of the system.

A key issue relating to Parsons's mode of argument is what sort of explanation his analysis provides. To describe the functional needs of a system is to adopt a quite different approach to that of conventional causal explanation, and although Parsons can be seen to have done both in different parts of his work (Turner 1999b: 9), his primary focus was on identifying the contribution that social arrangements made to the reproduction of social order. By deploying this type of argument Parsons can be seen to be following Durkheim's practice, but in Parsons's hands the approach became increasingly highly formalised. Subsequent to the publication of *The Social System* Parsons reworked the pattern variables into the identification of four key functions, presented as 'that best of all possible diagrams, the four-cell box' (Mennell 1974: 151), with the distinction between means and ends along one axis and on the other the distinction between things that are internal to the system and those that are external. This came to be known as the AGIL scheme because of the concepts contained in its boxes, 'Adaptation', 'Goal-attainment', 'Integration' and 'Latency'. As a result of this concern to further develop 'propositions that admit of logical, not empirical, proof' (Parsons 1999c: 185, 183), Parsons's theorising became more and more remote from the empirical investigations that it was intended to inform. For Gouldner, this 'taxonomic zeal' produced an approach that used 'four-fold tables as a logic machine to chop out mountains of conceptual distinctions'. Also lost in the process was the sense of agency with which Parsons had set out, because the ends pursued by individuals come in the Parsonian schema to 'derive *from* social systems' (1971: 205, 206, emphasis in original). As a result, Parsons was open to the criticism that he had 'engaged in theoretical "overkill" on the problem of order', because he 'solved the problem too well' (Menzies 1977: 110) and in the process reduced individuals to the passive performers of the roles into which they have been socialised. The logical orderliness of the model with its interconnections between the various parts of the system presented a picture of social coherence that many amongst Parsons's audience simply did not recognise.

The development of Parsons's thinking has a relentless logic to it. One of his starting points had been his acceptance of Weber's critique of economic determinism, and his mature reflection that '*All* such single-factor theories belong to the kindergarten stage of social science's development' could have been voiced 40 years previously. In the intervening period his conviction grew that 'within the social system, the normative elements are more important for social change than the "material interests" of constitutive units', and it was in this sense that he was prepared to accept the label of 'cultural determinist' (1966: 113, emphasis in original). In order to reach the analytical framework of his mature works, Parsons 'had to indulge in considerable flights of imagination and particularly in *analogy by association*' (Rocher 1974: 165, emphasis in original), even though he is frequently associated with a lack of imagination because of the criticisms aimed at him by Mills (2000). More serious is the charge that Parsons prioritised the construction of a logically rigorous analytical system and neglected the relationship of this system to empirical evidence. The connection of Parsons's general theory to his empirical work 'is in all but a few cases less than systematic' (Hamilton 1983: 130), and as a result of his concentration on conceptual analysis Holmwood has written that '[t]he sad, but necessary, conclusion to be made about Parsons's sociological writings is that virtually his entire contribution stands or falls with his general theoretical framework'. Holmwood's comment is made in the context of a comparison of Parsons and Weber which is favourable to the latter because of his far greater involvement in 'substantive sociological argument' (1996: 127). Parsons's project was an immensely ambitious one and aimed to build on the work of Weber and the other sociological classics in order to advance the scientific standing of the discipline. One of the most important things that his attempt revealed is that sociological knowledge is not in any simple sense cumulative.

List of Parsons's key sociological writings
Dates of original publication are given in ( )

The Structure of Social Action two volumes (1937)
The Social System (1951)

Toward a General Theory of Action (ed. with E. Shils) (1951)
Family, Socialization and Interaction Process (1956)
Economy and Society (1956) (written with N. Smelser)
Essays in Sociological Theory (1964)
Societies: Evolutionary and Comparative Perspectives (1966)
The Evolution of Societies (1977)

6

Charles Wright Mills: sociology as an imaginative craft

Introduction and overview

Charles Wright Mills was only 45 when he died of his fourth heart attack, at home in New York on 20 March 1962, having been born in Texas on 28 August 1916. His gravestone's epitaph, 'I have tried to be objective. I do not claim to be detached' (in Mills and Mills 2000: 341), was fittingly drawn from his own writings. It captures his ambition to live up to the high standards of social science at the same time as making the point that doing so is quite compatible with active involvement in the world. He perceived the big political issues of his day to be the misuse of power on a national and global scale and the conflicts to which this gave rise. In a tumultuous life he was never far from controversy. He interviewed the revolutionary leaders Fidel Castro and Che Guevara, and wrote a passionate defence of the Cuban revolution that was sufficiently anti-American in tone to lead to his receiving a death threat (Mills and Mills 2000: 346–7). His life-long argument was with what he perceived America had become: culturally shallow and dominated politically by a self-serving and dangerous elite. Horowitz's description of him as 'a conservative radical' (1983: 329) reflects the contradictions of a man who lamented the corrosion of traditional American values but who recognised that the forces that were changing the world would not allow any simple return to the past. His task therefore became one of trying to grasp the nature of the changes that political, economic and social structures were undergoing with a view to imagining a different future and making interventions that might help to bring these about.

Mills's unorthodox life and work defy easy classification; as Miliband noted, he 'cannot be neatly labeled and catalogued' because he was 'a man on his own' (1969: 11) rather than a follower of any particular school of thought or a member of any organisations that might subject him to their discipline. Mills understood himself to be 'a certain type of man who spends his life finding and refining what is within him' (in Mills and Mills 2000: 37), and sociology provided an ideal vehicle for this journey of self-discovery, in the same way that he felt it could for anyone trying to make sense of their life. Mills was sympathetic to the white-collar worker of mid-twentieth-century America whom he characterised as someone who did 'not know where he is going' and who responded by being 'in a frantic hurry' (1956: xvi). That Mills himself lived at a frantic pace is well known, but in contrast to the white-collar workers who were the subject of his monograph he sought to resist the modern social system's propensity to take ever-greater advantage of people's 'manipulatability'. Sociology provided a useful tool in this endeavour, by explaining how things have come to be as they are and by showing that things have the potential to be different. It would, he argued with his collaborator Hans Gerth, 'be provincial of Americans not to think about the diverse possibilities latent in all modern social structures' (Gerth and Mills 1954: xvii, xv), although as time went on he found himself increasingly frustrated by his compatriots' provincialism. Towards the end of his life he took his message abroad, and urged his South American audience to 'imagine all the range of alternatives that might exist' (1967b: 156), fearful that they might seek to follow the American path of social development that he regarded with such concern.

Mills stands out as an important figure in sociology because of both what he said and the way in which he said it. He is renowned for the passion with which he argued the case for sociologists to be imaginative in practising their subject, and a central part of *The Sociological Imagination* was devoted to his trenchant criticism of Parsons on the grounds that Parsonian 'grand theory' represented to Mills a betrayal of the true purpose of the discipline. In many ways the contrast between the styles of sociological argument deployed by Parsons and by Mills could not be starker. Mills certainly cultivated this perception. The two men had divergent sociological careers, reflecting their very different backgrounds and personalities (Seidman 1998: 172). In terms of key concepts, Parsons emphasised the importance of shared values, while Mills highlighted the phenomena of social divisions and conflict. Parsons correspondingly epitomised the sober-minded professional sociologist working systematically and in co-operation with numerous others, whereas Mills wanted to 'get on with it' (in Miliband 1969: 11) and could not conceal his impatience with his peers. He viewed himself as 'an outlander' (in Horowitz 1983: 84) generally at odds with colleagues, and his sharply polemical way of expressing his ideas contributed to his being regarded as 'a lone, sometimes quixotic figure' (Seidman 1998: 182). This was perhaps inevitable for someone whose enduring image as 'the sociologist in anger' (Cuzzort and King 1989: ch. 8) reflects his combative mode of engagement in public debate over the major political issues of the day. His career was an uneasy combination of 'a life of scholarship with that of the partisan intellectual' (Kivisto 1998: 36). Shils's review of *The Sociological Imagination* portrayed Mills as 'a rough-tongued brawler' (in Eldridge 1983: 109) whose scholarly activities were compromised by his capacity for splenetic attack. To his detractors, Mills's sociology was 'vulgar' (Bell 1991: 142), an epithet that Mills returned (Horowitz 1983: 102). To his supporters, he was a magical hero whose ostracism stemmed from the ruffling of feathers that his controversial insights and commitment to plain speaking necessarily caused (Horowitz 1967a: 1).

Behind the 'explosive' (Bell 1991: 138) quality that was a prominent feature of Mills's writing but was equally conspicuously absent from Parsons's work, the two thinkers had several things in common (Holton and Turner 1988: 191–4). One was that they both drew on the sociological classics to steer the discipline in a new direction away from the descriptive and atheoretical approach that Mills dubbed 'abstracted empiricism' (2000: ch. 3). In collaboration with Gerth, Mills made available to English-speaking audiences translations of Weber's writings, although this collection and their introduction to it (Gerth and Mills 1970) emphasised Weber's interest in power and politics, and thereby portrayed 'a strikingly different Weber than that presented by Parsons' (Seidman 1998: 173). The influence of Weber on Mills is readily apparent, not only in the latter's continued focus on power and domination in the contemporary world, but also in his concern to confront big issues through a comparative and historical perspective. The central questions of sociology that Mills identified bear the unmistakable imprint of Weber's thinking, the 'profundity and clarity' of which Mills praised. By urging sociologists to ask 'What varieties of men and women now prevail in this society and in this period? And what varieties are coming to prevail?' (2000: 6, 7), Mills echoed the concerns expressed by Weber at the end of *The Protestant Ethic*. Weber's mention there of the 'nullity' (1976a: 182) towards which rationalisation was propelling social development has a parallel in Mills's anticipation of the banal social order in which the typical person could be characterised as a 'Cheerful Robot' (2000: 171). In terms of his engagement with the processes of long-term social change Parsons had a similarly broad vision, but his perspective presented 'an unambiguous celebration of modernity' (Turner 1999b: 1) whereas for Mills such thinking smacked of 'historical provincialism', discounting as it did all the signs that 'The Modern Age is being succeeded by a post-modern period.' The scale of Mills's ambition to capture 'the human variety' (2000: 151, 166, 132) of social relations in all their diversity is illustrated by his unfulfilled plan to write between six and nine volumes on comparative sociology (Horowitz 1983: ch. 14). This project was barely started when he died, but although his work was left incomplete his legacy was mould-breaking.

The capacity to see things differently was a crucial part of what Mills referred to as the 'craft' of social science, especially of the sociological imagination which he regarded as 'a quality of mind' (2000: 195, 5). If practised well, this craft enabled people to make connections between their own biographies and broader patterns of historical development, and the power of these insights is indicated by their wide appeal. Such ideas resonated with the mood of the times as social protest against the status quo escalated. Mills's style of argument has been described as 'deceptively simple' (Marshall 1990: 196), and this is an important part of its appeal. Readers can readily accept the distinction between 'the personal troubles of milieu' and 'the public issues of social structure' that Mills referred to as 'an essential tool of the sociological imagination and a feature of all classic work in social science'. Mills recognised that the connection between the two is less readily apparent, and for this connection to be revealed, he argued, it is necessary to develop a sociological imagination. He saw this as a tool that could be used to challenge the fatalism that characterises the outlook of many individuals within the large and impersonal systems that dominate the modern world. Mills presented it as a paradox that people have a strong 'sense of being trapped' in an epoch when, 'The facts about the newer means of history-making are a signal that men are not necessarily in the grip of fate, that men *can* now make history' (2000: 8, 3, 183, emphasis in original). Mills was seeking to raise people's awareness that things could be different, but there was more to his argument than this simple but important point. He sought also to show how the sociological imagination entails the application of skills that need to be learned and practised methodically if such alternatives are to be given appropriate consideration.

Among the skills advocated by Mills was the cultivation of 'the habit of cross-classification' (2000: 213) in order to generate typologies. It was by the use of a simple four-cell typology of workers that he identified the type who, despite being denied the opportunity to participate in the 'objective structure of power', was 'cheerful and willing' (in Eldridge 1983: 39), the figure he later recast as the Cheerful Robot (1956: 233). It was noted in Chapter 5 that Parsons used the same method of analysis to develop his own types, but Mills sought to distance himself from Parsonian 'grand theory' by grounding his analysis much more directly in empirical evidence and also by expressing his ideas in more straightforward language. In Mills's opinion, the principal shortcomings of Parsons's approach were that it failed to 'get down to observation' and that it failed 'to describe and explain human conduct and society plainly' (2000: 32). Accessibility to a wider audience than that made up by professional academics was an important objective for Mills. As Lemert notes, he 'did not intend that the sociological imagination be a competence of only the more highly educated' (1997a: 13), and one of the methods that he used in order to reach beyond the realm of academia was to dispense with technical jargon. Mills undoubtedly had a command over language that Parsons lacked, and his 'talent for phrase-making' (Wrong 1999: 23) is evident throughout his work. One example is his use of the term 'crackpot realism' (1960: ch. 13) to describe the world view of military leaders in the context of the nuclear arms race between the USA and the former Soviet Union, and it is indicative of Mills's style of presentation that the book in which this term is found is provocatively entitled *The Causes of World War Three*. For some critics Mills got carried away by his rhetoric, and it has been remarked that 'He was too clever in his writing. He showed too much interest in the well-turned phrase and possibly too little in the well-tuned fact' (Cuzzort and King 1989: 194). A more favourable judgement is that Mills's work was 'accessible without being condescending to the general reader' (Eldridge 1983: 112). It is typical of Mills that even his pursuit of the apparently innocuous goal of stating things clearly has had the capacity to generate lasting controversy.

Thinking big and being bold

The need to think on a big scale was rooted in Mills's sympathy for the ordinary person, 'the generalized Little Man', whom he regarded as the unwitting 'victim' of 'big ugly forces' (1956: xii). In order to make sense of the position of ordinary people and the personal difficulties that they encountered in their everyday lives, Mills argued that it was necessary to look at the bigger picture of public issues to which these individual experiences were connected. The roots of this perspective lie in the tradition of American radicals such as Veblen whom Mills described as 'the best critic of America that America has produced' (1953: vi), although Mills was far too independent-minded to be confined within any one intellectual tradition (Miliband 1969: 11). As Tilman has noted, Mills's 'eclecticism early assimilated elements from nearly every major school of social thought' (1984: 18), and his writings were able to incorporate influences from Weber, Marx and Freud as well as the Pragmatists (on whom he wrote his PhD thesis (Mills 1966)) without treating any of them as an orthodoxy to be followed with undue reverence. A central theme of his work to which he returned constantly was the threat posed to reason and freedom by contemporary developments (Hearn 1985), and he saw sociology as having the potential to help people to become 'free and rational as individuals'. He did not, however, share the faith of Enlightenment thinkers that the progress of freedom and rationality necessarily went together, and his observation that 'increased rationality may not be assumed to make for increased freedom' echoed Weber's concerns about the rationalisation process. In the extreme, Mills argued, 'the chance to reason of most men is destroyed, as rationality increases and its locus, its control, is moved from the individual to the big-scale organization'. The need to expose this prospect of 'rationality without reason' (2000: 184, 167, 170) lay behind Mills's commitment in his work to 'do it *big*' (in Mills with Mills 2000: vii, emphasis in original); this was, he suggested, the only intellectually responsible course of action to take in such circumstances.

According to Wakefield, the motto that informed Mills's whole approach to life was 'Taking it big' (2000: 8), and it is instructive that a bio-graphical sketch describes Mills as a 'large man [who] thought in broad and bold terms' before going on to note that 'he exaggerated to make his point' (Mitchell 1979: 127). Exaggeration had an important part to play in Mills's work. He observed that 'often you get the best insights by consid-ering extremes', and one of his tips for stimulating the sociological imagination was 'If something seems very minute, imagine it to be simply enormous' (2000: 213, 215). There is some resonance between these ideas and the deliberate accentuation of one side of a social phenomenon that goes into the construction of a Weberian ideal type or the polarisation of an issue into the either/or of Parsonian pattern variables, but Mills went further than this by highlighting in his arguments the extent to which his views were at odds with received wisdom. A famous example of this is Mills's study of *The Power Elite* in which he stated bluntly that '[t]he top of the American system of power is much more unified and much more powerful ... than is generally supposed' and went on to characterise the system constructed by 'the higher circles' of industrial, political and mili-tary leaders as one marked by 'higher immorality' (1959: 29, 343). Mills regarded the book as aiming 'a blow at the smooth certainties and agree-able formulas that now make up the content of liberalism' and in doing so he deliberately employed 'caricatures' of 'bureaucrats and politicians and millionaires'. The object of his attack was nothing less than 'the classic lib-eral image of modern American society' (1969: 229, 230, 236) whose con-temporary exponents had 'abandoned criticism for the new American celebration' (1959: 25). Mills was scathing about the various means that they employed to discount concerns about the growing concentration of power in a country whose democratic credentials were routinely con-trasted favourably with the authoritarianism of totalitarian societies.

The social trends that Parsons had sought to comprehend through the concept of differentiation were to Mills much more ominous, and this reflected the contrasting conceptions of power that the two thinkers held. The emergence of increasingly specialised leaders in the economic, political and military fields that Parsons (1999c: 225) took to be a necessary feature of normal social development was for Mills something that posed a threat to basic American values. In *The Power Elite* Mills argued that 'there is a move-ment from widely scattered little powers to concentrated powers', and he invited his readers to consider where that process might ultimately lead. In his view American society had by the 1950s 'moved a considerable distance along the road to the mass society. At the end of that road there is totalitarianism, as in Nazi Germany or in Communist Russia', and although he recognised that 'We are not yet at that end', that 'We have not yet reached the extreme case', the implication of his line of reasoning was clear: America was becoming dominated by an elite whose grip on power was reducing ordinary citizens to the status of a manipulated mass. In this process the old order in which power was more diffused was coming to be replaced by a situation in which those at the bottom of society were 'increasingly powerless'. This trend towards the disempowerment of the mass of the population was in Mills's view the corollary of the usurpation by members of the power elite of positions by which 'they are in com-mand of the major hierarchies and organizations of modern society. They rule the big corporations. They run the machinery of the state and claim its prerogatives. They direct the military establishment.' Mills conceded that had these powerful leaders been members of unconnected groups then the liberal view of elites being 'so scattered as to lack any coherence as a historical force' might have applied, but he claimed that this was not the case. Rather there were mounting indications of 'an ever-increasing inter-locking of economic, military, and political structures' with the result that 'the leading men in each of these three domains of power – the warlords, the corporation chieftains, the political directorate – tend to come together, to form the power elite of America' (1959: 304–5, 304, 320, 324, 4, 16, 8, 9). These were 'The High and Mighty' (Mills with Mills 2000: 162) of the book's original title, and to Mills their emergence needed to be exposed even though the facts to be faced were 'decidedly unpleasant' (Mills 1969: 250), not least the fact that there were striking parallels between the USA and USSR (Horowitz 1983: 309).

What gave these developments a particularly sinister ring for Mills was the extent to which they were going unnoticed. This was not in Mills's view attributable solely to the apologetics of academics and commentators who played down the existence of a power elite and a powerless mass. Mills was fully aware of the problems of studying the extremes of the social structure, and he noted that while the middle classes are quite readily observable to sociologists and other investigators, 'the very top of modern society is often inaccessible, the very bottom often hidden' (1959: 363). This meant that *The Power Elite* could not contain sufficiently extensive and robust facts and figures about the concentration of power that Mills knew would be required to convince the most sceptical members of his audi-ence, although the book does refer to evidence about numerous aspects of the position of American business, political and military leaders that Mills drew from an extensive range of sources. These sources included not only his own fieldwork but also popular journalism as well as more academic publications. The references to these sources run to no fewer than 48 pages, as might be expected of a book that Mills's correspondence reveals was five years in the making and written with a desire to rebut the accusation (attributed to Parsons) that his work was 'impressionistic' (Mills with Mills 2000: 155, 158). Mills went further in rebutting the criticism that his argument lacked sufficiently compelling supporting evidence by claiming that what he had advanced was 'an elaborated hypothesis, anchored, I believe, at key points to acknowledged fact'. He noted that it was possible to question the validity of any so-called facts, doing so by recounting how 'If you have ever seriously studied, as I have, for a year or two some thousand hour-long interviews, carefully coded and punched, you'll have begun to see how very malleable these thousands of bits of fact really are' (1969: 233). His position was that 'We neither take the world for granted nor believe it to be a simple fact. Our business is with facts only in so far as we need them to upset or to clinch our ideas. ... We do not want merely to take an inventory, we want to discover meanings' (1959: 364). Mills argued that for this to happen it was necessary to engage in a reasoned dialogue about the interpretation of the available evidence, however incomplete that evidence may be.

Mills treated works like *The Power Elite* as a series of 'conversations' between the author and various audiences who come to be engaged in a process of unspoken dialogue. He regarded his topic as particularly suited to 'this essay-like way of reasoning together', because 'it enables us to bring together an effective variety of viewpoints' and by doing so the parties to the dialogue can further their understanding of the subject. This included the author, who by clarifying the ideas set down 'becomes aware of ideas he did not even know he had' (1959: 363–4). This observation can be linked to the more general tenet held by Mills that people's grasp of their situation was frequently unreliable. In *The Sociological Imagination* Mills proposed that 'individuals, in the welter of their daily experience, often become falsely conscious of their social position' (2000: 5). He also argued that individuals may be unable to identify 'the "real" motives' behind their actions because 'When we are motivated by impulses that are disapproved, we sometimes cannot stand the image of ourselves, so we keep these motives out of our awareness' (Gerth and Mills 1954: 119, 128). It followed from these propositions that it is problematic to take people's accounts of themselves as sufficient to understand their actions, and Mills reported that he had 'never studied any group that had an adequate view of its own social position' (1969: 230). This included the power elite, whose members were often 'uncertain about their roles', partly because they may over time come to accept as true 'the rhetoric of public relations' that con-structed their exercise of power as service of the public. Such individuals might in all sincerity believe the 'equalitarian rhetoric' that denies the progressive concentration of power, but that did not for Mills make them right to do so. Instead he referred to 'the higher ignorance' (1959: 4, 5, 14, 350) of the power elite to draw attention to the extent of the discrepancy between what they said about themselves and the reality of their situation.

The Power Elite completed what has been called Mills's 'great stratifica-tion trilogy' (Horowitz 1983: 282). It built on *The New Men of Power* and *White Collar* in which members of the working and middle classes had, respectively, also been presented as misperceiving their positions. Mills found it useful to employ the concept of 'false consciousness' throughout his career. In an early account of the middle classes he wrote (in an awkward style resembling the 'socspeak' (2000: 220) that he would later criticise) that '[i]rrational discrepancies between the objectively defined bases of a stratum, the subjectively held policies of its members and their commonly accepted values do not necessarily point to a problem of method. They may indicate the "false consciousness" of the stratum we are examining' (1967c: 275–6). Later in *White Collar* he referred to 'the mask-like character of liberalism's rhetoric of small business and family farm' in a world that had by and large replaced the independent entrepreneur with the paid worker. For Mills the United States had 'been transformed from a nation of small capitalists to a nation of hired employees', but people's per-ceptions had not adapted to the growth of the large corporation. Indeed, the ideology of a nation of small capitalists was so uncontested that 'in the minds of many it seems the very latest model of reality' even though there were by the 1950s 'four times as many wage-workers and salary workers as independent entrepreneurs' (1956: 35, 34, xiv). Mills recognised that in the modern world of white-collar work an employee could be 'job-conscious, plant-conscious, corporation-conscious or industry-conscious' rather than 'class-conscious' (in Tilman 1984: 104). What Mills called 'status panic' led workers to strive for prestige through their work position, and because of the fine gradations of white-collar hierarchies 'the individual may seize upon minute distinctions as bases for status'. Mills's further observation that 'these distinctions operate against any status solidarity' (1956: 254) confirmed that he had no faith in the Marxist expectation of growing class consciousness and mutual support. Rather it was Mills's view that work-ers, both white-collar and blue-collar, had been depoliticised by the pursuit of status and by consumerism, to which they turned in what he regarded as a futile search for individual fulfilment.

Mills's bold social criticism was also a forthright engagement with conventional Marxist thinking. He drew considerable inspiration from Marx's ideas, but saw no point shoring up untenable positions. It was in this spirit that he wrote bluntly of Marx, 'He assumes that capitalist history will do away with false consciousness. Obviously it has not' (1963: 114). In a very early publication, written in his mid-twenties, Mills had drawn attention to the way in which conservative forces could undermine efforts to develop radical consciousness by casting doubt on the motives of trade union leaders: 'A labor leader says he performs a certain act because he wants to get higher standards of living for the workers. A businessman says that this is rationalization, or a lie; that it is really because he wants more money for himself from the workers' (1967e: 448). Mills's subsequent analysis of this issue in *The New Men of Power* portrayed a situation in which the odds were stacked against trade unions because of the power of the mass media to cast doubt upon their case. As he put it, 'By their omissions and in their whole manner of dramatizing the American scene, particularly their heavy accent upon individual effort and individual ends, the mass media are biased against the labor world.' In such a climate trade union leaders did not necessarily recognise themselves to be the 'modern rebels' (1948: 34, 8) that Mills labelled them. This reflected the contradictory character of their role. It has been stated that Mills 'worked hard to avoid the rhetoric of the conventional Left' (Horowitz 1983: 216) and resisted deploying the language of class consciousness. Instead he highlighted the conflicting pressures on such leaders:

> even as the labor leader rebels, he holds back rebellion. He organizes discontent and then sits on it, exploiting it in order to maintain a continuous organization: the labor leader is a manager of discontent. He makes regular what might otherwise be disruptive. (1948: 9)

Mills did not share the faith of those who saw workers and their organisations as the route by which Americans would arrive at solutions to their problems, at least not while the leaders of these organisations were compromised by their acceptance of subordination in their dealings with the power elite.

The exercise of imagination

Mills's account of how unions were not 'levers for change' made it clear that this pertained to the organisations run by *'current* labor leaders' (1967a: 108, 104, emphasis in original) and was not presented as a timeless verity. His sense of historical change was also evident in his observation about the power elite that '[i]t has not always been like this' (1959: 8). He regarded sociologists who could not draw on the lessons of history for such comparative purposes as 'simply crippled'. Conversely, if they were able to answer the question 'Where does this society stand in human history?', they were well equipped in Mills's view to challenge accounts of a social order that dealt only in finding reasons for arrangements needing to be as they are. To Mills things could always be different, and sociology had a crucial role to play in imagining those alternatives. This point applied to alternatives at the level of the individual as well as the whole society, since the resolution of personal troubles was in Mills's opinion bound up with the public issues of the day. His examples of unemployment, war, divorce and urban sprawl were things that people did not need to feel were beyond their control. The sociological imagination had the capacity to counter fatalism among individuals 'whose mentalities have swept only a series of limited orbits' by awakening in them '[t]heir capacity for astonishment' and encouraging them to 'acquire a new way of thinking' (2000: 215, 6, 7–8). What *The Sociological Imagination* showed, in Miliband's view, was 'that social analysis could be probing, tough-minded, critical, relevant, and scholarly' and could be used to challenge the systematic 'brainwashing' (1969: 3) to which Mills argued people were exposed. Mills's style was premised on the assumption that he was correct in his assertion that ordinary people were increasingly subject to subtle and pervasive processes of 'manipulation' (1959: 316) of which they were unaware, and to which mild-mannered treatises would be an ineffective remedy.

Two words that capture Mills's spirit are 'flamboyance' and 'audacity' (Wakefield 2000: 6), and his 'characteristic élan' (Horowitz 1983: 213) is one of the things that makes *The Sociological Imagination* such a remarkable book. It contains a number of memorable passages, including his often-quoted proclamation that 'The sociological imagination enables us to grasp history and biography and the relations between the two within society. That is its task and its promise' (2000: 6). This was no small claim for Mills to make. In his view many people's grasp of historical change was limited, as he had sought to show in his discussion of the mismatch between the prevailing impressions of an occupational structure dominated by small independent businesses and the reality of the preponderance of employment by large corporations. People did not come easily to sociological thinking because 'even when the conditions of everyday life change swiftly, even when they come to see that their children face a world which they as children never faced, they come only grudgingly to a consciousness of epochal change' (in Horowitz 1983: 327). Mills characterised the situation of 'an "ordinary man" ' as one in which it was difficult 'to transcend the milieux in which he happens to live' (2000: 184). The ability to think beyond one's familiar surroundings was something that Mills identified as crucial to the cast of mind that sets the social scientist apart. Alongside preparedness to engage with the 'big-range thinking' (Horowitz 1964: 22) about issues such as the power elite and nuclear weapons, the development of the sociological imagination also required 'that you must learn to use your life experience in your intellectual work'. Mills's recommendation to the would-be social scientist to 'capture what you experience and sort it out' (2000: 196) is the advice of someone who did just that in his own work. The journey from small town to metropolis and from farming to white collar work described in *White Collar* is, as he acknowledged, Mills's personal and family history writ large (Gillam 1981: 5; Wakefield 2000: 9). Mills must also have been mindful of his own marital history when arguing that divorce is a public issue as well as a personal trouble. Public concern was understandable 'when the divorce rate during the first four years of marriage is 250 out of every 1,000 attempts' (2000: 9), but he also had direct knowledge of the personal difficulties as he and his two former wives were among these statistics (Mills with Mills 2000: 343ff). Mills's account in *The Sociological Imagination* of the shabby treatment of the 'unattached scholar' (2000: 112) by academic cliques is more thinly veiled autobiography.

Mills expected sociologists to reflect seriously on how their past and present circumstances influenced their understanding of social life. He was generally disappointed. His examination of textbooks on social problems found that they had been written by people who shared a non-metropolitan background, almost all of them having been 'born in small towns, or on farms near small towns, three fourths of which were in states not industrialized during the youth of the authors'. The failure of these writers to transcend the small-town mentality into which they had been socialised resulted in their expositions on social pathology focusing on 'the facts' and neglecting 'larger stratifications' or 'structured wholes' beyond the individual and his maladjustment to local social norms. These authors' commitment to fact-gathering as an unproblematic activity combined with their lack of analytical sophistication reminded Mills of Mannheim's phrase 'isolating empiricism' (Mills 1967f: 528, 533, 527, 526). The same shortcomings were later lampooned by Mills in his more general critique of 'abstracted empiricism' whose practitioners worked within 'curiously self-imposed limitations' and produced only 'detailed studies of minor problems' (2000: 55, 74). Mills had no time for 'textbook tolerance of the commonplace' since this reflected the priority afforded by the medium to the systematic transmission of accepted information over the more challenging promotion of 'discovery' (1967f: 525, 529). As he expressed it elsewhere, his position was that

> We do not want to so busy ourselves with details that we take the world in which they exist for granted. ... Facts and figures are only the beginning of the proper study. Our main interest is in making sense of the facts. (1959: 364)

Mills wanted to do things differently, both by reaching a wider audience than that of the classroom and by engaging with his readers in a more active way. As a result of his goal of 'creating a "public sociology" ' Mills 'spoke to a broadly educated public' not only through his books, journal articles and lectures but also by writing for 'the major national liberal and Left magazines and newspapers' (Seidman 1998: 174). Altogether this output amounted to no fewer than 205 items (Horowitz 1967b: 615–32). In Mills's view, sociology did not need to be the rather dull and unimaginative discipline that he believed it had become, and the key to its revitalisation lay in a fundamental reconsideration of how sociologists practised their subject.

The matter of style figured prominently in Mills's critique of his contemporaries. His opinion was that 'Style is not exactly a strong point of American social science; in fact most sociologists avoid style.' This had not always been the case, since Mills enthusiastically approved of Veblen's 'hilarious' style; it made 'fresh standards explicit' and thereby allowed us to 'smash through the stereotyped world of our routine perception and feeling and impulse'. Furthermore, Mills argued, Veblen's 'phrases stick in the mind, and his insights, if acquired early, often make a difference in the quality of one's life' (1953: vi, vii). There is a joke of a sort (at Parsons's expense), what Horowitz calls 'barbed wit' (1983: 195), in Mills's suggestion that 'one could translate the 555 pages of *The Social System* into about 150 pages of straightforward English' (2000: 31). There was humour as well when Mills characterised as 'crackpot realists' those military leaders who hold that the difficulties of managing peaceful relations between nations mean that it is easier to prepare for nuclear war, 'the simplification of known catastrophe'. Earlier in the same work he had commenced a section 'Once upon a time' (1960: 94, 95, 17) as a way of conveying the fairy tale like absurdity of crackpot realism. In general, the vulgar excesses of Veblen's idle rich lent themselves more readily to levity than did the topics that Mills addressed but his description of himself as 'a very cheerful type' (1969: 249) comes through in other ways in his writing. The 'playfulness of mind' that he identified as distinguishing 'the social scientist from the mere technician' included '[a]n attitude of playfulness toward the phrases and words with which various issues are defined' (2000: 211, 213). Such playfulness lay behind inventions such as the term 'banalization' (Gerth and Mills 1954: 380), coined to describe the dumbing down of complex ideas, or the use of apparently contradictory terms such as 'the sad-happy life of the very rich' (1959: 345). Mills recognised the capacity of well-crafted language to make his audience stop and think, and according to Gitlin he 'worked hard for two decades to perfect his style' (2000: 231). He was not always successful in this attempt, but at times he penned phrases (most notably those in his books' titles) that now have instant recognition.

If Mills's books have engaging titles, they also have arresting first lines. For example, by beginning his study of America's middle classes with the claim that 'The white collar people slipped quietly into modern society' (1956: ix), Mills was inviting his readers to ponder why this major social group had not arrived with more of a bang. Eldridge has noted generally of these openings that they 'attempt to seize the reader's attention. They make a statement, which, whether we agree with it or not, challenges us to read on' (1983: 42). The same is true of the metaphors employed by Mills in his texts, such as his depiction of educational institutions as 'mere elevators of occupational and social ascent'. That these led ultimately to 'the higher circles' and to the 'command posts of modern society' (1959: 318, 3, 5) reveals how Mills was untroubled by using a mixture of engineering, geometrical and military points of reference within the same analytical framework. To Edmondson, passages in *The Power Elite* are effective enough to give 'a description so vivid that the reader envisages the event as happening before his or her very eyes' (1984: 24). To critics of Mills, his rhetorical style was a ploy to divert attention from the shortcomings of his evidence, what Parsons referred to as 'empirical one-sidedness and distortion' (1999c: 223). Lazarsfeld likewise would have wanted more in the way of evidence from his former colleague who had singled him out for criticism as a prominent exponent of 'abstracted empiricism'. In response to Mills's claim in the opening line of *The Sociological Imagination* that 'Nowadays men often feel that their private lives are a series of traps' (2000: 3), Lazarsfeld has been imagined asking 'How many men, which men, how long have they felt this way, which aspects of their private lives bother them, when do they feel free rather than trapped, what kinds of traps do they experience, etc., etc.?' (Elcock 1976: 13). He could have done so safe in the knowledge that Mills would not have had answers to such detailed questions. Commenting on Mills's works, Eldridge has observed that '[t]here are times when he appears to follow the legendary self-advice of the preacher: argument weak here, shout louder' (1983: 44), and notes that Mills sometimes saw himself in the role of the preacher.

The imaginative quality of Mills's sociology meant that his ideas frequently raced ahead of empirical substantiation. He wrote enthusiastically in a letter of the potential for crime fiction to provide 'a wonderful instrument with which to think about the world of the USA', his reasoning being that '[t]he job of crime fiction ... is the same as the job of all social science worth the name: to make society become alive and as understandable and as dramatic as the best fiction makes the individual seem' (in Mills and Mills 2000: 232). Mills experimented with various literary forms, such as when he 'wrote his mass market paperback book about Cuba (*Listen, Yankee*) as a series of letters from an imaginary Cuban revolutionary trying to communicate with his U.S. neighbours'. He also wrote letters about Soviet–U.S. relations to 'Tovarich, his imaginary friend in the Soviet Union' (Mills with Mills 2000: xiii, 221), although these were not published at the time. To one reader *The Sociological Imagination* made the discipline sound 'just like fiction', suggesting 'that there was a good deal of overlap between sociology and novel writing' (Oakley 1994). Mills himself noted the similarity between the descriptions of American small town life offered by sociologists and novelists, and preferred the latter on the grounds that 'despite the rituals of proof they contain, the endless "community studies" of the sociologists often read like badly written novels; and the novels, like better-written sociology'. That said, in his opinion neither quite hit the mark because 'They have both generally been more interested in status than in power' (1959: 368), either local or national, something that was for Mills a fundamental weakness. In the face of the modern world's concentration of power he believed that what he called 'The cry for "community"' (2000: 172) was an unconvincing response to the prospect of a society populated by alienated but cheerful robots. He had little time for works that reproduced 'the lament over the loss of community' (1959: 322) because they lacked the structural view of power that he regarded as necessary for people to appreciate how the old social order had been transcended.

Mills anticipated a bleak future if the trends that he discerned were allowed to continue, but his writings contain little by way of alternative scenarios. He may not have been interested in offering a 'saving myth' (1969: 237), but several writers have detected elements of utopianism in his thought (Horowitz 1983: 6–8; Parsons 1999c: 233–4; Seidman 1998: 182; Wallace and Wolf 1995: 133). According to Gillam, 'Throughout *White Collar* … Mills writes not as a true historian but rather as a social critic. He quite literally inserts a golden age – a nineteenth century utopia of rationality and freedom – that dramatizes what has since been lost. This fails as scholarship but succeeds as radical mythology' (1981: 12). The same could be said about *The Power Elite*, in which Mills bemoaned modern society's metropolitan character, where the anonymity of city life contrasted unfavourably with that of small communities in which people 'know each other more or less fully, because they meet in the several aspects of the total life routine' (1959: 320). To the extent that he hankered after the lost world of the independent craft worker it is correct to say that Mills's social vision is characterised by 'a nostalgic populism' (Therborn 1976: 19), but his rising fame gave him increased opportunities to travel beyond the USA and the influence of these experiences on his perspective can be detected in some of his later writings (Horowitz 1967a: 7). His growing interest in and knowledge of the poorer countries of the world led him to entertain the possibility that the populations of underdeveloped societies did not need to reproduce the mistakes of the 'overdeveloped society' that America had become. Instead of the situation in which *'the style of life is dominated by the standard of living'* Mills suggested that it was possible to imagine an alternative which he called 'the properly developing society' in which 'men would have a choice among various styles of life'. The audience that he encouraged to 'liberate your cultural imaginations from all these other models' (1967b: 150, 156, emphasis in original) was in Brazil (Horowitz 1967b: 631), illustrating that by his last years he was speaking to a truly global audience.

Plain speaking

Mills's style was driven by what he considered his audience needed to hear, even though he acknowledged that they did not always welcome what he had to say. Intellectuals who followed his advice to 'think in a really free and wide-ranging way' were bound, as he put it, 'to stir up trouble' (in Mills with Mills 2000: 276). He recognised that before this could happen the attention of an audience had to be gained and then held, so making of the first questions confronting a writer 'For whom am I trying to write?'. Mills spoke of 'reading publics' in the plural, and also drew attention to the diversity of audiences by referring to the need of a writer to consider 'what kinds of people he is trying to speak to' (2000: 219, 221). One reason why Mills was so concerned about the development of mass society was that it would have no spaces for the exchange of opinions and engagement in debate that helped to prevent 'passivity and apathy on the part of the common man' (Tilman 1984: 140). Against this background Mills came to regard writing as 'a form of cultural struggle' (Eldridge 1983: 44) conducted in different settings. He suggested that his works were not all of a piece by making the distinction 'between scholarly publications such as *White Collar* and *The Power Elite*, written primarily for academic social scientists, and "pamphlets" written for propagandistic purposes. In the latter category would fall *The Causes of World War III* and *Listen, Yankee* which appealed to less specialized audiences' (Tilman 1984: 18). Mills also used the term 'preachings' (in Horowitz 1967a: 2) to describe his works that were aimed at a more popular audience.

This is an interesting but problematic distinction. First of all, there are several things that might be considered characteristics of any good writing, whatever its intended audience. What Mills wrote in the preface to *The Causes of World War Three*, that a writer 'hopes that every book he writes will become a contribution to a dialogue', arousing 'controversy, debate, and not a few calm reconsiderations' (1960: 14), would not have been out of place in his more 'scholarly' works. In *The Power Elite*, for example, he wrote that 'reasoning together is … a very important part of the proper way of arriving at the truth' (1959: 363), and his extended reply to the critical reviews of that book confirmed his interest in other people's responses. Furthermore, in this reply he stated that his primary concern was to 'try to get it straight' (1969: 249). This remark could just as easily have been made about *Listen, Yankee* which Horowitz has called 'Mills' one man crusade to present the truth about the Cuban Revolution to the American public' (1966: 26). In addition to the promotion of debate and the pursuit of truth, Mills was also concerned in everything that he wrote with the 'sore point [of] intelligibility'. His depiction in *The Sociological Imagination* of social scientists' necessary involvement in 'the struggle between enlightenment and obscurantism' (2000: 27, 178) reflected his commitment to plain speaking, as did his stated preference in *The Marxists* for 'Plain Marxism' over 'Sophisticated Marxism' (1963: 95). Mills's project of 'public sociology' required that ideas were presented in 'living language' because its audience was not a narrow educated elite but ordinary people, 'plain folks' (Horowitz 1983: 194, ch. 9). The sociological imagination as Mills understood it was intended to be acquired 'by individuals and by the cultural community at large' since 'the elements of contemporary uneasiness and indifference' to which it offered a solution were identifiable well beyond those social scientists whose sense of malaise was arguably 'more acute' (2000: 14, 13, 19). If intellectuals were to escape from being 'powerless people' (in Horowitz 1983: 161) they needed in Mills's opinion to develop the capability of speaking to a wider audience, because any problem being investigated needed to address '[t]he popular awareness of the problem' (2000: 206). The political relevance given to academic work by debate among a wider audience could not be achieved unless it were couched in readily understandable terms.

It might be argued that the distinction that Mills sought to make between academic and popular publications revolves around the relative importance attached to each of the two activities, theorising about social arrangements in order to better understand and explain them and criticising those arrangements from a particular standpoint. Cuzzort and King employ such a distinction in expressing their view that 'Mills was more effective as a social critic than as a social theorist' (1989: 194) and while it is not in doubt that Mills was engaged in both theorising and criticising, what is less certain is that he successfully resolved the tension between the two. One option was to abandon scholarly style for a more popular format, as he did in works like *The Causes of World War Three*, a mass-circulation paperback that contained virtually no references, but quickly sold 100,000 copies. Another popular work, *Listen, Yankee*, sold 400,000, but this mass appeal was achieved at the expense of academic credibility (Horowitz 1983: ch. 13). For several observers this development had been on the cards for some time. According to Bell, it was characteristic of much of Mills's writing that 'no point is ever argued or developed, it is only asserted and reasserted. This is fine as a rhetorical strategy, but it is maddening for anyone who does not, to begin with, accept Mills's self-election as an ideological leader' (1991: 140–1). No reader of *The Power Elite* could fail to notice what Parsons called the 'sharply caustic' (1999c: 223) tone employed against the targets of his criticism, and although supporters of Mills might point to the appropriateness of prose that was 'hard-driving' and 'muscular' (Gitlin 2000: 231) on the grounds that it constituted 'tough thinking for tough times' (Lemert 1995: 4), the vigour with which he pressed his case had the potential to alienate parts of his audience as well as to convince others. According to Berger and Berger, 'Mills's book was greeted by a storm of criticism at the time of its publication' (1976: 299), criticism that came from a variety of standpoints.

This is not simply an issue of disagreements with the political stances that Mills adopted, although that was clearly part of the problem for some readers. But even readers broadly sympathetic to his political outlook concluded that his style brought into question the analytical power of his academic output. For example, Wrong wrote that 'Mills's gift is largely for synthesis, for sketching the outlines of the whole, rather than for careful, close reasoning. His books are full of exciting vistas, imaginative suggestions pointing to overlooked connections in social life, but he invariably fails to follow these up in any rigorous fashion' (1999: 28). To such critics the problem was not so much that Mills's language was loaded, but more, that it was imprecise. In this vein 'the obvious self-confidence and the straightforward directness' of Mills's account of social change framed in terms of the 'mechanics' of the process has been contrasted with 'the more convoluted, as well as much more elaborate and subtle, social reflections of the Frankfurt School' (Therborn 1996: 58). A similar point has been made about Mills's 'selective and eclectic use of Marx' (Binns 1977: 130) which allowed him to adopt 'all that is intellectually excellent in Karl Marx' (Mills 2000: 6) but to prefer the concept of the power elite to the Marxist notion of the ruling class which he summarily dismissed in a footnote (1959: 277). Non-Marxists have also been critical of the concept of the power elite (Rex 1973: 182). The lack of theoretical sophistication that some commentators detect in Mills's works reflects his preparedness to take the ideas of Marx and Weber and 'pragmatize' (Horowitz 1983: 201, 179) them, a process that inevitably involved a degree of popularisation or 'banalization', to use Mills's own term. Horowitz's observation that '[t]he price of freshness of language was often precision in meaning', was made in relation to Mills's predilection for vague phrases like 'the main drift' (1983: 216–17), but it could be applied more generally to the way in which he used key concepts.

There is an irony in the fact that Mills 'envisioned himself as a poor polemicist' (Horowitz 1983: 103) given that it is his polemical style by which he is best remembered. In Wrong's view Mills 'made his most telling points when he is opposing a point of view which has been stated with sufficient clarity and intelligence to make it impossible to dismiss it in its least convincing form' (1999: 27–8), the most famous example of which was his critiques in *The Sociological Imagination* of 'grand theory' and 'abstracted empiricism'. Just as Parsons had selected 'the ablest proponents' (1968: 18) of the ideas that he sought to go beyond, so did Mills resist the selection of soft targets, although Parsons and Lazarsfeld were unlikely to have appreciated the implied compliment contained in his dissection of their work as he urged them, respectively, to 'get down from their useless heights' and to abandon their 'methodological inhibition' (2000: 33, 50). Merton refers to this as Mills's way of showing his 'reluctant admiration' (in Mullan 1987: 286) for Parsons and Lazarsfeld. Some light is shed on the question of why Mills 'responded to critics only rarely' (Horowitz 1983: 103) by his extended comment on the various reviews of *The Power Elite* in which he took issue with what he termed his 'liberal, radical and highbrow' critics. There is a sense that Mills felt that his reviewers had not really made sufficient effort to understand his argument, and that until such time as fellow academics did so there were more pressing things to get on with. Amongst the criticisms to which he took exception was the puerile imputation to him of the motive of 'resentment' of the fact that other people are millionaires and he is not. He showed particular irritation with the suggestion that he was saying nothing new, remarking that those reviewers who sought '[t]o blunt the edge of an argument' by suggesting that it was merely 'old stuff' were dealing in 'the common coin of the lazier reviewer's mint'. This was especially irksome to Mills given that he had, he thought, stated the 'extreme position' on unfolding trends by trying 'to focus on each trend just a little ahead of where it is now' (a position that sat uneasily alongside his claim that his critics had 'an incapacity to face facts as they are'). More generally Mills's piece gives the impression of someone uncomfortable with 'the angry character of many of the reviews' from people seeking 'to take a crack' (1969: 238, 231, 232, 250, 229) at him. This is consistent with Mills's mention in a private letter at the time of how the ' "criticisms" of *The Power Elite* hit me very hard indeed' (Mills with Mills 2000: 227). Perseverance while feeling assailed from all sides required depth of character, however much the hostile response to his plain speaking might have been anticipated.

Mills's published works do not convey the full complexity of the person. Gitlin has described him as 'a bundle of paradoxes' who amongst other things 'was a radical disabused of radical traditions, a sociologist disgruntled with the course of sociology, an intellectual frequently sceptical of intellectuals, a defender of popular action as well as a craftsman, a despairing optimist, [and] a vigorous pessimist'. Gitlin also notes that he was 'a man of substance acutely cognizant of style' (2000: 229). In similar vein Domhoff and Ballard have referred to Mills as a 'sparkling popularizer [who] was at the same time a well-trained and well-read professor of sociology who did a great deal of original research' (1969: 1). What Horowitz calls Mills's 'contradictions' make all the more remarkable his 'powerful appeal to the public conscience, or at least the educated public of the day' (1983: 6). It is an overstatement to attribute to Mills the role of founder of 'the new sociology' (Horowitz 1964), not least because many of his ideas were not unique to him; T. H. Marshall's 1946 reference to 'sociologists choosing either "the way to the stars" or "the way into the sands" ' (Runciman 1970: 22) can be read as an anticipation of distinction between grand theory and abstracted empiricism, for example. Nevertheless, his influence on those that have followed him has been far-ranging, including on the work of the ' "uppity generation" ... of ex-student-protestors' (Skocpol 1988: 630–2) and that of the practitioners of 'Muckraking Sociology' (Marx 1972). The apparently perverse aim of increasing the uneasiness of his contemporaries was prompted, he said, by the promise of 'new beginnings' that it might usher in. He was guided by what he called 'the politics of truth – the use of research to clarify significant issues and to bring political controversy closer to realities' (2000: 20, 64). Rather than engaging in controversy in so many different arenas he might healthily have heeded Lincoln's astute recommendation to fight '[o]ne war at a time' (Foote 1986: 160), but he was too much of 'a man in a hurry' (Kivisto 1998: 36) for that.

List of Mills's key sociological writings
Dates of original publication are given in ( )

The New Men of Power (1948)

White Collar (1951)

Character and Social Structure (1954) (written with H. Gerth)

The Power Elite (1956)

The Sociological Imagination (1959)

Power, Politics and People (1963) (collected essays written 1939–62)

Sociology and Pragmatism (1966)

7

Erving Goffman: sociology as an eye for detail

Introduction and overview

Erving Goffman was born in Canada to Jewish immigrant parents on 11 June 1922 but lived and worked for most of his life in the USA. He died of cancer aged 60 on 20 November 1982. Although Goffman in his research focused on apparently mundane aspects of the everyday social world, what he produced was 'undoubtedly serious work' (Atkinson 1990: 78). He had a rare eye for detailed and sharp ethnographic observation that directed attention to the features of social interactions that are all too readily dismissed as unimportant. Typical of his work is the chapter of his book *Forms of Talk* that is devoted entirely to the study of radio talk. The material it discusses is constituted of everyday announcements such as 'The loot and the car were listed as stolen by the Los Angeles Police Department' (1981a: 249). What such material illustrates is that communication is a skilled activity and that what people actually communicate is frequently not what they intend to. This point applies not only to spoken communication but to all forms of involvement in what he termed 'the interaction order' (1997), including the gestures and body language that make up an essential part of engaging with others in face-to-face situations. What we do in social life is necessarily open to competing interpretations, and even apparently straightforward actions such as driving a car through a red traffic light might have numerous other explanations besides the obvious one of deliberately breaking the law, such as brake failure or the need to get out of the way of an ambulance. Goffman's discussion of this example stops after the identification of 24 possible explanations, but it is clear that this is not an exhaustive list.

One of Goffman's purposes in using this example was to highlight the problematic nature of the idea of an 'objective "fact"', and to emphasise that a person's actions need to be understood in relation to 'the world he is in', that is, placed in the context of their *'situation'* (1971: 131–2, emphasis in original). The eclectic mixture of empirical material that Goffman used in his work to support his arguments raises fundamental questions about what constitutes acceptable sociological evidence and reasoning. Treviño has noted that 'no other sociologist has ever marshaled such a wide assortment of references in explicating his work', drawing on sources that range 'from the scientific to the popular, from manuals of etiquette to newspaper articles'. Furthermore, Treviño points out that a good deal of his material is anecdotal, prefaced with phrases such as ' "I have seen," "The following scene was reported to me," "I am told," or "I cite a personal example" ' (2003: 5, 26). Some is even acknowledged by Goffman to be made up by him and thus not 'real' (1981a: 55) at all. Such unorthodoxy in relation to the sources that he used combined with his extensive deployment of irony and other rhetorical devices led to Goffman's work being regarded with scepticism in some quarters, but Goffman saw himself as engaged in much more than 'just rhetoric' (in Treviño 2003: 16), which to him was a term better suited to the abstract formulations of grand theory of which he remained unimpressed. He understood his enterprise as one of revealing the hidden orderliness of everyday life and of the complex processes that lead to this outcome most of the time. Goffman's project required that he penetrate the veil of secrecy that people routinely use to limit outsiders' knowledge of their lives, although he was careful to exercise 'information control' (1969: 144) in relation to his own private life, about which very little is known (Winkin 1999: 19).

Goffman's sociology appears to be the antithesis of that of Mills. In contrast to Mills's 'desire to be a Big Thinker' located at the intellectual and political 'heart of things' (Becker 2002: 5), Goffman drew his inspiration from seemingly trivial interactions that took place in geographically or socially marginal settings, such as the crofting community in the Shetland Island of Unst that featured in *The Presentation of Self in Everyday Life*, or the Washington DC psychiatric institution reported on in *Asylums*. Not for nothing has Goffman been called the 'discoverer of the infinitely small' (Bourdieu 1983). When presenting his ideas, Goffman's style of expression was understated and ironic, leaving readers to draw their own conclusions in a way that Mills rarely did. Goffman did not pose as a 'Tribune of the people'; rather he was amongst those sociologists 'who prefer a more quietist approach' (Anderson *et al.* 1985: 146). Goffman was the very opposite of Mills in that he presented himself as 'detached' (Marx 1984: 653). Goffman's arguments and their full implications have to be teased out because 'His language is cool and precise. His claims are modest. He suggests his points rather than trumpeting them' (Collins 1980: 172–3). This does not mean that Goffman eschewed social criticism. He set about this task in a very different way to Mills, but both developed a 'social critique of America in the 1950s' (Lemert 1997b: xxiv) that raised profound questions about individuals' motives and about the extent to which people deceived themselves and others. Goffman was also suspicious of the claims of grand theorists (Williams 1998: 162). His judgements on fellow academics could be 'acerbic' (Drew and Wootton 1988: 2), as is evident in his reference to 'the high level of trained incompetence' (1997: 235) achieved by psychologists. Like Mills, Goffman railed against 'the rigid methodological prescriptions of conventional textbooks' (Collins and Makowsky 1998: 238). A further similarity to Mills was his status as an outsider, which was arguably attributable more to the fact that he 'refused to play by the rules of the game' (Kivisto 1998: 118) than it was to the reactions of others to his Canadian-Jewish roots (Burns 1992: 9; Lemert 1997b: xxi). Publications such as *Stigma* indicate that Goffman's sympathies were with society's outsiders.

One unfortunate effect of Mills's focus on the connection between personal troubles and public issues is that sociology can come to be regarded 'as a discipline largely, or even solely, concerned with social problems'. Jenkins points out that this is unduly restrictive, because 'not every sociologically interesting aspect of the human world is either an issue or a problem' (2002: 28). Goffman's work provides a good example of sociology that is not constrained by an agenda of issues and problems. His focus was on things that are 'funny' in either or both senses of that word, humorous and peculiar or discrepant. Typical of this is his account of how 'Seamen, whose home away from home is rigorously he-man, tell stories of coming back home and inadvertently asking mother to "pass the fucking butter".' Accounts such as this make the point that what is considered normal in one context is socially unacceptable in another. Goffman's analyses of how people's behaviour in a 'front region' are in sharp contrast with that in 'a "back region" or "backstage" ' (1969: 26, 109, 114) make the same point, that actions are performances aimed at particular audiences. Consequently, social interaction needs to be considered an achievement, an accomplishment, since what is surprising is not how often, but how rarely these interactions break down. When they do, the resultant misunderstandings and embarrassment are the stuff of everyday humour. According to Winkin, 'wry humour is ... constantly at work' (1999: 34) in Goffman's writings, while Fine has bracketed Goffman with Veblen because of their similarities in the use of irony and satire. This theme is developed by Fine who notes that the serious purpose behind Goffman's humour was 'to *persuade* an audience', not to entertain them; its subversive effect was to challenge 'a taken-for-granted world' (1999: 182, emphasis in original). What Goffman's observations reveal about the everyday world of commonplace interactions is that we necessarily make a great number of assumptions in our dealings with other people, and the revelation of these is an unsettling experience. As Giddens puts it, Goffman highlighted 'the unfamiliar in the familiar, to produce an intellectual estrangement from what is most common and habitual in our day-to-day activities. ... Goffman is quite brilliant at demonstrating that what appear to be quite trivial and uninteresting aspects of day-to-day behaviour turn out to be fraught with implications for interaction' (1987b: 114, 134–5). By approaching them in new ways, things familiar to us are rendered strange. This process has the potential to produce both amusement and serious reflection.

Goffman employed a variety of metaphors in order to analyse the strangeness of familiar social arrangements. The one with which he is most often associated is the metaphor of the theatre in which he 'develops a view of social life as an intricately staged theatrical production in which social actors attempt to pass themselves off to audiences as the characters they are pretending to be' (Rigney 2001: 151). Goffman's studies such as *The Presentation of Self in Everyday Life* bring out what can be learned by the detailed examination of people's 'performances' (1969: ch. 1), but he recognised the risk of overextending the use of this particular metaphor, and later found it necessary to remind his readers that 'All the world is not a stage' (1975: 1). Another metaphor drawn upon by Goffman is that of 'Society as Game' (Rigney 2001: ch. 7), and from the outset of his career he showed particular interest in the ways in which social life contained various elements of 'a con game' (Cuzzort and King 1989: ch. 12). In one of his earliest papers, 'On Cooling the Mark Out', Goffman used the example of victims' reactions to confidence tricks to explore the processes by which people adapt to failure and disappointment. This allowed him to note the similarities between 'defeat at games' (1962: 503) and various other endings in our lives such as redundancy or bereavement, all of which require time for the process of psychological adjustment to occur. Analysis in terms of games also revealed the strategic character of much social interaction, by which people seek to gain advantage over others or to limit their exposure to risk. Goffman's exploration of 'the calculative, gamelike aspects of mutual dealings' (1970: x) showed that understanding encounters requires that attention be paid to the rules that structure the interaction as well as the content of the communication between the players. A third metaphor employed by Goffman for viewing social life is that of ritual (Branaman 1997: lxiii). In the world Goffman portrayed, 'ritual is essential because it maintains our confidence in basic social relationships' (Manning 1992: 133), and this provides the rationale for his dissection of the greetings, apologies and other ritual features of everyday encounters. These three metaphors of drama, game and ritual were accorded varying degrees of prominence in different works by Goffman. Sometimes he combined them, as when he referred to the self as 'a kind of player in a ritual game' (1967: 31). Another example of their overlap is given by Collins (1990: 113) who treats Goffman's frontstage/backstage distinction as a key element in the ritual separation of dominant and subordinate groups.

Goffman's sociology can reveal the hidden logic of much behaviour that is at first sight puzzling. In *Asylums* Goffman described how the patients of 'Central Hospital' could be observed carrying around on their persons a large number of items such as 'books, writing materials, washcloths, fruit, small valuables, scarves, playing cards, soap, shaving equipment (on the part of men), containers of salt, pepper, and sugar, bottles of milk'. Goffman's explanation of women's voluminous handbags and men's equivalent, 'a jacket with commodious pockets, worn even in the hottest weather' was simple: 'Failure to provide inmates with individual lockers'. The broader point was that 'the craziness or "sick behaviour" claimed for the mental patient is by and large a product of the claimant's social distance from the situation that the patient is in, and is not primarily a product of mental illness' (1968a: 222, 223, 28, 121). Goffman's work generally is full of 'examples of action which is apparently irrational but which can be made sense of once the interactive context in which it takes place is known' (Crow 1989: 13). These observations arose from an approach in which Goffman sought to understand the everyday lives of his subjects as they themselves did. His accounts point to the conclusion that '*anyone* would behave like this in the circumstances' (Edmondson 1984: 153, emphasis in original). If his methodology was unconventional, so too was the way in which he developed his argument; this 'was essentially literary, using surprising paradoxes and colourfully juxtaposed examples from his carefully compiled card index of exotic cases drawn from both fact and fiction' (Boswell 1992: 175). The resultant insights are not easy to take on board, since they run counter to some of our dearest preconceptions. As Hochschild has noted, Goffman points to the irony whereby 'moment to moment, the individual is actively, consciously negotiating a personal and apparently unique course of action, but in the long run all the action seems like passive acquiescence to some unconscious social convention' (2003: 90). Goffman's message, in other words, is that his understanding of selfhood and identity 'is different from that by which the reader is likely to live'. His style 'demands *personal* changes from the reader' (Edmondson 1984: 152, 153, emphasis in original), even though it is done in such a way that it is not immediately apparent that reading Goffman will have this effect.

Funny things and serious matters

Everyday life is full of activities that we generally do not think about too deeply. When we subject these activities to closer scrutiny, their strangeness that is normally not appreciated becomes disconcertingly apparent. Goffman argued that the details of everyday interactions had been seriously overlooked by 'students of modern society' who treated them 'as part of the dust of social activity, empty and trivial'. The orderly and predictable character of these interactions led him to propose that 'Surely it is time to examine "Hello" or "Excuse me", or their equivalent … in spite of the bad name that etiquette has given to etiquette, it is time to study these performances.' His suggestion that interchanges may be either 'supportive' or 'remedial' was then followed by the description of numerous examples, and his accounts of the former include the description of how 'when two individuals are introduced by a third a little dance is likely to occur; faces light up, smiles are exchanged, eyes are addressed, handshakes or hat-doffing may occur, and also inquiries after the other's health'. His further remark, that 'this is only natural' is deceptive, however, since Goffman's purpose was to challenge the assumption that things which normally go unremarked can be so simply explained. Rather, he believed that 'universals are exactly what good ethnography brings into doubt' (1971: 90, 106, 122). If he is correct in his argument that 'Universal human nature is not a very human thing' (1967: 45), then phenomena that are routinely treated as the expression of human nature warrant closer scrutiny. In a later work Goffman returned to the topic of handshakes and noted that although they may be understood as a way for us to ' "express" our pleasure in renewing contact with a friend not seen for a time', they may have other, quite different meanings. Handshaking may occur at greetings and departures but it 'is also found in introduction routines, congratulatory practices, dispute settlements, and contract finalizations'. It is a part of the ritual of face-to-face activity, a non-verbal affirmation of the sincerity of what is being said. This is strange enough in itself, but Goffman made the further observation that additional 'significance of the act is to be found in the fact that in American society only male to male cannot employ a "social" kiss as a functional equivalent' (1981b: 61–2). Such rituals and the rules surrounding them were for Goffman highly revealing of how in everyday life we are constantly honouring the individuals around us.

The apparently trivial practice of shaking hands was for Goffman an important mechanism by which trust is reinforced, one of several 'forms of ritual … that sustain mutual confidence and respect' (Giddens 1987b: 135). Its connection to what Goffman called 'the arrangement between the sexes' was that its possible replacement by social kissing reflects the cultural subordination of women by men. Social kissing can be considered a 'ritualized gesture', one among many, part of a battery of courtesies by which 'males are very likely to express … that they define females as fragile and valuable, to be protected from the harsher things of life and shown both love and respect'. He argued that because men pose a potential threat to women by virtue of the fact that males are typically 'bigger and stronger than females', complex social arrangements have arisen in order to reassure women that respect for their femininity places a cultural prohibition on men exploiting their physical advantage over women. This maintenance of the gender order is given concrete expression in the provision of separate toilet facilities for women and men in workplaces and commercial establishments, 'done in the name of nicety, of civilization, of the respect owed females'. Goffman identified several other examples of sex-segregated spaces and enclaves, which he presented as further evidence in support of his counter-intuitive argument that women are a disadvantaged group who 'are held in high regard' (1987: 57–8, 68, 65, 58) by those who as a class occupy superior positions, men. Although he did not refer to it, there is an echo of Mills's ironic characterisation of women's treatment by men as 'darling little slaves' (1967d) in Goffman's account of the gender order. One 'political consequence' of the idealisation of femininity to which Goffman drew attention was women's marginalisation in the labour market because of 'the substantive work that women find they must do in the domestic sphere'. From Goffman's sociological point of view, the most interesting question was, 'How in modern society do such irrelevant biological differences between the sexes come to seem of vast social importance?'. If, as he argued, it is a 'rather questionable' proposition that 'our form of social organization has any necessary features' (1987: 73, 52, 67), then explanations framed in terms of functional requirements for gender differentiation simply would not do.

The answer that Goffman gave to his question about the basis of gender differences was constructed around the concept of 'idealization'. This did not imply approval on Goffman's part for arrangements that he recognised were 'sexist' and resulted in women being 'treated unfairly', or at least were 'a mixed blessing'. Rather, the term idealisation was used in the sense that females were treated as a category of people characterised 'as pure, fragile, valued objects, the givers and receivers of love and care'. The characteristics attributed to males complemented these as mirror-images, so that 'Frailty is fitted to strength, gentleness to sternness, diffuse serving to project orientation, mechanical unknowingness to mechanical competencies, delicacy relative to contamination vs. insensitivity to contamination, and so forth' (1987: 74, 56, 73). This list bears a passing resemblance to Parsons's characterisation of women's role in families as that of the 'expressive, "cultural" expert' and men's as that of the 'instrumental, technical expert' (Parsons and Bales 1956: 51), but whereas Parsons 'was always as explicit as he could be about what he wished to say', Goffman was deliberately 'deep' and 'hid away what he was doing' (Collins 1988: 41–2). By being cryptic he invited incredulity about the social world that he described, in particular about the 'idealized, mythologized' (1987: 58) characterisations of others with which people operated. Goffman's account presented the gender order as composed of 'ritual-like bits of behaviour which portray an ideal conception of the two sexes and their structural relationship to each other' within which displays of ' "natural" expressions of gender' are the product of people behaving with reference to conventions that have been subjected to 'standardization, exaggeration and simplification'. In *Gender Advertisements* Goffman argued that advertisers might be considered to have taken this process further, into the realm of 'hyper-ritualization', but that this was merely a question of degree, not a fundamentally different process: 'advertisers conventionalize our conventions, stylize what is already a stylization' (1979: 84). In other words, idealisation involves the cultivation of behaviour that is guided by stereotypes, sometimes 'extreme stereotypes' (1969: 49), even though the actor may be well aware of the illusory nature of the performance.

The bizarre qualities of gendered idealisations frequently caught Goffman's eye. His essay on the confidence trick contained the observation that men's typical beliefs about their 'masculinity', including images of themselves as 'shrewd ... when it comes to making deals' (1962: 485), constituted an important part of the reason why a steady supply of victims of confidence tricksters was available. In *The Presentation of Self in Everyday Life* Goffman described 'the tendency for performers to offer their observers an impression that is idealized', an example of which was the propensity of American college girls to 'play down their intelligence, skills, and determinativeness when in the presence of datable boys'. He cited the practice of girls deliberately misspelling long words in letters to boyfriends, thereby allowing themselves to be corrected, as one of several ways in which 'the natural superiority of the male is demonstrated, and the weaker role of the female affirmed' (1969: 44, 48). In *Frame Analysis* Goffman suggested that such 'fabrications' were not necessarily consciously reproduced through his observation that

> Men often treat women as faulted actors with respect to 'normal' capacity for various forms of physical exertion. Women so treated often respond by affirming this assessment. On both sides there may be unquestioning belief and a long-acquired capacity to act accordingly without guile or self-consciousness. (1975)

This statement might have been left to stand on its own in other works by Goffman, but on this occasion he chose to follow it with a direct prompt to the reader, by asking (albeit rhetorically), 'Nonetheless, cannot the question be put as to whether "real" incapacities are involved or merely institutionally sustained belief?' (1975: 196–7). The implication of this question was that stereotypes may become so ingrained in the minds of performers and of members of their audience that the idealisation takes on a life of its own.

For Goffman, gender differences were the result not of biological determination but of 'a sustained sorting process whereby members of the two classes are subject to different socialization'. As a result of this social-isation women and men 'are given different treatment, acquire different experience, enjoy and suffer different expectations'. Goffman acknowl-edged that there is variation between societies in terms of their 'concep-tion of what is "essential" to ... ideals of masculinity and femininity', but his reference to 'persons who are sorted into the male class and persons who are sorted into the other' (1987: 53) conveyed his recognition that the former typically constituted a cultural norm in relation to which feminin-ity is treated as inferior. Thus *Gender Advertisements* revealed not just dif-ferences between men's and women's positions but 'the ritualization of subordination' (1979: 40) to which women are subject. Gender provided 'an exemplary instance ... of social classification' that was constructed around the 'neat and tidy device' provided by biological differences between the sexes. This was the case even though attributing gender differences to a biological basis was 'a questionable doctrine' because it overlooked the myriad ways in which beliefs about gender were not sim-ple reflections of biology but could be seen to be 'extending it, neglecting it, countering it'. Simplifying differences between people into the binary opposition of male/female may be necessary for the same reason that other familiar social classifications operate with only two classes, namely that it 'provides a ready base for differential treatment' in a way that more complex classifications cannot. In this context Goffman referred to 'other binary social divisions – white/black, adult/child, officer/enlisted man, etc.' (1987: 52, 77, 53, 55), each of which is also immediately recognisable as a crude stereotypical contrast to which reference is nevertheless routinely made in everyday life.

Exploring the process of idealisation encourages the reconsideration of what we take to be normal. The norm against which we measure other people and ourselves was revealed to be very much abnormal in the statistical sense of the word by Goffman's description of the ideal male: 'in an important sense there is only one complete unblushing male in America: a young, married, white, urban, northern, heterosexual Protestant father of college education, fully employed, of good complexion, weight and height and a recent record in sports'. Goffman argued that it was possible to speak of all American males sharing 'a common value system' in which these attributes were prized, with the result that 'Any male who fails to qualify in any of these ways is likely to view himself – during moments at least – as unworthy, incomplete and inferior.' This passage in Goffman's book *Stigma* suggests that the great majority of people are vulnerable to

feelings of inferiority and stigmatisation. This was a significant development of the argument relative to the opening discussion in which stigma
was portrayed as something associated with the plight of unusual people.

Goffman began the book by reproducing a letter written to a lonely
hearts column by a 16-year-old girl who 'was born without a nose' and
whose inability to attract a boyfriend led her to contemplate suicide. She
signed the letter 'Desperate'. This is an extreme example of stigma,
defined as 'the situation of the individual who is disqualified from full
social acceptance', but the potential for stigmatization extends far wider
than such cases of 'abominations of the body' (1968b: 153, 7, 9, 14). As
Burns notes, those mentioned in the opening passages include

> the blind, the deaf, the crippled, the maimed, deformed, disfigured, diseased,
> prostitutes, and the mentally ill; also blacks, Jews, 'ethnics', lower class persons,
> homosexuals, illiterates, on to people with colostomies, mastectomies, to diabetics,
> stutterers, etc., and winding up with the old, along with ex-convicts and ex-mental
> patients. (1992: 218–19)

As he extended this list, Goffman progressively undermined readers'
previous certainties about 'the notion of "normal human being" ', and
by the latter part of the book he was able to advance the idea that 'the
role of normal and the role of stigmatized are parts of the same complex,
cuts from the same standard cloth', albeit that this was voiced as nothing
more than a suspicion. Goffman had started out distancing himself and
the reader from the ostensible subjects of the book by referring to the
way in which 'we normals' relate to stigmatised others, but ended by
discussing the ubiquity of deviance and of the 'shameful differentness'
(1968b: 17, 155, 24, 167) with which the reader could all to readily
identify through some personal experience or other. According to Becker,
the 'brilliance' of Goffman's writing here lay in the way his analysis
succeeded in, 'Exchanging the conventional contents of a concept for a
sense of its meaning', thereby enlarging 'its reach and our knowledge'
(1998: 145).

A further dimension of Goffman's argument was to highlight what he
referred to as 'the foolishness of the normals', thereby questioning where
discredit is actually due. Goffman reproduced several accounts from one-
legged girls that revealed the insensitivity to which they were routinely
subject and the intelligent creativity of their responses. One girl recalled
that 'Questions about how I lost my leg used to annoy me, so I developed a stock answer that kept these people from asking further: "I borrowed
some money from a loan company and they are holding my leg for
security!".' Although the style in which Goffman presented his ideas
differs significantly from Durkheim's more sober prose, the conception of

'the normal deviant' with which he operated and his interest in the processes by which people come to be classified are unmistakably Durkheimian. The argument that 'Society establishes the means of categorizing persons and the complement of attributes felt to be ordinary and natural for members of each of these categories' gives primacy to society over the individual in the way that Durkheim also did. Attitudes that may appear to be 'the stigmatized individual's personal point of view' turn out on closer inspection to be those of the group to which he or she belongs, and Goffman argued that 'this is only to be expected, since what an individual is, or could be, derives from the place of his kind in the social structure'. It is presented as 'a basic sociological theme' that 'the nature of an individual, as he himself and we impute it to him, is generated by the nature of his group affiliations' (1968b: 161, 162, 155, 11, 137, 138). The idealisation of these groups frequently generates ludicrous stereotypes, and although he used the expression in another context, Goffman's remark about how we engage in 'seriously kidding ourselves' (1997: 235) captures nicely what he felt.

Metaphors of social life

Goffman returned to the theme of people's stereotypical classification by group in his discussion of how games have a serious as well as a fun side to them. He recounted that 'In the classic phrase of England's gentry, "Anyone for tennis?" did not quite mean *anyone*; it is not recorded that a servant has ever been allowed to define himself as an *anyone*, although such doubtful types as tutors have occasionally been permitted to do so.' Alongside this pointed observation about how games effect the social exclusion of some people, Goffman made the further comment that others may be subjected to compulsory inclusion, compelled to 'participate in recreation that is not fun for them'. This lack of autonomy revealed their status as 'something less than persons'. Goffman's identification of 'children, mental patients and prisoners' as examples of 'these unfortunates' who 'may not have an effective option when officials declare game-time' was part of his wider purpose, 'to see how far one can go by treating fun seriously'. One of the results was the revelation that 'Games ... are world-building activities' in which distinctive meanings are generated. Sometimes this constitutes an act of resistance to authority, as is the case in wall games where 'school children, convicts, prisoners of war, or mental patients are ready to redefine an imprisoning wall as a part of the board that the game is played on' (1972: 28, 17, 25, 20 emphases in original). These groups demonstrate people's capacity to create meaningful worlds even in the unfavourable environment of what Goffman called 'total institutions', where individuals 'together lead an enclosed, formally administered round of life'. Sports and games provided potential 'escape worlds' (1968a: 11, 271) for the inmates of Central Hospital, and they also provided one of the key metaphors by which Goffman sought to illuminate social life. His observation that 'Games seem to display in a simple way the structure of real-life situations' (1972: 32) provided the rationale for trying to make sense of the serious business of interaction in a range of contexts, including those that appeared far removed from the realm of fun and recreation.

Many of Goffman's publications pursued the theme of the game-like character of social interaction and it allowed him to draw creatively on 'the vocabulary of strategies, ploys, rules, negotiation and bargaining, moves and counter-moves' (Anderson *et al*. 1985: 155), and also tactics, gambits and players (Williams 1998: 158). Although the game metaphor is most explicit in works that Goffman wrote in mid-career such as *Encounters* and *Strategic Interaction* (Branaman 1997: lxx–lxxiii; Manning 1992: ch. 3), its foundations were laid early on. His essay on 'the confidence game' made sense of upward and downward mobility in terms of 'the game for social roles' in which not everyone could win, although losers might be awarded 'consolation prizes'. The metaphorically defeated person was described as 'losing one of his social lives'. People who become 'socially dead' in this way also tend, Goffman suggested, to be physically segregated, 'brought together into a common graveyard that is separated ecologically from the living community ... [as] a punishment and a defense'; residents of such places are 'effectively hidden'. His further remark that 'Jails and mental institutions are, perhaps, the most familiar examples' (1962: 483, 494, 503, 504) anticipated his subsequent research into total institutions in which the process of 'mortification' of inmates was explored in some depth. In *Asylums* Goffman traced the process whereby the 'recruit' is stripped of the support previously available and subjected to 'a series of abasements, degradations, humiliations and profanations of self. He is systematically, if often unintentionally, mortified'. Goffman used an extensive list of the actions that make up 'admission procedures' to convey something of their overwhelming force: 'taking a life history, photographing, weighing, fingerprinting, assigning numbers, searching, listing personal possessions for storage, undressing, bathing, disinfecting, haircutting, issuing institutional clothing, instructing as to rules, and assigning to quarters'. The use of uniforms to identify the team to which an individual has been assigned is one of several aspects of this process that resemble a game, serving to impress on newcomers the importance of learning the 'house rules' by which the game will be played. Socialisation into these rules may be effected by an initial 'will-breaking contest' (1968a: 24, 25–6, 51, 26), and Goffman described in detail how this is subsequently reinforced by an often elaborate system of privileges and punishments.

The vivid description of such 'degradation rituals' (Burns 1992: 148) that *Asylums* contains make it unsurprising that it 'caused an intellectual furore' (Worsley 1997: 234). The book raised serious doubts about the benefits of incarceration through 'a passionate and sensitive portrayal of people whose every movement is monitored and judged' (Manning 1992: 106). Goffman's description of the orderly arrangement of relationships in total institutions as 'a magnificent social achievement' is all the more effective as a critique for its oblique quality, in that it forces the reader to ponder which of the various interpretations that might be put on such statements are the ones that Goffman actually intended. The style of the book was deliberately indirect, for rather than highlighting his conclusions Goffman allowed them to emerge almost incidentally. Much of what he wrote confirms the standard belief that total institutions operate to undermine the patient's self-concept as 'a full-fledged person', but the limitations of this process are revealed by odd remarks, such as his observation, made in passing in a footnote, that people admitted to mental hospitals come to discover that 'many other patients are more like ordinary persons than like anything else' (1968a: 104, 141, 57). This surprisingly persuasive technique does not rely on points being laboured but rather involves the suggestion of alternative perspectives to those with which the audience would be more familiar. As Burns describes it, 'Beginning with the title, which one soon discovers is heavy with irony, the sheer skill in writing wins over the reader' (1992: 141). An important part of this presentational strategy was Goffman's ability to cast doubt on conventional perspectives, and he did this by implying that his method of inquiry had allowed him access to a privileged vantage point from which a more sensible understanding could be gained. His declaration in the preface to *Asylums* that 'Any group of persons – prisoners, primitives, pilots or patients – develop a life of their own that becomes meaningful, reasonable and normal once you get close to it' (1968a: 7) meant that social distance had to be overcome before valid evidence could be collected. This was the rationale for his spending a year in the company of Central Hospital's inmates.

Goffman rarely went into great detail about his methods of investigation, although he did express the opinion that a year was the minimum amount of time necessary for an ethnographer to be sure that 'you've really penetrated the society you're studying' (in Manning 1992: 154). By immersing himself into the everyday life of a psychiatric hospital with over 7000 patients, Goffman was seeking 'to try to learn about the social world of the hospital inmate, as this world is subjectively experienced by him'. His belief was that this could be done by gaining experience 'in the company of the members to the daily round of petty contingencies to which they are subject', and he effected this by adopting 'the role of an assistant to the athletic director, when pressed avowing to being a student of recreation and community life'. He premised his strategy on the assumption that 'the inmate world' and 'the staff world' would be at odds with each other, and so kept his distance from the staff, avoided carrying a key (by which he might be identified with them), and 'passed the day with patients'. The paragraph summarising his methods concludes with the matter-of-fact statement that 'I did not sleep on the wards, and the top hospital management knew what my aims were.' Not only did Goffman provide the briefest of supporting cases for the method he adopted, he disarmingly pointed out that its limitations were 'obvious' and several. He noted that he was unable to report first-hand on what it was like to be a patient because he had not himself been committed; had he been so, his 'range of movements and roles, and hence my data, would have been restricted even more than they were'. Second, he reported that he 'did not employ usual kinds of measurements and controls', refusing to pursue statistical methods because 'gathering data on the tissue and fabric of patient life' ruled out both the time and the identification with authority that this would have entailed. Third, he acknowledged that his perspective was 'partisan', in terms of taking the side of the patient as against that of the psychiatrist, whose profession he conceded he 'had no great respect for', and also in terms of his status as 'a middle-class male' (1968a: 7, 8) which potentially blinkered his perception of how patients from lower social classes experienced the regime.

Goffman's self-effacing presentation of his approach is far removed from the confidence with which Durkheim advanced the merits of his chosen methods, but it was done with a purpose. As Collins has noted, 'Modesty, for Goffman, was a weapon of attack, and his overall stance was an aggressive, even haughty one' (1988: 41). The same technique of admitting one's weaknesses but using the opportunity to highlight the even greater shortcomings of rival approaches was drawn upon in *Relations in Public*. Here Goffman acknowledged that his method of 'unsystematic, naturalistic observation ... has very serious limitations', but countered this with the 'defence that the traditional research designs thus far employed in this area have considerable limitations of their own'. By this stage in his career Goffman was prepared to be far more explicit about what these latter limitations were, and his critique was spirited:

> Fields of naturalistic study have not been uncovered through these methods. Concepts have not emerged that reorder our view of social activity. Frameworks have not been established into which a continuously larger number of facts can be placed. Understanding of ordinary behaviour has not accumulated; distance has. (1971)

He accused those who operated with conventional methods of devising concepts 'on the run' and, in a passage reminiscent of Mills's critique of abstracted empiricism, he lampooned those who operated with a belief in 'A sort of sympathetic magic' characterised by 'the assumption ... that if you go through the motions attributable to science then science will result'. Goffman's judgement on this was that 'it hasn't', and he was particularly scornful of studies in which, 'The work begins with the sentence "We hypothesize that ..." ' (1971: 20–21) and proceeds to imply that the discovery of patterns of social interaction is simple. Goffman's formulations 'One can say', 'One can therefore suspect', 'One can assume' (1968b: 154–6) and 'This suggests that' (1969: 77) may serve the similar purpose of introducing the reader to key arguments but they do so in less alienating language.

Edmondson has commented that Goffman's style is one whereby 'The reader is *offered* an extension of his or her social understanding' (1984: 152, emphasis in original) as a way of moving towards the reordered view of social life that he was seeking to advance. As an example of this she refers to the passage in which Goffman referred to the 'commonsense models' of behaviour that contrast 'the real, sincere, or honest performance; and the false one that thorough fabricators assemble for us, whether meant to be taken unseriously, as in the work of stage actors, or seriously, as in the work of confidence men'. Goffman's subsequent unpacking of the contrast between 'reality and contrivance' does so by posing doubts that a reader could readily accept made sense, as a stepping stone to a more radical conclusion. He first sought to gain agreement that 'perhaps there are not many women who play the part of wife to one man and mistress to another; but these duplicities do occur, often being sustained successfully for long periods of time'. What this suggested to Goffman was that 'while persons usually are what they appear to be, such appearances could still have been managed. There is, then, a statistical relation between appearances and reality, not an intrinsic or necessary one.' Goffman had at the outset of *The Presentation of Self in Everyday Life* noted the 'obvious inadequacies' of the metaphor of social life as a drama that made it inappropriate to equate events in a theatre with happenings in 'real life', and he presented his approach as nothing more than 'one sociological perspective from which social life can be studied'. Although these qualifications were voiced, Goffman nevertheless claimed that his approach provided 'a framework that can be applied to any concrete social establishment, be it domestic, industrial or commercial'. It was, moreover, 'a coherent framework that ties together bits of experience the reader has already had'. By the end of the book Goffman had explored numerous examples of how everyday life could be understood in terms of the allocation of roles to actors, their performance of these roles on different stages to different audiences, responding to cues as scripted and using various props to enhance the impression management that they sought to achieve with dramatic effect. On the basis of this analysis he concluded that 'the dramaturgical approach may constitute a fifth perspective' (1969, 76–7, 9–10, 233) alongside four others that had already been established to understand social establishments in technical, political, structural and cultural terms.

What Goffman was seeking was an analytical framework that could 'be employed as the end point of analysis, as a final way of ordering facts'. As he saw things these frameworks did not need to be exclusive, and he identified a number of ways in which the metaphor of the theatre coincided with others. It is instructive that *The Presentation of Self in Everyday Life* has a whole chapter devoted to 'teams', and his remark that 'if an individual is to direct others, he will often find it useful to keep strategic secrets from them' reveals a cast of mind that found it useful to combine thinking about society as theatre with society's game-like character. Goffman's theme of society as ritual is likewise alluded to in his comment that 'Power of any kind must be clothed in effective means of displaying it, and will have different effects depending on how it is dramatized' (1969: 233, ch. 2, 234). Some commentators have interpreted passages such as this as indications of Goffman's view of people as essentially manipulative, but Branaman makes the important point that 'Goffman does not oppose manipulation and morality in his depictions of social life' (1997: lxvii), and cites in support of this interpretation Goffman's favourable quotation of Durkheim's views on the sacredness of the individual. Respect and deference being given to the individual is for Goffman a necessary symbol of 'the mutual dependence created by membership in the team' (1969: 88); the solidarity that necessarily underpins teamwork and collective endeavour would not be possible without such rituals (Collins 1990: 113). Rituals may be performances and they may have game-like qualities, but for Goffman it is only because they are observed that 'Social life is an uncluttered, orderly thing' (1967: 43). To mix metaphors is commonly regarded as an error, but in Goffman's writings the practice was adopted deliberately because, as Manning notes, 'it shows that the limitations or partiality of metaphors can be transformed into strengths rather than weaknesses' (1992: 37) by reminding readers that the purpose of metaphors is to encourage consideration of the similarities between two phenomena but also the limits beyond which the comparison cannot usefully be taken. This was Goffman's point in concluding that 'Scaffolds ... are to build other things with, and should be erected with an eye to taking them down'. The idea that 'all the world's a stage' was not to be taken literally, or even 'too seriously' (1969: 246), just seriously enough to suggest the strangeness of what to us is familiar.

Understatement and implicit messages

The method of immersing ourselves in a metaphor was justified by Goffman in terms of what it revealed by allowing us to see things differently, to reorder our thinking. In *Encounters* he noted that using the metaphor of a game to study social life had 'limitations', but also promised rewards since immersion in this perspective meant that 'We return to the world as gamesmen, prepared to see what is structural about reality and to reduce life to its liveliest elements' (1972: 32). Goffman thus intended engagement with metaphors to make us reconsider how we understand the world; his 'argument was that this reflexive use of metaphors was an essential tool of sociological work' (Williams 1998: 158). Goffman believed that it had the potential to reveal, for example, that 'what is prison-like about prisons is found in institutions whose members have broken no laws' (1968a: 11). Had he written *Asylums* as a more conventional monograph reporting exclusively on his research findings relating to Central Hospital, rather than developing the argument as he did by indicating how other institutions were in many ways prison-like, the book would have had much less impact. As Edmondson has noted, the book is carefully crafted with regard to 'The rhetorical effects of order', the sequence in which ideas were presented. She points out that in his discussion of total institutions 'Goffman begins with prisons, in whose destructive characteristics the (liberal) reader may find it easy to believe, *then* he goes on to mental hospitals ... the process of reading itself conduces to changes of attitude on the reader's part.' Hospitals are not prisons, but they can by this juxtaposition be shown to have more in common than might otherwise be imagined. The more general methodological point is that 'startling comparisons can surprise the reader into perceiving and drawing inferences from phenomena he or she would not normally associate with each other' (1984: 155, emphasis in original). Amongst those struck by such devices is Giddens, whose comment that 'The social world never seems the same again after having read Goffman' (1987b: 8) was made in the light of the unsettling effects that his apparently innocuous observations can have.

Goffman's way of advancing sociological arguments has, predictably, been subject to criticism from various angles, and Lemert's comment that 'Goffman may not be for everyone' (1997b: xli) is somewhat understated in the way that much of Goffman's own work was. Plummer has listed several grounds on which Goffman's writings have been questioned: 'He broke all the rules. His sources were unclear; his fieldwork seems minimal – Goffman being happier with novels and biography than with scientific observation; his style was not that of the scientific report but that of the essayist; and he was frustratingly unsystematic' (1996: 234). Others have elaborated on these points. On the matter of sources, Burns is distinctly unimpressed with the first essay in *Strategic Interaction* in which 'the supporting evidence … consists of lengthy quotations from what has been written about espionage, smuggling and its detection, criminal conspiracies and so on, and is somewhat tedious and distinctly old hat. … Much of the time, the level hovers somewhere between *True Detective* and *Reader's Digest*' (1992: 59). Goffman himself referred to the 'mixed status' of the materials used to illustrate *The Presentation of Self in Everyday Life*, which ranged from 'respectable researches' to 'informal memoirs written by colourful people' (1969: 9). In *Behavior in Public Places* his apparently self-deprecatory stance was still more in evidence through his acknowledgement that his data came from an even wider variety of sources including 'some from manuals of etiquette, and some from a file where I keep quotations that have struck me as interesting. Obviously, many of these data are of doubtful worth, and my interpretations – especially some of them – may certainly be questionable' (1963: 4). There is a similarity between this use of disclaimers as 'a defensive textual technique' (Treviño: 2003: 22) and that of apologising in everyday life, about which Goffman observed 'that the offender's willingness to initiate and perform his own castigation has certain unapparent values', one of which was that 'he can overstate or overplay the case against himself, thereby giving to the others the task of cutting the self-derogation short'; apologies make the offender 'worthy of being brought back into the fold' (1971: 144). Having apologised for the shortcomings of his data, Goffman induced his audience to agree with the suggestion, implied in his stated assumption that 'a loose speculative approach to a fundamental area of conduct is better than a rigorous blindness to it' (1963: 4), that however flawed it may be, his approach is still superior to the alternative.

On the matter of his style, the novel-like quality of his writing has been noted by many commentators, not all of them favourably (Burns 1992: ch. 1). Burns's own view was that his style contained 'a scholarly (at times ponderous) gravity combined with an exuberant display of verbal dexterity (and, at times, of sheer verbosity) which kept him a safe distance from current conventions of academic writing', and he noted in particular Goffman's 'combination of clinical approach, sensational content, deadpan stylishness, and bizarre juxtapositions' (1992: 14). This style was in a sense dictated by his underlying theoretical approach because 'his view of social reality was such that he could write about it in no other way but one that approaches fiction' (Lemert 1997b: xxxvii). His works give off the impression that he was a 'resolute non-theorizer' (Waters 1994: 27) and he comes across as 'not as concerned with sweeping generalizations about the human condition as he is with the particulars of daily life' (Kivisto and Pittman 1998: 236). Like much of Goffman's subject matter, these appearances are deceptive. Giddens has rightly observed that 'There is a system of social theory to be derived from Goffman's writings, although some effort has to be made to unearth it.' The 'plain language' in which he wrote contributed to his theoretical purpose being obscured, as did the fact that 'Virtually all of his books are assemblages of essays, rather than integrated works' (1987b: 109–10). As Ditton has pithily observed, in Goffman's writing 'style regularly suppresses structure'; in terms of his wider purpose, more was concealed than revealed by his 'presentational eloquence and expositional charm' (1980: 2). A particular complaint of some readers relates to Goffman's writings as a whole being fragmentary rather than cumulative. For Smith, 'Goffman gave the impression of always wanting to race on to the next issue or topic rather than consolidate what he had achieved' (1999: 7), although he goes on to note that this can also be read as the mark of unbridled creativity.

It is possible to detect two aspects of what Collins has called Goffman's 'conceptual frontiersmanship', reflecting the fact that he had both a 'popular side' and a 'scholarly side'. As Collins describes it, the popular side of Goffman's writings derived from 'his showiness and his topicality', working to an agenda set by 'the things people don't talk about' and drawing on his latest source of data, whether that was fieldwork in a mental hospital or a Nevada casino or something less tangible, such as people's unspoken fears about 'international espionage amid the nuclear shadows of the CIA-infested 1960s'. This agenda was bound to be constantly shifting. By contrast, the 'traditional scholar' in Goffman continually returned to certain basic concerns in the light of the new empirical material with which he engaged, and although this involved him in the development of new concepts, he employed the same 'classically Durkheimian strategy' of 'experimental subtraction', exploring the realm of abnormal phenomena for what they reveal about 'the conditions for normal self and normal interaction' (1980: 170–4). If Collins is correct in this characterisation of Goffman then it helps to explain why it is that his work has generated such diametrically opposed interpretations. Depending on what is selected from his works and how it is read he can, for example, be 'interpreted as a conservative functionalist and as a radical social critic', two obviously incompatible views. Perhaps the most important issue of disagreement between commentators centres on whether Goffman is better described as 'cynic or moralist' (Branaman 2001: 99, 101), an issue that depends on whether actors engaging in impression management are seen primarily as manipulators of their audiences or as people participating in the rituals necessary for the establishment and reproduction of trust in a world where interactions are always open to competing interpretations. It is possible to argue, for example, that people may deceive their audience for altruistic rather than selfish motives (Cuzzort and King 1989: 283), but

Goffman's comment that 'As performers we are merchants of morality' (1969: 243) and others like it fail to clarify the matter either way. Perhaps (as was suggested above) Goffman rejected the idea that the issue could usefully be posed as an either/or choice.

It was not until the year before his death that Goffman took the opportunity to respond publicly to published criticisms (Williams 1988: 64), a fact which led Collins to comment that 'The polemic of academic specialists is not part of Goffman's repertoire' (1980: 173). He did, however, find ways of making statements about his overall position which at least gave clues to his wider intentions. On the charge that he directed attention away from patterns of class inequality he was prepared to concede the point, but then made the rather barbed observation that 'he who would combat false consciousness and awaken people to their true interests has much to do, because the sleep is very deep. And I do not intend here to provide a lullaby but merely to sneak in and watch the way the people snore' (1975: 14). A further parting shot at his critics came in his encouragement of 'a spirit of unfettered, unsponsored inquiry' among sociologists, including research into 'the social arrangements enjoyed by those with institutional authority – priests, psychiatrists, school teachers, police, generals, government leaders, parents, males, whites, nationals, media operators, and all the other well-placed persons who are in a position to give official imprint to versions of reality'. Expressed more briefly, he was encouraging his fellow sociologists to develop 'the art of becoming a pain in the ass' (1997: 261, 254). These quotations from Goffman's Presidential address which was published posthumously capture his skill in using two very simple devices: the list, and the juxtaposition of apparently incongruous entities. By deploying the latter, 'the culturally at hand is made odd and arbitrary, the culturally distant, logical and straightforward' (Geertz 1988: 106), while the former tempts the reader into trying to add to it.

The combination of these two devices could be very effective indeed, as when for example Goffman sought to elaborate on the idea of 'face work' by noting that 'We have party faces, funeral faces, and various kinds of institutional faces' (1963: 28). Not all of Goffman's imagery has entered the language as readily as his idea of 'face work', which is unsurprising given that his innovations amounted to a (metaphorical) 'dictionary of new concepts' (Plummer 1996: 233). Nor is it entirely clear what is added by the suggestion in his discussion of the arrangement between the sexes that 'we are all priests and nuns' (1987: 52), and there must be a risk of not being understood, or of being misunderstood, if the task being undertaken is as fundamental as 'sociological *re*-description' (Watson 1999: 139, emphasis in original). There must also be the risk in this project of causing shock and offence, at least as Branaman says to 'readers who take themselves and their realities too seriously and are unwilling to admit their dependence on dramatic props and social support' (2001: 103). If Lemert is correct in arguing that 'Goffman forces readers out of the convenient illusion that their experience is uniquely theirs' (1997b: ix) it is bound to be an unsettling process. By demonstrating 'how the social solidarity that we take for granted must be continually recreated in daily life' (Hochschild 1983: 214), Goffman shattered one of our most precious illusions, but he tempered this by also pointing out that believing in such illusions makes good sense. In his discussion of performances by professionals he observed that 'The audience can see a great saving of time and emotional energy in the right to treat the performer at occupational face value, as if the performer were all and only what his uniform claimed him to be.' This pretence saves urban life from the 'unbearably sticky' (1969: 57) result of not playing along with the illusion. Worldwide sales of *The Presentation of Self in Everyday Life* had topped half a million before Goffman's death (Smith 1999: 3), suggesting that this open secret is one that we are quite capable of living with.

List of Goffman's key sociological writings
Dates of original publication are given in ( )

The Presentation of Self in Everyday Life (1956/59)

Asylums (1961)

Stigma (1963)

Interaction Ritual (1967)

Relations in Public (1971)

Frame Analysis (1974)

Gender Advertisements (1979)

Forms of Talk (1981)

8

Michel Foucault: sociology as shocking

Introduction and overview

Michel Foucault was born in provincial France on 15 August 1926 and died of AIDS aged 57 on 25 June 1984. He preferred not to be known by the name his parents had given him, Paul-Michel. Paul was the name of his father, of whom 'he was not very fond' (Eribon 1993: 14). He also disputed attempts of commentators on his work to apply labels to him. His reluctance to be classified led him to remark, with characteristic irony, 'Do not ask me who I am and ... to remain the same: leave it to our bureaucrats and our police to see that our papers are in order' (1972: 17). His observation that 'In political thought and analysis, we still have not cut off the head of the king' (1978a: 88–9) reflects his fascination and frustration with the grip that the past could continue to exert on present thinking. On one occasion in 1975 he responded to an invitation to discuss Marx by saying 'Don't talk to me about Marx any more! I never want to hear anything about that man again. ... I've had enough of Marx' (in Eribon 1993: 266). By this stage in his life the former Communist had become sceptical of the capacity of class analysis to point the way towards human liberation and was looking with others for 'an alternative way of thinking' (Lemert 1999: 16). His 1970 inaugural lecture took issue with the focus on ordered and predictable regularities that was characteristic of structuralist thought and directed attention to 'everything that could possibly be violent, discontinuous, querulous, disordered even and perilous' (1999: 419). By taking this position he became a key influence on the development of postmodernism, in which strand of thought the contingency of social relations is emphasised. By adopting the attitude of 'countermodernity' (1986a: 39) Foucault was able to pose a whole series of awkward questions that related to modern anxieties about madness, crime and sexuality, and he did so in the knowledge that these questions had great potential to shock.

Foucault's works have the capacity to unsettle audiences because in questioning conventional thinking they touch raw nerves and highlight paradoxes. In his study of the history of sexuality, he suggested that 'What is peculiar to modern societies ... is not that they consigned sex to a shadow existence, but that they dedicated themselves to speaking of it *ad infinitum*, while exploiting it as *the* secret' (1978a: 35, emphasis in original). It was not only the content but also the style of his writings that could be unsettling, since he was uncomfortable in the role of teacher that involved 'exercising a relationship of power with respect to an audience' (in Davidson 2003: xv). In the extreme, Foucault and his colleagues' reservations about 'outdated academic methods and ... dreary and scholastic prestige' led to the publication of a book relating to the case of a nineteenth-century French peasant who had killed three members of his family that was deliberately devoid of the commentary that would normally be expected. *I, Pierre Rivière* uses the documents about the murders to shock the reader, but Foucault and his colleagues 'were unwilling to superimpose our own text on Rivière's memoir' restricting themselves to 'a number of notes at the end of the volume'. In his contribution Foucault was typically cryptic, remarking that things that are apparently contrary 'like crime and glory' are in fact 'near neighbours ... always on the point of intersection' (1978b: xi, xiii, 205). The reader is left to ponder Foucault's meaning by a style that deliberately avoided telling people what to think. Foucault was sceptical of writers who presented themselves as dealing in 'the revelation of truth' (1978a: 7), and suspicious of audiences who looked to them for ready-made answers. His own mode of engagement is disconcertingly different. His analysis of the 'disciplinary society' (1979: 216) raises numerous fundamental questions, for example, but it does not spell out what his answers to them are.

Their shared interest in the prison-like character of many modern institutions is one of several parallels between Foucault and Goffman. Like Goffman, Foucault published research informed by 'spending long periods of time observing psychiatric practice in mental hospitals' (Sheridan 1980: 5; see also Foucault 1988a: 11). It was Goffman who noted the capacity of people in organisations to deviate from 'the official view of what they should be putting into and getting out of the organization and, behind this, of what sort of self and world that they are to accept for themselves', but the passage would not be out of place in Foucault's account of the limits that exist to the exercise of institutional power over individuals. What Goffman referred to as people's 'multitude of homely little histories, each in its way a movement of liberty' were of central interest to Foucault who also adopted a critical stance in relation to so-called normalisation. Striking similarities exist as well in Goffman's account of people's 'under-lives' as stories of resistance to 'disciplinary practices', expressed as 'little islands of vivid, encapturing activity' in the 'dead sea' (1968a: 267, 332) of the total institution. Foucault would also have concurred with the surprising corollary noted by Goffman, that social processes can have the effect of making 'every man his own jailer' (1967: 10); Foucault's description of how 'each individual' is tending to become 'his own overseer' (1980: 155) is a direct parallel. In addition both discouraged optimism that disciplinary power would generate a 'reactive solidarity' through which oppressive hierarchical classifications might be challenged and liberation achieved. Goffman's downbeat conclusion was that he did not have a superior alternative with which to replace asylums despite having drawn attention to their oppressive character, and his expectation was that closing them down 'would raise a clamour for new ones' (Goffman 1968a: 265, 334). This was echoed in Foucault's pessimistic suggestion that we should not expect the progressive reform of institutions simply because they had failed to achieve their stated objectives. Much depends, as Goffman had it, on 'the ideological use to which ... facts have been put', on how 'the institutional workings of society' are made to 'seem sound' (1987: 56, 52), which was central to Foucault's analysis of discourses. A further connection is that both thinkers raised questions about what constitutes truth. Much of Goffman's evidence was of the 'I have been told' (1969: 48) variety, drawing attention to the questionable foundation of knowledge about which Foucault also expressed fundamental concerns.

Not all aspects of the two thinkers' ideas coincided, and Foucault himself rejected the suggestion by some American reviewers of his work that he was 'trying to do the same thing as Erving Goffman in his work on asylums ... but not as well' (1996: 299). One particularly important difference was that Foucault worked primarily with historical materials, and used the strangeness of the past as a means by which doubt could be cast upon the complacent assumptions of the present. In pursuit of his dream of promoting 'a new age of curiosity' he sought to use evidence about bygone episodes so that we may 'find what surrounds us strange and odd' (1997: 325). This enables us to better answer the key question 'What are we to-day?' (1988b: 145). He did not intend this 'history of the present' (1979: 31) to be a comfortable experience; rather his approach constitutes 'an affront to our habits of thought' (Lemert 1997c: 102). Foucault used the technique of juxtaposing the past and the present so that attention is drawn to the distinctiveness of the present, by revealing what we take for granted about current arrangements and by exposing historical discontinuities and unexpected parallels. Foucault's approach was designed to contribute to the process of 'wearing away certain self-evidentnesses and commonplaces about madness, normality, illness, crime and punishment' (1991: 83). By doing so attention was directed to the paradoxes inherent in our understandings of the individual as 'enslaved sovereign, observed spectator' (1974: 312), and of the processes whereby we have become 'historically determined ... autonomous subjects' (1986a: 43). Foucault's interest in the language through which ideas are expressed made him highly sensitive to 'the ambiguity of the term "subject" ' (Philp 1990: 67), and his work has been described as 'a continuous reflection upon "the human subject" ' (Barth 1998: 252). His stated objective of creating 'a history of the different modes by which, in our culture, human beings are made subjects' (1982: 208) arose out of the controversial position that 'man is an invention of recent date. And one perhaps nearing its end' (1974: 387). If, as he argued, 'history serves to show that-which-is has not always been' (1990: 37), this perspective could be applied to our thinking about ourselves and to the disciplinary bases of our knowledge of ourselves.

Foucault's accounts explored how modernity ushered in a world in which people had become subjects in two senses, individuals with distinct identities who were at the same time subject to disciplinary control. As Lemert has noted, 'Foucault destabilized yet held together the term *subject* in order to define the ideology whereby its one meaning, subjecthood, was used to mystify its political effect, subjugation' (1995: 83: emphasis in original). Foucault's analysis of the ambiguities of key terms also applied to the word 'discipline', which referred not only to the practices through which social regulation was effected, but also to academic specialisms such as psychology and sociology, the development of which had made such regulation possible. His position was 'anti-disciplinary' (Seidman 1998: 247) because he was critical not only of modern mechanisms of social control but also of their intellectual underpinnings. The human sciences had sponsored the emergence of what Foucault called 'the society of the teacher-judge, the doctor-judge, the educator-judge, the "social worker"-judge', since the power of all of these professions rested on their claims to knowledge about normality, 'the universal reign of the normative' (1979: 304). He even spoke of his approach being 'anti-science', and famously remarked that 'I am well aware I have never written anything but fictions' (1980: 145, 193). This false modesty was intended to raise questions about accepted truths, and it implied a commitment to critical thinking in which he endeavoured 'to know how and to what extent it might be possible to think differently, instead of legitimizing what is already known' (1992: 9). Foucault's ideas did not fit easily into established ways of thinking because he was seeking to confront what Bauman has called 'the dull routine of rule-governed debate and the stultifying grip of agendas' (1992: 83). He rejected existing discourses because following their rules did not give the points of leverage that he sought. In contrast to Habermas's belief in 'the force of the better argument' (qtd in Delanty 1999: 107), Foucault took the view that 'language, or discourse, tends to operate in an unarguable manner' (Billig 1996: 14). For Foucault no common ground existed on which rival discourses might be brought together; he suggested rather that accounts of the social order were periodically challenged from a radically different perspective linked to an alternative configuration of power.

In his effort to promote such a challenge, Foucault subjected to scrutiny many of the central ideas on which mainstream social science had been founded. He questioned the idea that science could discover some 'essential kernel of rationality' that would help to promote freedom. This questioning was linked to his suspicion of the logic of either/or choices, as when he rejected the idea that 'one has to be "for" or "against" the Enlightenment' (1986a: 43). Such ideas are not easy to grasp. He recognised that advances in knowledge came 'at the cost of a certain difficulty for the author and the reader' (qtd in Rabinow 1997: vii), although critics are divided on whether he could have made things easier for his audience (if not for himself). Some sense of this division may be gleaned by considering the many adjectives that have been used to describe Foucault's work; these include 'brilliant' (Halperin 1997: 5), 'refreshing' (Moss 1998: 16), 'provocative' (Dreyfus and Rabinow 1982: 201), 'iconoclastic' (Philp 1990: 67), 'elliptical' (Lemert 1995: 63), 'cryptic' (Ritzer 2001: 160), 'prolix' (Dean 1994: 2), 'distinct and challenging' (Barth 1998: 252), 'vague' and 'subtle' (Baert 1998: 131), and 'profoundly original and hopelessly opaque' (Marshall 1994: 187). Foucault's style is in White's opinion intended to be 'thorny': 'His interminable sentences, parentheses, repetitions, neologisms, paradoxes, oxymorons, alternation of analytical with lyrical passages and his combination of scientistic with mythic terminology – all this appears to be consciously designed to render his discourse impenetrable to any critical technique based on ideological principles different from his own' (1979: 81). Against this it can be noted that in certain fields of study 'the so-called Foucault effect is almost overwhelming', reflecting the influence of 'a man of uncommon curiosity and keen insight' (Lindgren 2000: 305). Foucault left us, as May has commented, 'with mixed messages' (1996: 192). This is not only because of the fact that at the time of his death his planned six volumes on the history of sexuality, described by Seidman as 'Without doubt, his master work' (1998: 236), were uncompleted (Marshall 1994: 187). Foucault's ambiguity can also be attributed to his research practices; the method that he employed in his studies was subject to 'subtle, and sometimes gross, shifts and reconfigurations' (Dean 1994: 14), leaving readers unclear about how the various parts of his work relate to each other. Likewise it has been observed that 'Foucault's prodigious writings display no unified theoretical model', but this did not prevent him becoming 'one of the most important and popular thinkers of the twentieth century' (Katz 2001: 117). It is undeniable that he reached a huge audience, even if (and perhaps because) the messages that different members of this audience took away with them were at variance with each other.

The history of the present

A good example of how Foucault's style of presenting his ideas opened up
the possibility for diverse and mutually exclusive interpretations is provided by the sentence with which he concluded part Three of *Discipline and
Punish* in which he asked, 'Is it surprising that prisons resemble factories,
schools, barracks, hospitals, which all resemble prisons?' (1979: 228).
Commenting on the subsequent discussion in the book Giddens has
remarked that 'Factories, offices, schools, barracks and other contexts where
surveillance and disciplinary power are brought into play are mostly not
like this, as Foucault admits, without developing the point' (1984: 153–4;
see also 1982: 222–3). This is a subtlety that could easily be missed. Barth
has likewise argued that 'It would be a mistake to understand Foucault as
suggesting that Western society is governed like a prison. Because of the
power of discipline, our society is precisely unlike the prison' (1998: 255),
but one can see how others might interpret differently the resemblance to
prisons to which Foucault referred. It can be suggested more generally
that the way in which Foucault set about his 'new questioning of modernity' (1990: 89) made settled interpretation of his work impossible. It is
certainly the case that his writings do not have a cumulative quality, particularly if the material contained in the many interviews that he gave
throughout his career is considered. Even a narrower focus on his major
monographs reveals striking discontinuities. As Gutting has noted, 'each
of Foucault's books has the air of a new beginning', with his attention
shifting from discourses to power and then on to the subject at different
points in his career. This fact helps to explain why his writings 'hardly
ever refer back to his previous works' (1994: 4, 3). He himself acknowledged that his 'humble path' had taken him on a number of 'detours'
(1990: 200), but this was not meant to imply that he saw his writings as
constituting a single, unfolding narrative. What he did speak of was the
benefit of being 'a rummager', and he proposed that his books could be
considered 'little tool boxes' (1996: 149) within which readers might find
the means to serve a number of purposes, including those unintended by
the author.

   One aspect of Foucault's work about which there is general agreement
is its capacity to offend our sensibilities. Lemert has pointed out that his
approach was associated with the deliberate creation of confusion, and
that appropriately 'his literary style and his ideas are filled with surprises.
Often he begins with a shocking claim that runs entirely contrary to what
most people think.' Foucault's *The History of Sexuality* is used by Lemert to
illustrate this point, since at the start of this book 'Foucault immediately
attacks ... two general concepts that are typical of modern thinking:
that power is the effect of strong elites consciously and overtly crushing

ordinary people; and, that Christian morality and its secular successors were determined to repress all talk of sex, not to mention sex itself'. Presenting a controversial argument that goes against what 'Most of us are inclined to believe' is, Lemert notes, one of Foucault's favoured 'literary tricks' (1997c: 48). It is used, for example, on the first page of *Madness and Civilization*, where the opening chapter begins by noting that 'At the end of the Middle Ages, leprosy disappeared from the Western world.' This simple statement will be surprising to anyone unaware that Europe had a past in which provision for lepers had to be made and in which leprosariums numbered 'as many as 19,000', with more than 2000 registered in France alone in the early thirteenth century. But the more shocking claim that Foucault made in this introductory passage is that the marginal spaces vacated by lepers came in a later period to be occupied by 'a new incarnation of disease, another grimace of terror, renewed rites of purification and exclusion'. The new inhabitants of these abandoned structures were the product of a very different culture, but were subject to the same process of exclusion: 'Poor vagabonds, criminals, and "deranged minds" would take the part played by the leper' (1971: 3, 7). Further aspects of this shocking story were revealed by Foucault as the book proceeded, elaborating on the general theme that the history of insanity has the potential to disturb the settled classifications of types of people with which we are used to operating.

It becomes apparent quite quickly that the title of Foucault's book is intended to raise questions about conventional understandings of the relationship between madness and civilization, and to suggest that the scientific credentials by which the former came to be classified deserve critical scrutiny, as do the criteria by which the modern mind identified civilized behaviour. The book's subtitle, *A History of Insanity in the Age of Reason*, similarly invites consideration of the connection, and of the irony of cruel and barbaric acts being practised on those classified as mad, carried out in the name of reason. By extensive reference to and analysis of documents of the time, Foucault revealed that madness was treated as simply one among many 'forms of social uselessness' (1971: 58), a description that has similarity to Goffman's notion of people becoming 'socially dead' (1962: 504). Foucault's account points out that it was not until the nineteenth century that separate asylums for the insane were set up, and that in the century and a half prior to this they had been confined as part of 'the poor, the vagabond, the unemployed'. What Foucault referred to as 'the great confinement' had surprisingly wide reach, as he remarked: 'It is common knowledge that the seventeenth century created enormous houses of confinement; it is less commonly known that more than one out of every hundred inhabitants of the city of Paris found themselves confined there, within several months.' They were caught by an edict of 1656 that founded Paris's Hôpital Général and which Foucault quoted to highlight how such institutions were not designed to discriminate but to accommodate 'the poor of Paris "of both sexes, of all ages and from all localities, of whatever breeding and birth, in whatever state they may be, able-bodied or invalid, sick or convalescent, curable or incurable" '. Although this pattern of confinement gave way subsequently to 'the birth of the asylum' in the early nineteenth century, it was nevertheless for Foucault a crucial development: 'in the history of unreason, it marked a decisive event' (1971: 57, 38, 39, 241, 64). It was the moment when a new perception of madness emerged along with new techniques of discipline and control.

Foucault's account is full of attention to particular details, not only of the practices of confinement but also of the words used to describe them. Developing a theme that would reappear in his later work, Foucault described how 'Madness became pure spectacle ... .Until the beginning of the nineteenth century ... madmen remained monsters – that is, etymo- logically, beings or things to be shown.' The move away from such arrangements was made possible by new ways of thinking about mad- ness, 'a whole new order of concepts' that the proponents of reform saw as helping 'to free the mad from a lamentable confusion with the felonious' and to bring to them the benefits of medical advance. Foucault cast doubt on these accounts of progressive change inspired by 'philanthropy' and a concern to secure 'liberation' because these were 'legends' and 'myths' in contrast to which 'The truth was quite different'. The 'justifications', he said, were at odds with 'The real operations'. The deliverance brought by the coming of the asylum was, according to Foucault, a paradoxical process since it intensified the intervention to which individuals were sub- ject. As he saw it, 'Madness escaped from the arbitrary only in order to enter a kind of endless trial for which the asylum furnished simultane- ously police, magistrates, and torturers.' Medical science promoted the asylum as 'a free realm of observation, diagnosis and therapeutics' but for Foucault what emerged was 'a juridical space where one is accused, judged and condemned'. These changes did not constitute the progress that they are conventionally portrayed in liberal accounts as achieving; they were in Foucault's eyes quite the opposite, 'that gigantic moral imprisonment which we are in the habit of calling, doubtless by antiphra- sis, the liberation of the insane' (1971: 69–70, 219, 221–2, 243, 247, 269, 278). The lessons of this historical episode are thus far-reaching indeed, because an instance of words being used to imply the exact opposite of their normal meaning has the potential to raise all sorts of doubts about the freedom and sanity of our own age.

According to Baert, *Madness and Civilization* 'was well received in acade- mic circles, and its literary and allegorical style applauded' (1998: 114–15), but it did not reach such a wide audience as many of Foucault's later works did. Almost one and a half decades separated its publication from that of the book for which he is most famous, *Discipline and Punish*, but there are strong similarities of style and subject matter even though Foucault's methodological standpoint had shifted in the interim. This shift 'from archaeology to genealogy' (Smart 1988: 41) saw Foucault move away from a more fixed conception of how knowledge is formed to a more fluid one in which more open-ended struggles are involved. *Discipline and Punish* was the product of seven years' work, and was artfully constructed (Katz 2001: 120). Its opening passage is truly shocking. Under the heading 'Torture', Foucault quotes at length over several pages from accounts of the public execution of 'Damiens the regicide' that took place in Paris on 2 March 1757, accounts which did not spare any of the details of death by hanging, drawing and quartering. This passage was followed immediately in the book by the timetable in which intricate details of the normal day's routines were set out for young prisoners in Paris eighty years later. This juxtaposition of two very different descriptions allowed Foucault to observe that although 'They do not punish the same crimes or the same type of delinquent … they each define a certain penal style. Less than a century separates them. It was a time when, in Europe and in the United States, the entire economy of punishment was redistributed.' Foucault chose not to discuss all of the features of the 'new age for penal justice' that emerged from the later eighteenth century onwards, but opted rather to 'consider one: the disappearance of torture as a public spectacle' on the grounds that it had come to be unduly neglected. The fact that 'Today we are rather inclined to ignore it' could, he suggested, be attributed to our preparedness to believe in the standard account of how punishment has become modified by 'humanization', or it could reflect the view that it is a relatively minor detail in the grand scale of things, 'when compared with the great institutional transformations'. Neither of these possible explanations was convincing for Foucault, who sought to show that 'the disappearance of punishment as a spectacle' was not a mere 'special case' unworthy of interest but was instead a puzzle that required further analysis. His further remark that the book was 'intended as a correlative history of the modern soul and of a new power to judge' (1979: 1, 3, 7, 8, 23) indicated that he would seek to show that this analysis was of more than purely historical interest, that it had the potential to shed light not only on the past but also on the present.

Details mattered for Foucault. In his analyses he was concerned to 'cultivate the details and accidents that accompany every beginning' (1986b: 80) as a way of revealing what was concealed by the conventional accounts with which we are familiar. In his view, conventional accounts of the development of modern institutions can be regarded as a 'retrospective justification' (1975: 125) by members of medical and other establishments, and these accounts in which history was portrayed as an orderly sequence of progressive changes deserved to be challenged. Foucault's method 'records the past of mankind to unmask the solemn hymns of progress. Genealogy avoids the search for depth. Instead, it seeks the surfaces of events, small details, minor shifts, and subtle contours' (Dreyfus and Rabinow 1982: 106). It is a method described by Foucault as 'gray, meticulous, and patiently documentary' (1986b: 76). In the case of the penal institutions that are the subject of *Discipline and Punish* Foucault's initial contrast between a bloody public execution and the rational orderliness of the routine of a nineteenth-century prison suggests confirmation of the explanation of change in terms of the replacement of barbarity by humane treatment. He acknowledged that this would be a reasonable conclusion to be drawn by a researcher who studied 'only the general social forms' as in his view Durkheim had. He then argued that his approach differed in important respects, not least by paying attention to things that 'seem marginal at first sight'. A particularly important finding generated by this attention to detail was that 'Torture is a technique; it is not an extreme expression of lawless rage.' In contrast to the view that Foucault could assume his readers would hold of torture he described it as 'neither irregular nor primitive'. To support this argument Foucault set out how 'To be torture, punishment must obey three principal criteria: first, it must produce a certain degree of pain, which may be measured exactly, or at least calculated, compared and hierarchized.' Foucault elaborated on this point by reference to examples of different methods of inflicting pain, before going on to identify the other criteria, that 'torture forms part of a ritual' in which the body of the victim is marked, and that 'from the point of view of the law that imposes it, public torture and execution must be spectacular', so that the lessons of the consequences of lawbreaking are clear to the audience. What seem to the modern mind 'excesses' (1979: 23, 33, 34) are, Foucault implied, nothing of the sort when considered from the viewpoint of the age.

It is even appropriate to think of the use of torture under the old regime as having a certain logic to it. As Poster has noted, 'Instead of condemning the barbarism of pre-modern society, its inhumanity, injustice and irrationality, Foucault will present the difference of the pre-modern system by demonstrating that, on its own terms, it makes sense and is coherent' (1984: 96). This was done not to romanticise the past but to undermine the certainties of the present. Poster suggests that this is similar to the way that Marx sought to cast doubt on the supposedly eternal categories of the political economy of his day, except that Foucault's scepticism was not accompanied by Marx's faith in the capacity of science to promote social progress. For Foucault the new regime of replacing the punishment of criminals with treating them, seeking 'to obtain a cure', was not founded on a superior body of knowledge. What it represented was a different configuration of power which was particularly distinct because it took place within a dramatically new architecture, that of the Panopticon. The impact of Bentham's design for buildings in which inmates could be observed without being able to see their observers was presented by Foucault as 'the architectural figure' that allowed for the process of individualisation to unfold. Such structures made 'each actor ... perfectly individualized and constantly visible' under the gaze of the supervisor. In his account Foucault identified 'the major effect of the Panopticon' as a device 'to induce in the inmate a state of conscious and permanent visibility that assures the automatic functioning of power'. Because it facilitates surveillance of unprecedented extent and efficiency, it can be described (with heavy irony) as 'a marvellous machine'. Nor is its potential limited to prisons, since the same principles can be applied to a range of populations: 'All that is needed ... is to place a supervisor in a central tower and to shut up in each cell a madman, a patient, a condemned man, a worker or a schoolboy.' The exercise of this new form of disciplinary power 'from the beginning of the nineteenth century in the psychiatric asylum, the penitentiary, the reformatory, the approved school and, to some extent, the hospital' suggested to Foucault parallels with the treatment of lepers and plague victims several centuries earlier, not least because they were both exercises in differentiating between 'the normal and the abnormal'. This line of analysis then 'brings us back to our own time' (1979: 200, 201, 202, 200, 199) by revealing the disreputable origins of our familiar social arrangements and by encouraging us to consider just how different the contemporary treatment of abnormality actually is.

Disciplinary narratives and discourses

The unsettling conclusions about the present towards which Foucault's analysis were designed to lead do not stop with the treatment of individuals who come to be classified in some way or other as abnormal. They extend to include the very idea of the individual that is a cornerstone of contemporary understandings of identity but that is, Foucault said, of relatively recent provenance. In his account he argued that in the past most people's distinguishing characteristics went unremarked: 'For a long time ordinary individuality – the everyday individuality of everybody – remained below the threshold of description. To be looked at, observed, described in detail, followed from day to day by an uninterrupted writing was a privilege', something that was reserved for members of the powerful minority. Only quite recently did the reversal of this 'political axis of individualization' occur, as a result of which the ordinary individual became 'a "case" '. Foucault's language here was deliberately social scientific because the social sciences were in his view instrumental in the shift. In particular, 'all the sciences, analyses or practices employing the root "psycho-" have their origin in this historical reversal of the procedures of individualization.' This process extended beyond children, patients, madmen and delinquents 'to individualize the healthy, normal, and law-abiding adult' (1979: 191, 192, 193). In contrast to the idea of individualisation as a process of liberation and the freedom to exercise choice, Foucault spoke of 'this kind of individuality which has been imposed on us'. He employed the paradoxical notion of the 'government of individualization' to refer to the way in which power in its modern form 'categorizes the individual, marks him by his own individuality, attaches him to his own identity' (1982: 216, 212). Foucault commented on how the modern individual is required to internalise these classifications, 'to act upon himself, to monitor, test, improve, and transform himself' (1992: 28). That he did not regard this development as something to be welcomed is apparent in his reference to 'the stifling anguish of responsibility' (1971: 247) that the modern individual suffers as a consequence.

Claims that science brings with it individual liberation were regarded by Foucault with disdain (Gutting 1994: 21). In the field of study devoted to human sexuality, for example, he was sceptical of the 'domain of knowledge' that had produced 'a collection of rules (which differentiate the permissible from the forbidden, natural from monstrous, normal from pathological, what is decent from what is not, etc.)' (1986c: 333, 334). From this perspective the assignation of a 'deeply negative' character to the 'stereotypical portrait of the homosexual' found in nineteenth-century texts was a form of 'problematization' that made sense only in relation to the pervasive process of 'normalization' (1992: 18, 12). This process was rooted in the discourses of medical and other scientific experts. Foucault's consideration of how it came about that 'scientific knowledge was endowed with its own rules', on which basis were developed 'techniques for "governing" individuals – that is, for "guiding their conduct" ' (1986c: 337–8), was part of a more general critique. His statement that his 'problem is to see how men govern (themselves and others) by the production of truth' (1991: 79) highlighted not only the importance of knowledge but also its contestable character. By speaking of truth as something produced rather than something discovered he could challenge claims made in the name of science. That was also the effect of his reference to 'the games of truth by which man proposes to think his own nature when he perceives himself to be mad; when he considers himself to be ill; when he conceives of himself as a living, speaking, labouring being; when he judges and punishes himself as a criminal'. If it can be revealed in this way that there is 'a history of truth' (1992: 7, 6), then the soundness of the knowledge produced in such contexts as a prison administered along the lines of the Panopticon can be brought into question. In *Discipline and Punish* Foucault had noted that 'the Panopticon was also a laboratory; it could be used as a machine to carry out experiments ... .To experiment with medicines and monitor their effects ... a privileged place for experiments on men, and for analysing with complete certainty the transformations that may be obtained from them' (1979: 203–4). The knowledge produced in this way might indeed be questionable.

A number of disconcerting conclusions follow from Foucault's argument that 'Each society has its régime of truth ... . The types of discourse which it accepts' (1980: 131). In the preface to *The Order of Things* he reported laughing by as he read a passage that shattered 'all the familiar landmarks of my thought – *our* thought, the thought that bears the stamp of our age and our geography'. The text in question was a 'certain Chinese encyclopaedia' reported on by Borges which divided animals into a number of categories. The first of these are presented alphabetically: '(a) belonging to the Emperor, (b) embalmed, (c) tame', but as it proceeds the list increasingly stretches the reader's credibility to breaking point. It continued, '(d) sucking pigs, (e) sirens, (f) fabulous, (g) stray dogs, (h) included in the present classification, (i) frenzied, (j) innumerable, (k) drawn with a very fine camelhair brush, (l) *et cetera*, (m) having just broken the water pitcher, (n) that from a long way off look like flies'. This taxonomy has an unnerving effect because, Foucault noted, it operates in such a way as to 'threaten with collapse our age-old distinction between the Same and the Other'. It serves as a means of demonstrating 'the exotic charm of another system of thought' and 'the limitation of our own, the stark impossibility of thinking *that*' (1974: xv, emphases in original). Even though the encyclopaedia entry was a literary myth, an invention of Borges, it served Foucault's purpose of encouraging us to reconsider the familiar classifications with which we attempt to impose order onto the world. It worked, in other words, to reveal 'the limitation of our own system of thought. Because we are locked in our own discourse we simply cannot see how the animal world could be mapped in this way' (Philp 1990: 70). Foucault used this story as a device to enter into a discussion of the human sciences from a particular angle, one by which their 'essential instability ... their precariousness, their uncertainty as sciences' (1974: 348) could be exposed. What needed to be challenged was nothing less than the scientific status of the knowledge produced by disciplines such as psychology and sociology.

Foucault's critique of the human or social sciences located them historically. He said that the emergence of these disciplines could be related to specific historical conditions. Thus 'the new norms imposed by industrial society on individuals were certainly necessary before psychology, slowly, in the course of the nineteenth century, could constitute itself as a science'. Likewise, 'reflection of the sociological type' could not have emerged except against the background of the threat to social order that first became apparent during the French Revolution. What was problematic for Foucault about these new disciplines was that they had attempted to make 'man' into 'the object of science' and open to analysis 'in accordance with models or concepts borrowed from biology, economics, and the sciences of language'. They had done so, moreover, in a remarkably short period of time, as Foucault implied in his reference to 'all this knowledge within which Western culture had given itself in one century a certain image of man'. Claims that this knowledge was scientific were contested by Foucault because in his view the human sciences 'are not sciences at all', however much their claims were framed in terms of concepts like human nature. Foucault rejected the narratives of disciplines that imposed a spurious universality onto their subject matter. What he disparagingly called 'psychologism' and 'sociologism' were guilty of 'anthropologization' (1974: 345, 347, 361, 366, 348), by which the assumptions embodied in contemporary culture about the individual subject or self are projected onto all societies. In this vein in a later discussion he questioned the use of the notion of rationality as an 'anthropological invariant' (1991: 79). In contrast to the confidence with which statements were made in the name of science by psychologists and sociologists, Foucault brought doubt. His argument was that the human sciences 'are rooted in non-rational, contingent and frequently unsavoury origins' (Philp 1990: 70), and as such any knowledge that they produced could not live up to what was claimed for it. The human sciences were too much the product of modernity, understood as 'an attitude ... a way of thinking and feeling', too much caught up in modernity's 'heroization of the present' (1986a: 39, 42), to bear the claims to superiority over rival discourses that their proponents made for them.

Foucault was not a social scientist and never aspired to become one. Working from the outside, the human sciences 'were his object of study ... it was the effective operation of these disciplines – how and around what concepts they formed, how they were used, where they developed – that was Foucault's prey' (Rabinow 1986: 12). Foucault described his analysis of these 'domains of knowledge' as an 'experiment' that revealed their status as 'vested knowledges' (1997: 6–7). He was in no doubt that the human sciences had played an important role in moulding the modern world through the reshaping of individuals that 'the disciplining of societies' entails. The pursuit of social scientific knowledge had been prompted by the paternalistic project of 'leading people to their salvation ... in this world'. This project was pursued through the promotion of 'health, well-being (i.e. sufficient wealth, standard of living), security, protection against accidents'. It was done under the gaze of the increasing numbers of officials who oversaw the activities of 'private ventures, welfare societies, benefactors and ... philanthropists' as well as institutions with longer histories that adapted to this new function, notably families and hospitals. For this to happen, individuals had to submit themselves to this 'new form of pastoral power' which required 'the development of knowledge of man'. Foucault's rejection of this whole project is conveyed in his subversive suggestion that 'Maybe the target nowadays is not to discover what we are, but to refuse what we are.' Foucault's objection was to the whole rationale of the social sciences as the handmaidens of a type of society. By contributing to the processes through which individuals became subjects these disciplines were complicit in bringing about a new form of 'subjection' (1982: 219, 215, 216, 213) of the population.

Foucault's questioning of the social sciences concerned not only their purpose but also the way in which they operated in relation to evidence as if it were open to unambiguous interpretation in the style of what he called 'global, *totalitarian* theories' (1980: 80, emphasis in original). His inaugural address sought to gain his audience's attention with the words 'I would like to recount a little story so beautiful I fear it may well be true.' He recounted the story to expose 'one of the great myths of European culture' that the knowledge that it embodied was open to universal application. His declaration that 'This notion does not, in fact, stand up to close examination' (1999: 415–16) is instructive because it indicates how Foucault proposed to proceed with his investigations, namely by paying careful attention to detail. His style of writing is open to criticism for being 'often "too" literary ... strewn with gnomic utterances, tantalizing hints, and a taste for verbal drama rather than logical argument' (Merquior 1985: 56), but the fact that these presentational devices are at odds with the conventions of social science does not mean that his work is unsociological in every sense of that word. He has been described as someone who 'contributed to historical sociology ... from some distance' and from 'a number of rather oblique angles' (Dean 1994: ix, 2). His emphasis on attention to detail is arguably among the most important of these. His method required this because he set about his work in a particular way: 'instead of running through the library of scientific literature, as one was apt to do, and stopping at that, I would need to examine a collection of archives comprising official orders, statutes, hospital or prison records, court proceedings and so on' (1997: 5). Much of his work is concerned with close analysis of these documents, which he described as 'a vast accumulation of source material' (1986b: 76). In *Discipline and Punish* he quoted approvingly Marshal de Saxe's words, 'Although those who concern themselves with details are regarded as folk of limited intelligence, it seems to me that this part is essential ... . It is not enough to have a liking for architecture.

One must also know stone-cutting.' For Foucault, 'Discipline is a political anatomy of detail' (1979: 139), and he advised those seeking to challenge it to pay attention to 'the micro-mechanisms of power' (1980: 101). Modern discipline and the intellectual disciplines that made it possible had created the prison that, as Philp puts it, 'shuts the prisoner up (in both senses)' (1990: 77). Against this, Foucault sought to give prisoners a voice (Smart 1988: 17). His suggestion that he was a 'person who lends an ear to hear a muffled voice from below history' (qtd in Callinicos 1999: 264) positioned him outside of mainstream social science discourses. To many people in his audience (including some sociologists amongst them) this is an important part of his appeal.

Leaving things open

Foucault's work defies simple classification and is not easy to locate in relation to the sociological enterprise as a whole or even particular thinkers within it. This was deliberate on Foucault's part. His dislike of being pigeon-holed came to the surface in his complaint that 'In France, certain half-witted "commentators" persist in labelling me a "structuralist". I have been unable to get it into their tiny minds that I have used none of the methods, concepts or key terms that characterize structural analysis' (1974: xiv). Other labels were treated as equally unsatisfactory. The careful wording of Foucault's title as professor of the history of systems of thought was significant, as Weeks (2000: 106) has noted. His method of subjecting established classifications to close scrutiny could be applied to academic disciplines as well as those embodied in historical documents, and with the same result: 'it disturbs what was previously considered immobile; it fragments what was thought unified; it shows the heterogeneity of what was imagined consistent with itself' (1986b: 82). In any event, Foucault had no time for undue reverence for intellectual traditions, and he lamented the predicament whereby 'We are doomed historically to history, to the patient construction of discourses about discourses, and to the task of hearing what has already been said' (qtd in Sheridan 1980: x). Foucault did not align himself with established traditions of thought, and contended that 'conventional categories really don't fit him' (Bové 1988: viii). If they had done so his adherence to them would have compromised his ability to encourage the new ways of thinking that he regarded as crucial to the search for routes out of what he called the 'society of normalisation' (1980: 107). This was the rationale for the disruptiveness and sometimes shocking boldness that characterises his work.

One of the ways in which Foucault sought to engage with his audience was through experimentation with different styles. Foucault's use of shocking material can have unanticipated consequences, as Deleuze shows by noting that his discussion of 'A whole chain of phenomena, from anti-masturbation machines for children to the mechanics of prison for adults, sets off an unexpected laughter.' On more than one occasion, Deleuze suggests, Foucault employed 'a literary and humorous way' of presenting ideas that related to 'serious disciplines' (1988: 23, 98). He was also unusual amongst academics in the extent to which he sought to convey his ideas through interviews, which according to Bové contain 'Many of Foucault's most telling statements' (1988: vii). They served an important purpose in their presentation of Foucault's ideas in a more accessible format than that typical of his books (although it can be noted that the concluding chapter of *The Archaeology of Knowledge* is structured as a dialogue, with Foucault responding to the comments of an interlocutor). Kritzman has observed of Foucault's interviews that their form as a dialogue enabled him 'to engage intimately in a critical reflection on the crucial shifts in his philosophical, political and cultural perspectives. No other European intellectual since Jean-Paul Sartre has been so committed to the interview as a cultural form' (1990: vii). This does not mean that they are comfortable reading, as is the case for example with those that 'occur in an admonitory mode', with Foucault seeking to correct misunderstandings of his ideas that came when others sought to locate him 'in line with their own intellectual, political and professional needs' (Bové 1988: vi). Again, this is an aspect of the presentation of Foucault's work that is not restricted to his interviews. Philp notes of Foucault that 'he frequently spends more time making clear what he is not saying than with stating his own position' (1990: 68). In *The Archaeology of Knowledge*, for example, his identification of what 'My aim is not' and of what 'my aim is most decidedly not' (1972: 15) precede his statement of what he is about. Foucault regarded himself as participating in 'discussions' rather than 'polemics', involved in a dialogue rather than waging war, engaging with 'a partner in the search for the truth' rather than confronting 'an adversary, an enemy who is wrong'. The polemicist was characterised as someone seeking 'to bring about the triumph of the just cause he has been manifestly upholding from the beginning' (1997: 111–12), that is, someone who did not bring an open mind to the discussion of differences.

Foucault was also interested in the literary style of the confessional. In one interview he appeared to reveal something about his inner self by observing that 'learning can be made an erotic, highly pleasurable activity' and by inviting his questioner to 'Imagine what it would be like if people were crazy about learning the way they are about sex' before concluding his comments cryptically, '[in an undertone] I don't include myself' (1996: 136). Confessions were for Foucault revealing about the importance of the process of self-examination in the making of modern subjects, and it was his view that 'We have ... become a singularly confessing society' (1978a: 59), since confessions have become ubiquitous and extend far beyond activities associated with more conventional understandings of wrongdoing such as criminal and sinful acts. There is a confessional quality to Foucault's account of what drove him to undertake the research for his studies of the history of sexuality. He notes that he reminded himself 'that it would probably not be worth the trouble of making books if they failed to teach the author something he hadn't known before, if they didn't lead to unforeseen places, and if they didn't disperse one toward a strange and new relation with himself' (1986c: 339). The certainties that he sought to question included those that he himself brought to the problems under investigation, and he noted that his studies led him 'through certain paradoxes and difficulties'; these are unavoidable if one is seeking 'to get free of oneself' or is at least 'straying afield' (1992: 13, 8). He reported in a similar fashion that his developing analysis of power had proceeded 'in a very zig-zag fashion'. Marxist ideas continued to provide him with a point of reference long after he had broken with the Communists, although this was a means of distancing himself from that past. He came to conclude that systems of thought such as Marxism foreclosed debate rather than opened it up, and that 'the attempt to think in terms of a totality has proved a hindrance to research'. Foucault's sense of historical discontinuity and of the contingency of social relations meant that he was unconvinced by what he regarded as rigid conceptions of societies as integrated totalities with deterministic relations between their component parts. His preferred style of argument was one that 'put forward a few "propositions" – not firm assertions, but simply suggestions to be further tested and evaluated' (1980: 94, 81, 132–3). Only these could in his view capture the great heterogeneity of social forms that totalising discourses suppressed.

Baert contends that the difficulty of placing Foucault in relation to other thinkers needs to be located in the context of Parisian intellectual life 'in which claims to originality are crucial to one's reputation' (1998: 118). Foucault's indebtedness to Nietzsche's ideas is evident in many of his works, most obviously those relating to power and knowledge. Deleuze has suggested that the similarity extends to their method of working: 'The key thing, as Nietzsche said, is that thinkers are always, so to speak, shooting arrows into the air, and other thinkers pick them up and shoot them in another direction. That's what happens with Foucault' (qtd in Katz 2001: 117). According to Deleuze, 'nothing in Foucault is really closed off', as is indicated by his use of Nietzsche's imagery of 'the iron hand of necessity throwing the dice of chance' (Deleuze 1988: 43, 86). Foucault's sense of the open and contingent character of social change is also conveyed in his remark that 'the things which seem most evident to us are always formed in the confluence of encounters and chances, during the course of a precarious and fragile history' (1990: 37). This sense of history as an open process in which 'things can be changed' (qtd in Smart 1992: 220) took the argument much further than Weber's critique of determinism did, even though there are important similarities between two thinkers (Crow 1997: 162–3). Weber would not have agreed with Foucault's position on the malleability of forms of rationality embodied in human practice; whereas Weber's theory of rationalisation resulted in his iron cage imagery, or the idea of a limited number of tracks along which societies might travel, Foucault argued that 'since these things have been made, they can be unmade, as long as we know how it was that they were made' (1990: 37). This highlights the point that Foucault was approaching the question more as a historian of ideas than as a sociologist, and on these grounds his work is open to the criticism that his 'model of the social is too much influenced by the literary model of the text: textual subversion cannot be taken to be an appropriate model for social action' (Delanty 1999: 108). It is, in other words, easier to change the ways in which we think and write about social life than it is to change social life itself.

It can be argued that such criticism misses the point of what Foucault saw himself as trying to do. As Philp has noted, Foucault 'would deny that he is offering a new theory of social and political order because, above all, his concern is with the destruction of such theories ... and to give free play to difference, to local and specific knowledge, and to rupture, contingency and discontinuity' (1990: 68). Foucault's preference for the ' "specific" intellectual as opposed to the "universal" intellectual' (1980: 126) was reflected in his concentration on particular institutions such as hospitals and prisons because the distinct patterns of power and resistance found there had been overlooked by theorists who sought (in his view mistakenly) uniform society-wide processes. Foucault's work thus poses very sharply the question of whether an argument deserves to be engaged with on the terms set out by the author. Typical of Foucault's practice of bracketing out certain questions was his statement in *The Order of Things* that he had confined himself to describing the transformations considered in that book and had deliberately 'left the problem of causes to one side' (1974: xiii). Those readers who seek answers to problems that Foucault opted not to tackle are likely to be left feeling that 'the unanswered questions are manifold' (Weeks 2000: 120). In this context it can be noted that many feminists have been surprised by Foucault's 'apparent indifference to some of the issues raised by gender', but their subsequent engagement with rather than dismissal of his ideas is linked amongst other things to the fact that 'Foucault is often his own most trenchant critic' (McNay 1994: 10) and whose style invites such engagement. According to Sawicki, 'Feminist appropriations of Foucault have resulted in path-breaking and provocative social and cultural criticism' (1991: 95). This can be taken as confirmation of the value of applying to Foucault's work more generally his remark in *The Order of Things* that 'I should like this work to be read as an open site' (1974: xii). The concomitant risk is that this very openness allows readers to find what they want to find and that, as Apperley puts it, 'Michel Foucault can be all things to all people' (1997: 10). Characteristically, Foucault's comment was that he was 'amused' by this (1997: 113).

List of Foucault's key sociological writings
Dates of original publication are given in ( ); English translations are given in [ ]

Madness and Civilization (1961) [1965]

The Order of Things (1966) [1970]

The Archaeology of Knowledge (1969) [1972]

Discipline and Punish (1975) [1977]

The History of sexuality (3 volumes) (1976, 1984, 1984) [1978, 1985, 1986]

Society Must be Defended (1997) (given as lectures 1975–76) [2003]

9

Ann Oakley: sociology as emancipation

Introduction and overview

Ann Oakley was born on 17 January 1944 in London, where she has lived and worked for most of her life. The sociologist Trent Lovett warns that 'nothing is simply knowledge' (1999a: 184). The fact that he is a character in one of her novels reinforces the point. It is a central theme of Oakley's that there are 'different ways of knowing' (2000: 3), and she takes a special interest in how certain types of knowledge come to have more credibility attached to them than others. She has a particular concern about the way in which academics in the pursuit of knowledge go through 'a sanitizing process which strips it of its most vital and interesting aspects – where it came from, just how it is mediated by the knower's own experience and rooting in the material social world' (2002: 2). Oakley's writings are not so 'sanitized': they detail how she has come to know what she knows and why she considers such knowledge important. Her view that knowledge production is highly gendered has inevitably courted controversy, but she is unrepentant about breaking with male-dominated academic conventions and quotes approvingly the view that 'well-behaved women rarely make history' (2004: 5). Challenging the established way of doing things in intellectual life is vital if it is to be recognised that 'knowledge is reached through *everyone's* experience of everyday life' (in Halsey 2004: 215, emphasis in original), a perspective that in Oakley's opinion sociologists ought to promote but have tended not to.

Oakley was the only child of Kay and Richard Titmuss, who during the wartime pregnancy confidently expected the child would be a boy (1997a: 200). Relations between family members figure prominently among the topics that she has researched, reflecting interests that can be traced back to her childhood. Her characterisation of modern Western societies as ones in which 'a chasm between "family" and "society" developed: women came to represent the first, men the second' (1982a: 142) corresponded to her own experience. Her father was the eminent Professor of Social Administration (what would now be called Social Policy) at the London

147

School of Economics, and was 'the active one' of her parents; her mother was allocated the role 'of devoted helper and dutiful wife'. The standards of the time identified this arrangement as 'a perfect division of labour – exactly what families exist for' (1997a: 11), but Oakley was sensitive to 'the contradictory forces and attitudes that made up relations between my parents' (1985: 15). There is a resonance in Oakley's life with de Beauvoir's identification of the implication for women of the tension between the 'feminine world' and the 'masculine universe', that 'they can settle down nowhere in peace' (in Oakley 1982a: 15). She continues to hold that 'Women are outsiders in a system which often appears to them to come from another planet' (2002: 3), and still strives to promote emancipation from this system. This places her at odds with writers whose work 'removes sociology from the field of practical public policy' (in Halsey 2004: 215), since in her opinion it is important not to lose sight of the fact that 'people in the "real" world continue to be disadvantaged and oppressed and to suffer from remediable problems' (2000: 306), a belief with which her parents would undoubtedly have concurred.

Oakley's strictures against 'theory for theory's sake' (in Halsey 2004: 214) do not imply an anti-theoretical stance. Other feminists may have engaged with Foucault's ideas more extensively than she has, for example, but their writings share several important themes. First of all, they both reject the separation of the personal and political domains of life, and both writers draw extensively upon personal experience. Foucault's comment that 'Each of my works is a part of my own biography. For one or another reason I had the occasion to feel and live those things' (1988a: 11) has a parallel in Oakley's frequent reference to aspects of her life. Her accounts draw directly on her experiences of housework, of childbirth, motherhood and miscarriage, and of gender disadvantage and oppression. She has commented about herself and other academics that 'there *is* a very close association between people's personal experience and what they do in terms of their area of work, their interests in that, and the methodology that they use' (in Mullan 1987: 193, emphasis in original). A second parallel with Foucault is her portrayal of women's position as 'subject' (1982a; 1992: x) in the twin senses of dominated and complicit in that domination. In conventional terms women appear powerless but can be seen to be 'powerful in other ways', although they do not necessarily use this to press for change; in the case of mothers, for example, she discusses 'normal motherhood' as 'an exercise in self-control' (1981b: 104). The subjective experience of being subject is captured by using the phrase 'doing good and feeling bad' to describe women's lot in 'our kind of society' (1982a: 81).

It was noted above that Friedan identified this as 'the problem that has no name' (1999: 359), and Oakley shares Friedan's concern with the hidden travails of 'apparently satisfied wives' (Oakley 1982a: 27). It follows that naming a problem is an important part of attempting to resolve it. Like Foucault, Oakley is dissatisfied with inherited classifications that obscure particular situations and conceal the oppression that they entail. Conventional classifications of work are problematic for her because their narrow focus on paid work make an important part of women's lives 'invisible' (1974: ch. 1). By re-naming the labour women expend 'inside the home for love' she can expose how 'The paradox of working more and earning less than men derives from the double meaning of work for women' (1993: 9). Subjecting the contemporary world to critical examination also leads Oakley (1984: 1) to endorse Foucault's project of writing the history of the present. Engaging in 're-interpreting the social world, both past and present, from a perspective which includes women' (Mitchell and Oakley 1976: 14) allows her to challenge contemporary and historical accounts from which women's contributions to social life have been written out.

Oakley presents a direct challenge to prevailing understandings, and as part of this process she seeks to rescue the discipline of sociology from the hands of those practitioners who suffer from what she calls 'the sociological unimagination' (1980: ch. 3). The echo of the complaint expressed by Mills about his contemporaries is deliberate. Oakley acknowledges his influence on her by noting that it was reading *The Sociological Imagination* as an undergraduate that 'made me want to be a sociologist', before going on to pay him the further compliment of employing his approach to critique his own work. Even though 'the whole of my professional life is his fault' (1994), Mills was not above criticism for the sexism of his terminology (such as 'intellectual craftsmanship') and for 'his own low level of awareness' (Oakley 1974: 24) of the male-dominated nature of the sociological thinking of his time. The more positive message that Oakley draws from Mills is the sense of excitement about sociology's potential to spur the imagination through the linkage of personal experience to broader political agendas, and the sense of betrayal when sociologists fail to realise this promise. Mills's legacy is also detectable in Oakley's extensive engagement with questions of methodology and the status of the knowledge that researchers generate. Her early investigations reveal that 'The trouble with sociology (as with many other academic subjects) is that it is not merely sexist on the surface but deeply and pervasively so' (1980: 2). It follows that attention needs to be paid to fundamental questions of academic purpose and procedure. The appeal to imagination leads Oakley to challenge not only the omission of key aspects of women's lives from the research agenda but also the problematic treatment of women in conventional research practice when they are made the object of study. Her bold thesis that interviewing women is 'a contradiction in terms' forces a reassessment of the status of evidence generated in the pursuit of objective scientific knowledge. Oakley's experiences of failure when trying to employ the techniques of 'masculinist social science' (1986a: 231) prompt a more general consideration of precisely what their shortcomings are. This has not entailed outright rejection of quantitative methods as a basis for producing knowledge, since Oakley argues that 'women and feminism need the service of these methods' (2000: 4) as well as the qualitative methods with which feminist sociology is more usually associated.

Oakley's rationale for this approach is pragmatic and critical of the adoption of dogmatic stances. In her view, if social science is to contribute to people's emancipation then its practitioners need to concentrate their attention not on semantics but

> on the business in hand, which is how to develop the most reliable and democratic ways of knowing, both in order to bridge the gap between ourselves and others, and to ensure that those who intervene in other people's lives do so with the most benefit and the least harm. (2000)

Preparedness to use quantitative data allows a broader range of questions to be posed and arguments developed than is possible when such an approach is rejected as irretrievably flawed on the grounds that it embodies thinking that is 'masculine' (2000: 3). Typical of the questions that Oakley seeks to pose is that of asking 'Are men good for the welfare of women and children?' (Oakley and Rigby 1998), and in answering it she and her co-author are not afraid to use statistical tools such as odds ratios. Similar ideas underpin her concern to ask 'Who's afraid of the randomized controlled trial?' (1990a). By including in her methodological repertoire research techniques more usually associated with medical science Oakley has been able to develop distinctive modes of argument and to address audiences that typically have been unreceptive to sociological perspectives. Medical scientists are wont to treat as ' "soft", and by implication inferior, material of social-scientific surveys' (1993: 21). Feminist sociologists understandably grew weary with the predictable belittling of their research by medical experts who pronounced that 'It's all common sense' (Roberts 1981: 14). Oakley responded by re-emphasising that she had 'never advocated "qualitative" to the exclusion of "quantitative" work, or the other way round' (2000: 21). In her view obstetricians 'need ... sociologists to convince them' that there is more to childbirth and post-natal depression than they have conventionally acknowledged, and if that process of engagement with medical experts requires approaching such wider phenomena as measurable then 'we've got to find the right way of measuring them, we've got to start somewhere' (in Mullan 1987: 200). The treatment of quantitative and qualitative approaches as a dichotomy between which a choice must be made embodies a faulty logic, since 'Either/or thinking puts an embargo on both/sometimes-the-one, sometimes-the-other, possibilities' (1992: xi). The world does not have the neatness of the dichotomising mind, and sociological research is all the poorer if this basic fact is overlooked.

The themes of how attempts are made to impose orderliness on a recalcitrant reality and of how such attempts are resisted and subverted are pervasive in Oakley's work. In her first book she advances the 'rather surprising contention' that sex and gender do not automatically correspond; the evidence of cultural anthropology is that 'one finds the same biological distinctions between male and female coexisting with great variations in gender roles'. Research by psychoanalysts also points to the same conclusion, that 'boys without penises may become "normal" males: girls with penises and without uteruses may become "normal" females' (1972: 158, 159). The embodiment in culture of such simplifications of the messiness of experience is the stuff of anthropology, on which Oakley draws freely, but she does not restrict her examples to exotic cases. The same conclusion can be reached by examination of everyday categories that are in use closer to home. In this vein Oakley refers to the way in which 'single-parent families ... represent a social situation full of ambiguities', one of many examples of the pervasive *'ambivalence* in the cultural values applied to women's roles' (1976a: 70, 60, emphasis in original). Another example of how real people confound cultural stereotypes of normal behaviour was provided by the government report published in the 1970s that declared (in Oakley's paraphrase) 'that the high percentage of people marrying is a cause for official concern', indicating as it did that 'the institution of marriage must be attracting many people who are unfitted for it' (1982b: 135). The more general point is that 'On the one hand, there are statements, arguments, ideas and suppositions about how the world is ... and, on the other, there are the lived realities of individual lives'. The discrepancies between these two mean that although 'the whole aim of theory is to tidy up the world, it is unlikely ever to succeed in this aim' (1986a: 230). Oakley's criticisms of theorising that 'degenerates into very arid concepts' reflect her view that some writers 'get carried away by theory and they lose sight of the *point* of the theory'. Her feminism prompts the use of a variety of forms of expression, including those that have the capacity to engage with emotions, 'valuing feelings and valuing those ways of perceiving the world that are not reasoned debates' (in Mullan 1987: 203, 202, emphasis in original). In her view 'there are many different ways to tell stories about science and about life' (1986a: 9). Her methodological position has prompted one commentator to suggest that it leads to the logical conclusion that 'Oakley makes sense only to Oakley' (Pawson 1989: 320), but this is clearly not the intention of someone who encourages sensitivity to 'intimations of a world beyond ourselves'.

Her work is dedicated to enabling others as well as herself 'to break out of our normal channels of thought and activity', and although the modest goal of 'changing the attitudes and behaviour of just a few' (1986a: 7) would count as success, all the indications are that she has achieved far more than this.

The sociological unimagination

An important part of sociology's appeal for Oakley is its potential to challenge common sense. In her view 'No assumption is worth having unless it can be challenged' (1986a: 7), and although this approach carries with it the risk of unpopularity, this is a necessary price of her prepared-ness to cause 'discomfort in some quarters' and her commitment 'to go on being awkward' (1993: xi, xii). The exposure of parochialism and blink-ered vision courts a hostile reception, but this is inevitable for anyone who accepts Elias's designation of a sociologist as 'a destroyer of myths' (1978: ch. 2). Much of Oakley's work involves confronting myths about mother-hood, housework and family life that collectively constitute a culture that women find at odds with their own experiences. Her study of childbirth, for example, concludes that there is a mystique surrounding motherhood, and that this 'idealization is linked with the fostering of romantic expecta-tions about childbirth'. It highlights 'the considerable gap that exists between expectations and reality: pregnancy, childbirth and motherhood are not the way most women expect them to be' (1980: 284, 280–1). Oakley could make this pronouncement with some confidence, since she herself had learned the hard lesson 'that mothers have no instant bonds with their babies' (1985: 136). Her development of a critique of 'the "myth" of moth-erhood' is not a denial of the rewards that mothers may experience; rather, it is motivated by a concern to give voice to those women who reported to her that being a mother 'has considerable deprivations too, and that the social glorification of motherhood in our society acts to conceal them' (1974: 174). Another pervasive myth referred to by Oakley is the 'myth of the division of labour by sex', which reinforces women's identification with domestic labour. Such myths need to be challenged because they reproduce the status quo: 'myth anchors the present in the past'. It needs to be demonstrated that 'as statements of fact they are untrue' because if left unchallenged 'Myth stated as fact becomes fact', or at least it 'appears real' (1976a: 156–7). Sociologists can play an important role in the expo-sure of such cultural biases. By doing so they contribute to the liberation of women from the difficulties generated by trying to live according to unrealisable ideals.

Oakley's assessment is that sociologists have more often been part of the problem than part of the solution. Conventional sociological accounts of gender 'spring from the intellectual's internalization of his own cultural milieu: he hopes that what he believes in – the family and marriage – is more than a mere figment of his imagination' (1976a: 184–5). Put simply, if sociology is sexist, it is because its practitioners tend 'to adopt the values of the wider society', and as a result, 'In much sociology women as a social group are invisible or inadequately represented: they take the insubstantial form of ghosts, shadows or stereotyped characters' (1974: 2, 1). Oakley returns repeatedly to this theme of disappointment with sociological writing. It relates not only to individual sociologists' shortcomings but to something more systematic: 'sociology has been in its modes of thinking, methodologies, conceptual organization and subjects of inquiry, one of the most sexist of academic disciplines, embodying in largely uncritical fashion the structure and values of the existing social order' (1980: 71). Such strictures have led many other feminists to distance themselves from the discipline of sociology altogether, and Oakley's experience of being 'vilified ... for being a sociologist' by sections of the women's movement led her to reflect on whether a feminist sociology was a desirable objective, or even a possible one. Her surprising conclusion was that not only do feminist ideas have a legitimate place in the discipline but that feminism opened up the opportunity for sociology to be reinvigorated. Her claim that 'the sociological perspective, in its most basic elements, is an inherently feminist perspective' was one that she acknowledged 'might seem to contradict almost everything else I have said', but it embodied an impeccable logic. Women might reasonably be expected to have particularly keen insights into the 'relations between people' that are at the heart of the discipline's subject matter because of the historical allocation to women of responsibility for managing this sphere of life. In addition, women have 'a specially urgent need' (1986a: 199, 210) for understanding the social processes that shape who we are as individuals due to their sharp awareness of the discrepancy between what is supposed to exist and their actual experiences. Oakley's view is that 'Those who are socially subordinate may find that their ways of thinking do not fit the language – or, rather, that conventional linguistic forms cannot adequately express their experiences' (1993: x). She describes marginality as a 'critical experience' (2002: 9). Lemert (1999: 19) makes a similar point in suggesting that some of the best social theorising comes from people at the margins, because their need to make sense of the world may be more pressing than it is for more privileged groups. Goffman likewise acknowledged that sociologists are not immune from taking for granted things that cry out to be studied by remarking that 'we have had to rely on the discontented to remind us of our subject matter' (1987: 51) when introducing his analysis of gender relations.

Oakley offers a sociological account of the failure of sociologists to realise the potential of their discipline. In much the same way that Mills had attributed the narrowness of vision of his professional contemporaries to their inability to transcend the assumptions of the small town culture into which they had been socialised, Oakley points to the ingrained insensitivity of her male peers to the systematic marginalisation of women of which she was only too painfully aware. When asked to explain sociologists' tendency to neglect alternative understandings of gender relations she replied, 'Because they're men! Because ... the dominant view of women in our society is still unchanged, and it's easier to participate in that view than to challenge it' (in Mullan 1987: 191). Her poem *General Smuts Pub* describes the experience of being (involuntarily) among a crowd of men drinking prior to a football match as something that required her to fight to make sense of a place 'as foreign to me and all feminists as outer space' (1986a: 220). The use of the device of encouraging one's audience to look afresh at familiar social relations through the eyes of an outsider is common in sociology and anthropology, and the same effect can be achieved by reference to foreign travel as is created by the imagination of how strange the world might appear to a Martian visitor. Sociology and related disciplines such as anthropology and history have the potential to challenge what insiders tend to take for granted because they necessarily generate comparative perspectives. Cross-cultural comparisons are particularly valuable, Oakley argues, because they help 'to undermine the logic of fatalism: it does not *have* to be the way it is, because it *can* be done differently' (1997c: xi, emphases in original). Sociologists' failure to live up to this promise of imagining alternatives to the status quo does not mean that the overall project of analysing the world sociologically deserves to be abandoned.

Putting gender relations onto the agenda of sociological research was not a matter of simply pointing out an omission that could be quickly rectified. It required, as Skocpol puts it, 'the chutzpah to undertake the virtually impossible' (1988: 635), and involved sustained struggle against opposition from members of the academic establishment. Oakley's proposal to undertake 'a study of women's attitudes to housework as work' required her 'to insist on the seriousness of my aim in the face of a lot of patronising jocularity about the academic absurdity of such a topic. The idea of doing a Ph.D. on housework in Britain in 1969 was laughable' (1985: 74). The ignorance underlying the 'distorted male-oriented perspective' that Oakley encountered, she attributed to three aspects of conventional sociology: 'the nature of its origins, the sex of its practitioners, and the ideology of gender roles, borrowed from the wider society, which is reproduced uncritically within it' (1974: 28, 21). Her strategy for confronting this 'distinctly sexist academic environment of the time' (1985: 78) involved simply 'going back to women themselves and looking through their eyes at the occupation of housewife' (1974: 28). Her next study, on motherhood, likewise sought 'to catch it and describe it and explore it through the eyes of some of those who experience it'. This reflected the fact that 'the women said it all much better, and much more clearly and directly, than a sociologist could ever do' (1981a: 1, 5). Such data contrast with the various myths surrounding women's lives, and thereby challenge them. It is instructive that her first publication was entitled 'The Myth of Motherhood' and it is instructive also that this appeared in the magazine *New Society* (1985: 75), where it would reach a wider audience than could a more narrowly focused academic journal. Her subsequent book *The Sociology of Housework* was also written with more than sociologists in mind since the audience envisaged included 'people who have a general interest in the housewife's situation, but no particular knowledge of sociology' (1974: vii). This stance set the pattern for what was to follow. Oakley describes her commitment to sociology as rooted in the discipline's capacity 'to find out about things *in order to make them better*' and to this end she aims to reach several audiences, including non-academic ones. Arguing that 'communication of research findings' is 'a very ignored part of the research process', she is committed to 'writing articles for *Mother and Baby, Woman's Own* as well as for *The British Journal of Sociology* and *The British Medical Journal*' (in Mullan 1987: 202, emphasis in original). She knew that doing so would raise the hackles of more conventional sociologists, but in her view this is merely one more expression of 'sexism in sociology', the academic counterpart of 'discrimination against women in society' (1974: 1) more generally.

Oakley's demonstration of the capacity of sociology to reveal the discrepancies that exist between idealised versions of women's lives and the more mundane realities opens up a whole range of possibilities. The rectification of the previous neglect of housework as a sociological problem had shown what insights the application of 'revised notions of women's place' could lead to, and Oakley's attention was drawn to another unduly neglected aspect of women's lives, that of childbirth. Sociology could correct the tendency of medicine and psychology 'to return reproduction and the character of women to the domain of nature'. Oakley looked to sociology as the means of approaching childbirth in 'the only valid way to arrive at an understanding of what happens, why and with what consequences' (1980: 72, 70, 2), but was starting effectively from scratch given the virtual absence of sociological studies of the subject. In a discussion reminiscent of Foucault, Oakley argued that this situation reflected 'the colonization of parenthood, and especially of motherhood, by professionals'; consequently the knowledge that was available was medical knowledge. This was generated by 'the whole edifice of routine medical surveillance of pregnant women' and was alien to women's way of understanding the world because in Oakley's view, its principal purpose was driven by 'the need for a patriarchal social order to get motherhood under control'. It was an approach that distorted women's experience by reworking their emotional attachment to their babies as something that 'must be named and organized, become the subject of experimentation and of bureaucratic rules' (1990b: x, xiii, xii). It is unsurprising that the medicalisation of pregnancy, that is, its 'reconstitution ... as a distinct type of social behaviour falling under the jurisdiction of the medical profession' (1984: 4), is quite compatible with widespread ignorance about the process among the prospective mothers to whom Oakley talked. She reports how one interviewee asked her the question, 'Is it right that the baby doesn't come out of the same hole you pass water out of?' (1986a: 241). This lack of knowledge was made all the more startling by the fact that this woman had attended antenatal classes but found that 'they didn't deal with those sort of questions' (Oakley in Mullan 1987: 195). The other face of the 'medical mastery' (1980: 9) that the medicalisation of childbirth has ushered in is the disempowerment of women and their relegation to the role of passive recipients of medical expertise.

These findings reinforced Oakley's sense of indignation about what happens to women during pregnancy and childbirth, and they also heightened her awareness of the difficulties that are encountered during fieldwork situations when researchers attempt to follow conventional research guidelines. These procedures encourage the researcher to relate to people being researched in what she regarded as a manipulative way, by being non-committal or evasive when the person being studied asks questions. This approach Oakley found both impractical and unethical. In her study of childbirth Oakley conducted 178 interviews with women who asked her no fewer than 878 questions (that is, on average, a fraction under five questions per interview). She reports that she 'found it very difficult to avoid answering these questions as honestly and fully as I could' (1986a: 241). It was for two reasons. One is that it seemed to her impractical to stall when asked by a woman 'which hole the baby came out of'; understandably, she 'felt it was absurd to say that questions like that should not be answered'. Second, she perceived this approach to be unethical, since she regarded the discussion of intimate details of a person's life to require a degree of reciprocity: 'you really cannot – it's inhuman – ask for somebody's co-operation with this kind of thing without giving them something in return' (in Mullan 1987: 195). Oakley's feminism prompted her to seek to repay her respondents with something more concrete than vague assurances that the project was 'in the interests of "science" ' and that the information that they gave to her would be useful for 'some book that might possibly materialize out of the research – a book which many of the women interviewed would not read and none would profit from directly' (1986a: 242). Oakley admits to having a 'naughty curiosity about other people's lives' (1985: 126), but she was also driven by the prospect of 'using sociology to improve the situation of women'. This was a particularly urgent task at a time when the world was 'getting demonstrably worse for women' (1986a: 210, 256). On other occasions Oakley has adjudged that, in some ways at least, 'things have got better' (1993: xii) for women, but the calculation is a complex one that requires engagement in argument about the criteria to be used in arriving at such an assessment. Such analyses of how things have changed lead directly on to the consideration of why they have changed, and of whether such changes are likely to endure.

Personal and political agendas

Oakley's identification of the 'political, personal and scientific reasons' (2002: 2) that lay behind her book *Gender on Planet Earth* could be applied to her writings more generally, albeit that the balance between these three factors varies somewhat from work to work. In *From Here to Maternity* she describes herself as 'a feminist, an academic sociologist, and a woman with children'. The inclusion of these three identities reflects her belief that 'academic research projects bear an intimate relationship to the researcher's life, however "scientific" a sociologist pretends to be. Personal dramas provoke ideas that generate books and research projects' (1981a: 2, 4). This personal dimension is acknowledged in other contexts, as for example when she notes that 'my stance on world affairs is filtered through the sieve of my own life: whose isn't?' (1985: 85). Personal experience directed her to particular research topics, and the Preface to *Housewife* includes (somewhat barbed) thanks to her 'own family for the experience of my own oppression as a housewife. Without this I would never have wanted to write the book in the first place' (1976a: x). Elsewhere she describes how her work has been part of her pursuit of authenticity. Her challenge to the ascription of conventional feminine roles means that her writings 'speak of my own struggle to get away from impersonation' (1993: xii). Her work has been part of her search for 'a concept of myself', as distinct from the set of roles ascribed to her. If the view is taken that 'Female, male, lover, spouse, parent, child … are names, mere names' (1985: 190, 204) then the quest for identity must transcend them. There is an obvious identification with the indignation of the respondent in her housework study who railed against being regarded as 'just a housewife' (1976a: 100) and who thereby provided an effective vehicle for Oakley to use in arguing that individuals are much more than the labels attached to them by other people.

Researching topics that are close to home is bound to have an effect on the researcher's sense of self and politics. Oakley reports that 'My work turned me into a radical' (1985: 124), and there is an autobiographical ring to her statement that 'The "deconditioned" housewife is ... a potential revolutionary'. Although it is written in the third person, the analysis reflects Oakley's own journey of discovery:

> A thorough comprehension of gender differences, their origins and implications, can develop out of the realization of the socially imposed tie between femininity and domesticity – a realization which is, at the same time, an awareness of how women are led to acquiesce in their own subordination. (1974: 197, 196)

This process of 'Breaking the circle' (1976a: ch. 9) in order to challenge the equation of women with the role of housewife is precisely the transition that Oakley went through. She reports that she 'took the plunge into family life' with her eyes 'completely closed', and only later realised through involvement in the women's liberation movement 'that my uncomfortable experiences were not mine alone'. It was while undertaking her research on housework that she attended a meeting mentioned by one of her interviewees, imagining herself in the role of 'participant observer, with neutral attitudes'. From this beginning she went on 'to find out a lot of things I needed to know and couldn't read in books or discover by myself alone' (1985: 70, 76). She came to perceive her experiences not as unique to her but rather as shared ones: 'my private conflicts were nothing more or less than the legacy that all women in modern industrialised society inherit' (1981a: 2). Who we are reflects in no small degree 'our personal connectedness with others' (1985: 190). An important source of her feminism has been discussion of 'aspects of oppression that women share' (Oakley and Mitchell 1997: xxi) as well as of the more politically awkward 'differences from one another' (Mitchell and Oakley 1986: 3) that quickly become apparent. Her later co-edited collections that take stock of feminist ideas and their impact have followed in the tradition of the first in presenting 'the case against sexism' (Mitchell and Oakley 1976: 7), but they do not shy away from the difficulties that arise from being a feminist. Confronting the 'paradox' that feminism pursues the goal of 'the elimination of gender roles' by promoting 'gender consciousness' (Mitchell and Oakley 1986: 3) is one of the issues with which Oakley and her collaborators grapple in assessing feminism's contemporary relevance.

Oakley's feminism commits her to seeking out a broad audience, to speak to others besides those who have formal training in sociology and to answer questions that are meaningful to their lives. Her capacity to present ideas with stark simplicity helps this. She reports having developed 'an intolerance for anything other than plain speaking' (2002: 3), and has always been committed to communicating straightforwardly. The simple truth can thus be stated that 'Our lives are organized around men' (1985: 117). Nor is there anything new in this situation; rather, 'Most human cultures are, or have been, sexist in one way or another' (Oakley and Oakley 1979: 172). Another simple but powerful observation is that change does not move in any simple progressive fashion towards greater equality. Oakley notes that one of contemporary feminism's achievements has been to challenge the widely held assumption that 'domestic technology liberates housewives'. Research findings that 'housework hours have actually risen with the invention of new household appliances' present a paradox that directs attention to 'the standards housewives set for themselves' (1982a: 171, 172). One of the respondents in Oakley's study of housework reported washing her flat's curtains fortnightly, cleaning thoroughly her carpets weekly and vacuum-cleaning some of them up to twenty times a day. Her housework constituted 'a 105-hour week'. Although this particular housewife acknowledged that she had 'high standards', Oakley argues that she and others like her were not the 'pathologically obsessed' individuals that figured in the psychiatric literature. Rather, 'it makes more sense to view their behaviour as a rational response to a problematic situation' (1974: 109–11) in which performing household tasks well is central to a positive sense of self but where the amount of time that can be devoted to housework is potentially limitless. The finding that the 40 women in Oakley's study spent on average 77 hours a week on housework could be explained by their belief in 'the "need" to change and wash the sheets ... two or three times a week and to get them "whiter than white" ' (1982a: 172). How women acquire 'the personal need to *be* a housewife' (1974: 196, emphasis in original) is thus a question of some import. It directs attention to the identification of influences such as the advertising industry that propagate misleading images of domestic perfection and fulfilment and thereby threaten to cancel out the potential for liberation from drudgery that technological advances make possible.

In contrast to the popular perception of progress towards gender equality and the supersession of outdated patriarchal social conventions, much of the evidence considered by Oakley points to the conclusion that it is often more appropriate to conclude that 'Life doesn't get better for women'. One of the obstacles to the improvement of women's lot is 'the belief that we're all liberated now' (1985: 191), and challenging this perspective requires recognition that it is not a view held exclusively by men. The achievements of second-wave feminism for which Oakley and her generation struggled are taken for granted by 'many young women' for whom they constitute an 'unacknowledged birthright'. In response to this, feminists have continued to produce research that 'takes a cool look at what's happened to women, concluding that rampant discrimination still exists' (2002: 75, 74), but this is not a particularly easy message to get across. Even if it is accepted that women's liberation has not been achieved, other arguments have been advanced regarding the unintended consequences of feminism that challenge its desirability. This backlash against feminism (Oakley and Mitchell 1997) draws on what Hirschman (1991) calls *The Rhetoric of Reaction* to argue that its goals are either unattainable or attainable only at unacceptable cost because of their wider consequences. Such arguments construct feminist aspirations as problematic, and Oakley and Mitchell see little new in this: 'the term *feminist* is the name now given to the disliked or despised woman, much as *man-hater, castrating bitch, harridan,* or *witch* were used before the advent of second-wave feminism in the 1960s' (1997: xix, emphases in original). Oakley regards this as one of the lessons of history: 'The social study of gender has long told us that women are a problem for any male-dominated social order' (1990b: ix). Her alternative message is 'women are an oppressed social group' (1985: 196) and that the problem lies not with the women themselves but in the way in which they come to be constructed as a problem.

This argument directs attention away from the oppressed and onto the oppressors. For Oakley it follows that 'if women cease to be the problem, because one sees how women are constructed out of the problems and how they must repudiate them for advances to be made, then men, somewhat inevitably, become the problem instead' (1985: 197). Put another way, the important question to ask is whose problem is to be considered: 'If women are a problem for society, then men are a problem for women.' She acknowledges that it appears paradoxical 'that men become more, not less, problematic whenever the political impetus of feminism plots a less gender-divided world' (1990b: x), but men's opposition becomes more readily understandable once their attachment to the benefits that they enjoy is considered. In her view 'There is ... no reason why men should renounce the comforts of patriarchy other than that the women to whom they are attached require them to do so'. Her judgement that anyone would be reluctant 'to exchange an easy life for a more difficult one without a good reason' (1985: 75) leads her repeatedly to the question 'Why should men change?'. The relentlessness of childcare and the fact that it is 'socially and financially unrewarded work' help to explain why fathers are reluctant to relieve mothers of their responsibilities; the desirability of maintaining the status quo is the conclusion more likely to be drawn by 'any man "in his right (i.e. patriarchal) mind" '. Many feminists underestimated the scale of the change that would be involved when seeking greater involvement of fathers with childcare, being misled by 'the invalid assumption on which equal parenthood rests, namely that men and women are able to live in harmony with one another' (1990b: xi). Family life is a site of friction because 'the vested interests of all men are inevitably in the continuation of patriarchy'. The conflict of interests between them means that 'men and women actually find it very difficult to live happily with one another' (1985: 158, 152). Oakley endorses Mills's analysis of divorce as a public issue as well as a personal trouble, and questions why it should be that 'Unsuccessful marriages are interpreted as problems, not solutions to problems' (1982a: 245). If as Oakley argues 'men are the enemies of women' then it follows that relationships between them are bound to be problematic. This case is made not simply in defence of women's interests, but appeals to broader criteria: 'Without men the world would be a better place: softer, kinder, more loving; calmer, quieter, more humane' (1985: 116). And if it is correct that women are at the cutting edge of progressive change, that 'they move into the future first' (Mitchell and Oakley 1986: 4), the question becomes not what is wrong with women but what to do about the problem of the patriarchal institutions, attitudes and practices that stand as obstacles to that advance.

In this context Oakley's decision to direct attention to the institution of the family is particularly instructive. Her challenge to the prevailing wisdom that men bring advantages to other family members has profound implications. It is incontrovertible that 'In most conceptions of welfare, the presence of a man in the family is presumed to benefit both women and children', but it is precisely the validity of this presumption that Oakley and Rigby set out to explore as an empirical question. By asking 'do men make a positive contribution to the welfare of women and children?' they highlight the shortcomings of research that treats the family as an unproblematic unit of analysis in which members gain equally from the resources available and benefit from a heightened level of social support. Their data reveal that 'Within father-present households, material resources are not necessarily allocated equally between mothers and fathers', that in terms of contributions to housework and childcare 'the *absolute* level of help from men is rather low', and 'that being married to or living with a man is not coterminous with being helped or supported by him'. The overall conclusion to which their and other researchers' findings point is that 'patriarchy ... is bad for women and children's health', although 'This fact is disguised by the rhetoric of heterosexual love and protection which encourages women to see men as their saviours' (1998: 102, 104, 111, 113, 117, 123–4, emphasis in original). It is only by exposing the shortcomings of such rhetoric that phenomena like lone mothers being 'better off poorer' (Graham 1987: 59) can be considered. One of the most useful functions performed by Oakley's work involves doing nothing more complicated than introducing the idea that it might be possible to demonstrate the existence of 'disbenefits of traditional father-present households' (Oakley and Rigby 1998: 123). In a similar way her earlier work sought to escape the constraints of received conceptualisations by suggesting that patriarchal men may be thought of as dependent as well as powerful ('babies in disguise' (1985: 56)), and that social support is not an unambiguous good because it 'may be experienced as more of a burden than a benefit' (1992: 27). If as Oakley suggests certain concepts 'provide a powerful mechanism for distorting women's experiences' (1993: xi), there is political value in challenging them and seeking to replace them with others that offer a truer perspective.

Novel forms of sociological argument

Sociology is at its most potent when its use succeeds in persuading people of the need to think differently. How best to achieve this outcome is an enduring concern of Oakley's. From her engagement in the production of 'an "anti-text" ... that could be set against the ideological message of orthodox literature on the position of women' (Mitchell and Oakley 1976: 7), through other studies such as *Social Support and Motherhood* that deliberately 'is not a book that reports the results of research in the way in which this is conventionally understood' (1992: xii), to the inclusion in *Gender on Planet Earth* of self-penned 'fictional reviews ... written by imaginary critics' (2002: 5), Oakley has experimented with a variety of presentational styles in search of more effective communication. She also laments that her *Essays on Women, Medicine and Health* is 'not the book that I would have written had I had the freedom to alter received wisdom of what "proper" books should look like'. Experience of publishing poems, novels and auto/biographical works on herself and her family alongside more conventional essays, articles, edited collections and monographs has led her to conclude that 'it is apparently too early in the revision of our notions of writing for poetry to be accepted as a legitimate invader of the terrain of "factual" writing. People are uncomfortable with the mixing of the two and with the implicit argument that fiction and fact may flow seamlessly into one another' (1993: xii, x). Yet if sociology is about challenging conventional wisdom then it is appropriate to consider questions about the discipline itself, including its conventions concerning how ideas are presented and for what purpose. Oakley's uncomfortable message is that those who look to sociology for 'easy answers' will be disappointed. This is not primarily because of methodological or conceptual shortcomings, but more because sociologists pose 'some of the most difficult questions of our time' (1992: ix). In a similar vein Oakley's account of her engagement with feminism suggests that it 'raises more questions than answers', as might be expected when what are confronted are '*human* issues, the unresolved problems of the *human* condition' (1985: 195–6, emphases in original). Oakley uses the phrase 'Journey into the Unknown' (1986b: 59) to describe women's transformative experience of becoming a mother, but it could equally well be applied to her experience of doing research that has taken her to destinations that could not be anticipated and which existing knowledge prepared her for only inadequately.

Thinking differently requires the exercise of one's capacity to imagine. Oakley's view is that 'All writing is an invitation to the imagination', and a variety of means are available to challenge and encourage readers to think in unaccustomed ways. From this point of view whether something 'is fictional or non-fictional matters not at all. All writing is a matter of new arrangements of words, and thus of new forms' (1985: 191). Her use of poetry alongside academic essays 'were different ways of communicating the same issues', issues which included 'motherhood's facts and fictions' (1993: x). This does not condone the view that anything goes; rather it advocates the imaginative use of a range of styles of presenting ideas in pursuit of improvements on standard practice. Dissatisfaction with much of what sociologists currently do is quite consistent with Oakley being 'optimistic about the chances of using sociology to improve the lot of women'. What is required to achieve this is an outlook unconstrained by convention: 'the real challenge *is* to innovate, and in producing new theoretical understandings and ways of working, liberate sociology from its own oppression as a didactic and chauvinistic science' (1986a: 210, emphasis in original). There is a parallel here with Foucault, who 'does not write in order to teach lessons' but who 'writes politically in that ... he challenges tradition and works to pose new questions by means of new methods. ... The reader is forced to do his own work' (Lemert and Gillan 1982: x, 32). Oakley would, of course, be careful to avoid the suggestion that her audience was typically male, but her style is akin to Foucault's in its preference for engagement and dialogue with her readers rather than seeking to instruct them in what to think. No one method enjoys a monopoly as a means of 'telling the truth', and so she experiments with 'different ways of writing'. This is done in the belief that they are 'reconcilable – parts of the patchwork quilt of the whole'. Feminist research has revealed 'creatively blurred ambiguities of the way in which women experience the world' (1993: x), and feminist sociologists need to be creative in the attempt to capture these ambiguities.

It was noted earlier that Mills possessed the knack of capturing the imagination in a pithy phrase. Oakley follows in this tradition. Several of her books have arresting titles because of the intriguing ambiguities that they contain: *Women Confined, Subject Women, The Rights and Wrongs of*

Women, Taking It Like A Woman. The last of these contains the observation that 'women are lost ... in the family' (1985: 201) which engages attention because it is open to more than one interpretation. The family also provides an illustration of the implications of thinking differently. Oakley encourages her readers to reverse the conventional couplet 'man and wife', and notes that 'wife and man' sounds distinctly odd because 'a reversal of terms destroys the meaning of the phrase, which is man (person) and wife (female-person-in-the-possession-and-under-the-control-of-man)' (1976a: 61). Twenty years after this was written Oakley used the phrase *Man and Wife* as the title of her book about her parents because it 'sums up the traditional arrangement' according to which they lived and which meant that upon marriage her mother Kay was obliged to give up 'a life of her own' (1997a: 1, 3). This theme is also present in Oakley's fiction. Her novel *The Men's Room* opens with a quotation from Simone de Beauvoir's *The Second Sex*, and proceeds with a wife reflecting that 'women must define their positions in relation to men' (1989: 1). In other places Oakley captures the humour of ambiguity, introducing her discussion of the history of antenatal care with the title 'Great Expectations', and proceeding to the more serious point that, in the light of the disadvantages of hospital deliveries, there is 'No Place Like Home' (1984: 9, 213). Getting the joke in entitling a chapter in a book on social scientific research methods 'Mean Values' (2000: ch. 5) requires some basic knowledge of mathematical terminology, but it too makes a serious point. The rhetorical questions, 'Feminism, Motherhood and Medicine – Who Cares?' (1986c) and 'Who Cares for Women?' (1993: ch. 6) are further examples of the diversity of ways in which Oakley has the capacity to deploy a few words to great effect.

Oakley's sensitivity as to how words are used comes out in numerous ways. Her first book was an extended discussion of 'the distinction between "sex" and "gender" ' (1972: 16). She returned to this subject a quarter of a century later, in a context where 'gender slips uneasily between being merely another word for sex and being a contested political term. ... in one of its guises "gender" is simply another word for "women" ' (1997b: 30). By opening *Subject Women* with the apparently ludicrous question 'Are women people?' Oakley provides a necessarily provocative starting point in her attempt to demonstrate that a woman is treated as 'a kind of person', one who is 'defined in relation to the prevailing standard of normality' (1982a: 1, 63). Women are people only if they give up the right to be themselves; they 'are not acceptable for what they are, but must fit themselves into certain routine shapes' (1985: 96). More can be revealed about the stereotypes to which women are expected to conform by showing that they vary considerably. Her analysis of how women in different times and places have figured more prominently in the management of childbirth includes the observation that 'Etymologically and historically, four words or roles have been closely related. These are woman, witch, midwife and healer' (1976b: 23). In her contemporary work, great importance is attached to the words used by the women whom she interviewed. In *From Here To Maternity* these are given more prominence than her own words: 'my intention has been to reverse the usual text–quotation relationship so that the women's own words make up the text of the book. Chapters 2–12, which reproduce the women's accounts, accordingly reverse normal typesetting practice; it is my comments and not the interview quotations that are italicised' (1981a: 5). This style of presentation can be called 'ethnography' (1980: 95), in order to distinguish it from the 'academic version of the research, ... *Women Confined*' (1981a: 5). In the subsequent work on *Miscarriage* the women whose experiences it recounts are described as 'really co-authors of the book, since their accounts of, and comments on, the experience of miscarriage appear throughout it'. They deserve this status because without them, 'the first British book of its kind on the subject' (Oakley *et al.* 1984: 12) would not have appeared.

The discovery that there was 'no study of childbirth from the woman's point of view' (Oakley 1976b: 21) set an obvious research agenda for Oakley to follow in the same way that the discovery of a dearth of studies of how women experienced housework had previously. In addition to the extensive use of selected quotations from interviews as a means of getting across her findings, Oakley uses the technique of presenting case histories in order that we might 'listen carefully to what women say'. The chapter in *Housewife* devoted to the detailed accounts of particular housewives contains material on four individuals drawn from the forty who had been involved in the study reported on more fully in *The Sociology of Housework*. These cases are presented as 'representative of the larger sample, although each ... highlights specific aspects of the housewife situation' (1976a: 103). The technique of presenting detailed accounts of particular individuals drawn from a wider sample is also used in *Social Support and Motherhood*, where the 'four women whose voices are heard' (1992: 188) were selected from 509 possible cases. Such material promotes the accessibility of ideas, because 'The concrete and the personal are always easier to grasp than generalities' (2002: 8). Putting the same point another way, and acknowledging Dorothy Smith's influence in arriving at the formulation, Oakley says that 'there is no theory about the world that does not begin in someone's everyday experience' (1992: xii). When researching the sociology of reproduction it makes sense to take 'the words of the reproducers themselves as the best descriptions available' (1980: 95). It is surprising that researchers did not follow this route sooner.

Breaking with research conventions prompts questions about why apparently sensible strategies have not been adopted before. Part of the answer in relation to the use of the qualitative data that interviews can generate is that simply reproducing people's words is unlikely to tell the whole story. This is not just a point about the inevitable need to pare down what people say to a manageable level, although this is an important consideration. Oakley's acknowledgement in her introduction to the four case studies of housewives that 'The interviews ... have been edited so that much of the original data on housework attitudes and routines is omitted' (1976a: 104) raises the issue of the criteria used to determine what to include and what to leave out. Similarly, the account of motherhood presented in *From Here to Maternity* is one that she rightly anticipated would be felt by some readers to be 'too bleak'. She notes that some among her audience might believe the selection to have been guided primarily by the belief that 'the best news is bad news: happiness doesn't hit the headlines' (1981a: 6), although she does not hold this opinion herself; in her view 'It is hard to avoid the fact that there is something really depressing about motherhood' (1993: 85). Alongside this point about selectivity is an equally important one about validity: it is risky to take what people say at face value. Even in the extended accounts of their lives that Oakley collected from housewives, 'A great deal of dissatisfaction with housework may exist in a concealed form' (1976a: 104). The analysis of research findings requires interpretation of people's descriptions of their realities. This problem is not unique to qualitative research. It is a more general truth that 'No facts "speak for themselves" ' (1997a: 1), and with this recognition we are led once again to consider the fundamental question of how we come to know what we know.

Oakley has approached from several directions the problem of how to relate to the existence of more than one way of knowing. Her analysis of in-depth interviewing contributed to an extensive and ongoing debate that links to wider discussions about the relative merits of qualitative and quantitative research methods and the relationship between them (Letherby 2003: ch. 4). It came as a surprise to some people familiar with this debate that she also has employed quantitative methods involving the randomised controlled trials favoured by conventional medical research, but her view is that quantitative methods have long had an important role to play in promoting women's interests. They are, for example, used to highlight the extent of gender inequalities in education, labour markets and health problems, and to Oakley it is odd if feminists do not acknowledge that 'the very charting of women's oppression required quantification'. In her view there has been a natural progression to her career and not a radical break between, as one of her critics put it, 'the old Oakley' and 'the new Oakley' (2000: 19, 21). It is instructive to note that both *The Sociology of Housework* and *Women Confined* begin with a 'Note on Tables and Tests of Significance' (1974: vi; 1980: ix), as does the more statistically ambitious *Social Support and Motherhood* (1992: vi–vii), even though in the first case at least the use of the chi-square test of significance 'might be criticized on the grounds that the sample is too small to justify it' (1974: 35). Concern with the representativeness of her research samples also figures prominently in her earlier as well as her more recent empirical investigations (1974: 39–40; 1981a: 5; 1992: 123). In general terms her approach has been premised on 'the integration of so-called "qualitative" and "quantitative" research methods'. Rather than seeing the two as opposites between which researchers have to choose, what she proposes is 'to reframe the relationship between aggregated data and individual standpoints as *dialectical*' (1992: 14, 187, emphasis in original). Both have a contribution to make towards the 'meticulous, systematic, transparent, sensitive striving for descriptions of "reality" ' (2000: 4) that is the object not only of social scientists but of human beings generally.

At the same time that Oakley has been engaged in these debates she has also written several novels. Her view of the connection between academic work and writing fiction is suggested in her comment that 'There are many reasons for writing novels, but trying to gain a sense of sanity and order out of an experience of delusion and disorder is certainly one of them' (1999b: 19). All of her work is written conscious of 'the artificiality of the boundaries we set ourselves'. If she is right that 'Human experience is often not as neat and tidy as we strive to make it' (1981a: 4) then academic work can take advantage of this. References to the works of various literary figures are to be found in her sociological writings, including Chaucer, Lewis Carroll and Dickens (Oakley 1976b: 29; 1982a: ix; 2000: 115–17). She is also adventurous in relation to her preparedness to engage with other academic disciplines, such as anthropology (1972), psychology (1980) and economics (2002). This apparent eclecticism of styles and subject matters reflects a desire to engage with a range of different audiences, in one place described as being 'anyone who cared to listen' (1986b: 3). She is, however, not minded to give priority to the task of marshalling 'convincing evidence of women's worth to convert the listless or the unlistening' (1986a: 256). In addition, she reports that her thinking contains 'a sort of stubborn insistence on the difference between biological sex and social gender' (2000: 15). Her comment about her Marxist feminist critics, that 'while I understand their position, I understand mine as well' (1986a: 199) also indicates that openness to new ideas and a concern to promote healthy debate requires the capacity to stand one's ground when confronted by criticism that cannot be accommodated. It is as much for this quality as any of its others that Oakley's research has been described as 'Model Knowledge-making' (Spender 1985: ch. 11).

List of Oakley's key sociological writings
Dates of original publication are given in ( )

Sex, Gender and Society (1972)
The Sociology of Housework (1974)
Housewife (1974)
Women Confined: Towards a Sociology of Childbirth (1980)
The Captured Womb (1984)
Social Support and Motherhood (1992)
Experiments in Knowing (2000)
Gender on Planet Earth (2002)

10

Conclusion

This final chapter is devoted to the consideration of how the various thinkers discussed in this book relate to each other and to the exploration of what can be learned from them, individually and collectively, about the nature of sociological argument. It might be concluded from feminist critiques of 'malestream' sociology that sociologists do not stand on the shoulders of their giant predecessors in the way that Newton implied is a necessary feature of scientific advance. Certainly it is the case that Oakley has a healthy disrespect for the tendency towards hagiography that pervades many accounts of the history of the discipline. The founding fathers are, after all, not infallible purveyors of timeless truths but merely 'DWMs (dead white males)' (Letherby 2003: 38). It is easy to detect, for example, 'an "old fogey" mentality in Durkheim's writings ... in the way they portray women' (Poggi 2000: 10). If one is committed, as Oakley is, to 'living in the present' (1985: 145), the relevance of these figures is not something to be taken on trust, uncritically. Yet Oakley is aware of their continuing influence, by providing the basis for the critique out of which current ideas have emerged as well as in terms of the more positive legacy that is concentrated upon in conventional accounts. If, as she argues, 'Knowledge is pushed forward a little at a time – inch by inch, not (usually) by quantum leaps' (1992: 305) then it is important to be aware of the history of our present thinking, to be familiar with how we have come to know what we now do. She quotes Comte's comment that 'a science cannot be completely understood without a knowledge of how it arose', and builds on this by arguing that the development of how the world is perceived needs to be placed 'in the context of gendered social relations' (2000: 4). One of her poems questions the ritual honouring of great men by suggesting 'Galileo, Copernicus, Newton, Harvey / were little men who picked their noses / like the rest of us' (1986a: 229). She returns to the theme in her description of 'the sculpture of Isaac Newton, a gigantic, muscular, crouched figure ... quite unlike the real Newton, born the size of a pint pot' (2002: 17). These observations demystify Newton, make him seem more human, and thereby cast doubt on our tendency to elevate great thinkers to a superhuman status.

The same deflation is one object in Oakley's various comments on sociology's 'founding fathers' whose 'intellectual achievements ... rested in a personal way on the basis of women's domestic oppression' (1974: 21–2). Marx is among those criticised on these grounds, since there was 'a contradiction between what he says about marriage, his theoretical point of view, and the way he lived his life. ... he wanted women to be his darling little slaves' (in Mullan 1987: 193). Oakley's comment on the letters of Marx and Engels is that 'Instead of two intellectual giants, we see two often infantile minds ... exchanging neurotic demands and promises and making snide, even outrageously rude remarks' (1986a: 223). In *Capital* Marx may have made much of the double meaning of the word freedom, but he overlooked the irony that ' "Labour" describes what women do to give birth to children and what men and women do to make goods and services for use or exchange in home or market place' (1992: 18). Oakley also enjoys the joke made at Marx's expense, reproducing the story that 'Marx's mother once said: "if only Karl had made *Capital* instead of just writing about it" ' (1986a: 256). Similar observations are possible about the personal and intellectual shortcomings of Durkheim and other prominent figures in sociology's history. The important general point is that 'The early sociologists established a number of traditions that have subsequently moulded the place of women in sociology' (1974: 23), traditions that feminist sociologists have been obliged to contest as part of their presentation of alternative ideas. The critique is not restricted to the founding fathers, but applies also to the development of their perspectives by later generations. For example, Oakley's comment that 'It's easier to think in roles but much lazier' (1985: 90) can be read as a challenge to a cornerstone of the Parsonian project, while her critique of 'The habit of thinking in dichotomies' (1992: xi) is necessarily at odds with Parsons's pattern variables. As she says in response to Parsons's attribution of the terms 'instrumental' to men's role in marriage and 'expressive' to women's, 'As anybody who has ever washed a floor, emptied the rubbish or cleaned a lavatory has known, there is nothing particularly "expressive" about housework' (1986a: 204). Nor does Oakley endorse uncritically the position of Parsons's great adversary Mills. Mills was notoriously combative, and the 'virile virtues' that he and other 'tough men' (Lemert 1995: 4) embodied do not sit easily with feminist thinking about the need to transform fundamental tenets of the very way in which we argue (Tannen 1998).

Critique must be distinguished from outright dismissal, since its purpose is to rescue and build upon those parts of perspectives that are worth saving. Oakley has used the expression that 'the baby need not be thrown out with the bathwater' (1998: 723) to support the case for retaining what is worthwhile in quantitative social science rather than rejecting it wholesale because of the evident shortcomings of certain practitioners. She uses the same phrase in relation to sociology to support the position that 'it is no use pretending that there is nothing of value in the entire field of male-oriented sociology as it has developed' (1986a: 208). Just because many sociologists have been offensively sexist does not mean that the discipline is irredeemably flawed. Nor does it mean that the work of those individuals is to be rejected in its entirety. Durkheim is mentioned at several points in Oakley's writings. She acknowledges, for example, that his 'hypothesis ... that anomie and social isolation are potentially suicidal states' has been 'validated' (1986a: 165) by later findings. She also notes (2000: 118–19) that Durkheim's arguments about suicide were among the many ideas of the founding fathers of sociology that were anticipated in the writings of women who preceded them by several decades, such as Madame de Staël, whose pioneering contributions have been overlooked in conventional histories of the discipline (McDonald 1994). The argument can thus be developed that although the legacy of the founding fathers has been 'a blinkered, and therefore partial, perspective on the nature of the social world', it does not follow that the discipline is closed to 'feminist reconstructions' (Sydie 1987: 10, 211). Wallace and Wolf's claim that 'feminist theorists have expanded the horizons of different perspectives' (1995: xi) echoes this point, employing the visual metaphor associated with Newton's remark about seeing further by standing on the shoulders of giants. Creative work requires that scientists adopt an outlook that combines recognition of the achievements of forerunners with being 'not content to remain in the shadow of great men' (Merton 1976: 34). Morgan provides an example of what rereading classic texts in this spirit allows when he points out that Weber's *Protestant Ethic* study contains only one reference to women, and that that is in what by modern standards is 'an extraordinarily patronizing passage'. His purpose is not to undermine Weber's credibility, but to highlight how the argument has the potential to be recast as 'The Protestant ethic and the spirit of masculinity' (1992: 55, 54) because of what on closer inspection it reveals about the gendered dimension of the story.

Close examination of the history of a discipline does, of course, have the potential to reveal the human frailties of the authors of classic texts as well as the strengths and weaknesses of their arguments. Newton achieved the status of being one of the 'giants of science' but Merton records how he was described as 'insidious, ambitious, and excessively covetous of praise'. This is an important antidote to the process whereby scientists have been 'idealized and, on occasion, idolized' (1976: 39, 41, 35). Among the sociologists considered in this book, several have had problematic aspects of their work attributed to ill-health. Marx claimed that the completion of the first volume of *Capital* was something for which he had 'sacrificed health, happiness and family' (in Nicolaievsky and Maenchen-Helfen 1976: 270). He hoped that its publication would 'give the bourgeoisie cause to remember my carbuncles' (in Benney 1978: 57), and his various ailments have been used to explain the singularly aggressive tone in which his arguments were couched (Blumbenberg 1972: 114). In a similar way Weber's 'unpolished methodological style' can be treated as 'a consequence of his prolonged illness' (Oakes 1977: 8). Oakley includes Weber among the several early social scientists whose 'psychological crises' reflected 'the struggles of men involved in giving birth to a "feminine" science' (2000: 130–1) as they grappled with the problem of how to deal with emotion in their analyses of social life. In a rather different fashion we might understand the 'fevered pace' (Horowitz 1983: 5) at which Mills worked as a reaction to his knowledge that his heart condition meant that he would not live to a ripe old age. His work offered another way to make a lasting impression. Oakley's poetic question, 'who would want a history of articles / typed and dissected, lost and uncredited[?]' (1986a: 212), provides a more sober perspective on mortality that is closer to Brinton's famous enquiry 'Who now reads Spencer?' (in Parsons 1968: 3). It was one of Weber's most incisive observations that scientists who have difficulty adjusting to the prospect of their work being surpassed are in the wrong job, and he was keen to distance himself from those 'big children' (1970b: 143) who believed that science had the capacity to make scientists and their audiences happy. Weber's famously pessimistic outlook is illustrated by the story Antoni tells of him: 'To those who might ask what his scholarly activity meant to him, he responded: "I want to see how long I can hold out" ' (1962: 121). The mood of disenchantment that pervades Weber's personality and writings was fed in part by his sense that it is the fate of academic achievements to be criticised and superseded.

The development of sociological arguments

One consequence of knowledge being built on what has gone before is that earlier achievements come to be discredited and ultimately forgotten. It was Weber's view that 'In science, each of us knows that what he has accomplished will be antiquated in ten, twenty, fifty years' (1970b: 138), and his observation certainly applies to the 'obscure contemporary mediocrities' (Löwith 1982: 21) with whose ideas he engaged, often at great length, but whose names are now unfamiliar. His own work is an exception to the rule. This is so much the case that Marshall can answer the question 'Who now reads *The Protestant Ethic and the Spirit of Capitalism*?' with the retort, 'Almost everyone, it seems' (1982: 9). Why Weber's writings have avoided the same fate as Spencer's is worthy of consideration. Weber's continued influence, and that of others concentrated on in this book, cannot be attributed to a consistently accessible style of engagement with audiences. Löwith has remarked that Weber and Marx have both 'written almost unreadable works' (1982: 21), and this judgement has also been passed on Parsons. It is possible to argue that their writings demand attention because of the profundity of the ideas that they contain, but this is a necessary and not a sufficient condition of securing a wide academic readership. What is required, and what each of the writers considered in this book has in addition to the powerful intellectual positions that they advance, is the ability to employ various rhetorical devices to their advantage. Such 'tricks of the trade' (Becker 1998) are crucial to the development of arguments and to getting them across to an audience.

Locating an argument as an important advance on an illustrious predecessor's work is a technique that has been used many times. The critique of Hegel that Marx advanced was all the more effective because its focus was on the work of 'that mighty thinker' (1976: 103), just as his critique of Smith and Ricardo built upon his acknowledgement that they 'stand with both feet on the shoulders of the eighteenth-century prophets' (1973a: 83) such as Rousseau. It was noted earlier that Marx was not included among the 'ablest and most clear-headed thinkers' that Parsons chose to critique in *The Structure of Social Action*, the implication being that he was to be located among the 'lesser lights' (1968: 18) who did not deserve the same degree of attention as Durkheim and Weber. Parsons later modified this stance by declaring himself 'very happy to acknowledge that, on the sociological level, Marx is one of the symbolic "grandfathers" of the theory of action' (1976: 361). This is consistent with Weber's identification of Marx and Nietzsche as the crucial influences on the scholars of his day, observing that 'Whoever does not admit that considerable parts of his own work could not have been carried out in the absence of the work of these two, only fools himself and others' (in Hennis 2000: 149). On occasion the reference to a past great figure whose tradition is to be developed requires rescuing them from neglect, as occurs in Mills's use of Veblen's work to strengthen his own critique of American society. Mills's claim that Veblen was 'the best social scientist that America has produced' (in Tilman 1984: 63) overstated the case, but it served to reinforce Mills's critique of Parsons on whom contemporaries were trying to lay that mantle. The general point is that 'New writers on a topic can be expected to check their position by the brightest stars' (Billig 1996: 14), however much they subsequently develop a distinctive position of their own.

Sometimes the acknowledgement of intellectual debt is framed more ambiguously. It was not Goffman but Collins who claimed that Goffmanian sociology 'is a continuation of the Durkheimian tradition' (1988: 43). That Goffman preferred not to locate his work explicitly in this way reflects the fact that he was 'worried about the prospect of specious and flawed forms of "intellectual pigeonholing" ' (Smith 1999: 5), and had an antipathy to 'the "hero worship" of any thinker, including himself' (Treviño 2003: 2). What he did offer were more veiled references, such as his opaque suggestion in his discussion of the gender order that 'traditional Durkheimian notions work here because in this business we are all priests and nuns' (1987: 52). Foucault's writings have a similar paucity of celebratory references to giant predecessors. According to Smart, 'Foucault generally tended to avoid unnecessary citations and references to the influence of major thinkers on his work, the rationale being that the traces were clearly there for all to see' (1988: 14). One exception to this pattern was Nietzsche, whom Foucault described as 'a revelation' (1988a: 13). Foucault followed Neitzsche in believing 'that thinkers are always, so to speak, shooting arrows into the air, and other thinkers pick them up and shoot them in a different direction' (Deleuze, in Katz 2001: 117). Foucault also sought to make space for those 'subjugated knowledges' (2003: 7) that too much reverence to established thinking threatens to crowd out. His purpose was to make audible the 'muffled voice from below history' (in Callinicos 1999: 264). It was for the same reasons that feminists needed to challenge 'the biases of "masculine" knowledge' in order to rectify the situation of 'women's invisibility' (Oakley 1998: 708). Traditions of knowledge can be an obstacle as well as a resource.

Sociologists' relationships with their intellectual forebears thus involve some combination of respect and criticism. Marx's comment that 'The tradition of the dead generations weighs like a nightmare on the minds of the living' was made in criticism of those whose over-reliance on 'the spirits of the past' (1973b: 146) constrained their ability to think and act differently. To avoid this in his own work he presented his approach as an inversion of Hegel. Hegel's use of the dialectic was erroneous because, Marx argued, 'With him it is standing on its head' (1976: 103). Precisely the same phrase has been used about Durkheim's celebrated recasting of the distinction between mechanical and organic solidarity: 'by depicting preindustrial societies as mechanical and industrial societies as organic, he was standing Toennies on his head' (Kivisto 1998: 95). Subsequently, in *The Rules of Sociological Method*, Durkheim repeated this technique of contrasting his ideas with previous thinking. As Lemert notes, he 'used a familiar prophetic device – "Up to now ..." / but, verily, I say unto you – to establish his little book as a classic' (1999: 25). The religious tone of Durkheim's perspective is evident (LaCapra 1985: 28), but it was tempered by his insistence that his findings were the product not of 'gratuitous hypotheses and unverifiable flights of the imagination' but of 'the discipline of the methodical doubt' (1964b: 399, 36). This choice of words is reminiscent of Marx's favoured motto, 'doubt everything' (Shanin 1984: 140). It is no coincidence that Marx also claimed that the strength of his perspective rested on the application of a method of investigation superior to that used by those whose ideas he sought to criticise. Where surface appearances are deceptive, the development of an alternative explanation will hinge on the methodological rigour by which hidden truths are revealed.

Claiming to have discovered hidden dimensions of social life has a long history in the presentation of sociological research (Crow 1999). This technique allows an audience to be presented with a new way of looking at the world, and the dramatic effect of doing so is heightened if making this revelation is deferred. It was noted in Chapter 2 that Marx was careful to reveal the secret of capital accumulation only once the deceptiveness of the surface appearances of market society had been demonstrated. Political economy was for Marx like astronomy: 'a scientific analysis of competition is possible only if we can grasp the inner nature of capital, just as the apparent motions of the heavenly bodies are intelligible only to someone who is acquainted with their real motions, which are not perceptible to the senses'. Marx started his account with the perspective of his rivals, and proceeded to see to it that their 'apologetic armour crumbles off, piece by piece, like rotten touchwood' (1976: 433, 932). Had he proceeded differently he would have conceded this advantage. As LaCapra notes, 'to begin a work with even a schematic "showing and telling" brings a loss of dramatic unity. The last act is given away in the first' (1985: 6). Marx was unusual in the length of time he kept his readers in suspense, but the same pattern of identifying a puzzle of which people were previously unaware before going on to solve it by an unexpected revelation is a common one. Durkheim's *Division of Labour in Society*, Weber's *Protestant Ethic*, Parsons's *The Structure of Social Action*, and Goffman's *Behavior in Public Places* are four very different studies that fit this mould, since each begins (quite literally) with 'The Problem' (Durkheim 1984: 1; Weber 1976a: 33; Parsons 1968: 3; Goffman 1963: 3) that the author seeks first to establish and then to resolve.

The skill involved in pretending that a problem is being grappled with when the presenter in fact knows precisely where the presentation will lead has been discussed in relation to other authors besides those considered in this book. One such is Weber's contemporary Simmel. According to Coser, Simmel gave his audience 'the impression that he was "thinking aloud" while he lectured, so that they imagined that they – the listeners – were, so to speak, assisting ... he deliberately gave the impression ... that he was struggling with his ideas when he had, in fact, worked out his thoughts long before' (1965: 34). Gaining and keeping an audience's attention in this way works with the written as well as the spoken word, even though, as Giddens notes, the former 'tends to be a "work" in a more protracted sense'. Writing is a process in which a great deal of attention may be paid to 'conventions of form, style and readership. "How" the reader is to take the text is "worked upon" by the author in its production' (1987b: 104, 106). Weber was mindful of the responsibility that this places on authors when he spoke of the need for academics to exercise 'self-restraint' (1970b: 146) in relation to the advancement of political as opposed to scientific arguments. Goffman was equally forthright in his criticism of the misuse of authorial privilege in his comments on the 'venerable tradition in philosophy that argues that what the reader assumes to be real is but a shadow, and that by attending to what the writer says about perception, thought, the brain, language, culture, a new methodology, or novel social forces, the veil can be lifted'. His objection was that this line of reasoning 'gives as much a role to the writer and his writings as is possible to imagine and for that reason is pathetic' (1975: 1). The importance of this point to Goffman is indicated by the fact that it comes in the opening passage of *Frame Analysis*, in which book he goes on to criticise sociologists who sought to pronounce on matters of other people's false consciousness from a position of presumed superiority.

Goffman preferred a style that was less directive of his audience. Frequently it appeared to involve doing little more than relating true stories to reveal the character of social life. *Frame Analysis* reproduces the report from the *Las Vegas Sun* that related how 'Police identified a 21-year-old Oklahoma City bill collector last week as the man who has been posing as a doctor to trick housewives into submitting to his advances' (1975: 160), and does so with an economy of analysis from Goffman himself. His style involved 'bringing to light many features of the ordinary experience of any person', albeit that his work bore the unmistakable hallmark of 'his own astringent view of the world' (Smith 1999: 6). This can be located in the tradition of Veblen, who as Mills notes made use in his analysis of the simple but effective formula, 'All this is incredible, but it is everyday fact' (1953: xiii). Oakley's recognition that it can be *'polemical'* to provide 'a statement of how things are, rather than of how people like to think they might be' (1981a: 6, emphasis in original) is similarly in this tradition. The importance of paying attention to everyday experience is also highlighted in Oakley's comment that 'conquering unfair tradition ... is a matter, not of grandiloquent statements, but of practical day-to-day details' (1985: 185). Elsewhere she expresses her concern 'to distance myself as a feminist social scientist from those who say that either capitalism or patriarchy is to "blame" for the present situation'. Such full-blown rhetoric is of limited analytical value. *Social Support and Motherhood* was written in order 'to expose complex problems rather than provide simple solutions'. She warns her audience that 'there is no point in turning to the end of this book to find solutions to the problems posed – the reader will be disappointed' (1992: ix). What is crucial in her view is the ability to identify what the best questions are to ask, and what are the most appropriate ways of going about trying to answer them.

Weber was also keen to discourage the idea that sociology could reach final answers. As he put it, 'Every scientific "fulfilment" raises new "questions" ', and he was aware that the rationale of engaging in such an unending activity was not immediately apparent. In his view, academics had a responsibility to recognise and face up to the implications of the ' "inconvenient" facts' that stand in the way of simple solutions. Rigid, fixed, dogmatic thinking can give only a false sense of security. In contrast, scientific analysis could be likened to the use of 'plowshares to loosen the soil of contemplative thought', and although this process might be personally uncomfortable, preparedness to think differently is the hallmark of creativity. The tools to carry out this activity are not always readily available. New ways of thinking cannot be forced, but 'occur to us when they please, not when it pleases us. ... Ideas come when we do not expect them, and not when we are brooding and searching at our desks.' There is no ready formula for the promotion of 'scientific inspiration' and 'imagination', although Weber's opinion was that it would not be forthcoming without 'inner devotion to the task' (1970b: 138, 147, 145, 136, 137). In addition to paying attention to this psychological factor, a sociologist might ask whether certain social positions and experiences also contribute to fostering the sociological imagination, or at least to shaping the form it takes in particular individuals. In the case of most of the writers studied in this book, much is known about their backgrounds and personal lives, and the significance of this information for the development of their thinking has been the subject of extensive debate, debate to which several of them have themselves contributed.

Personal and public agendas

One of the factors that features prominently in many sociologists' location of themselves is social class. Weber's reflection on his position as 'a member of the bourgeois class ... educated in their views and ideals' (in Mommsen 1994: 14–15), Foucault's reference to having been 'brought up as a provincial petty bourgeois' (1996: 133), and Oakley's identification of herself as 'a white middle class woman' (2002: 4) all illustrate this predisposition. The same conclusion could be drawn from Mills's statement that he was 'not aware of any desire to be more like the rich' (1969: 239), although he was also conscious of how social groups typically have inadequate understandings of their social positions. Mills's reference to 'the southerner come north to crash New York' (1953: xi) has an autobiographical ring to it, and Mills's mindfulness of his outsider status has parallels with Marx's and Durkheim's consciousness of their Jewishness, and Oakley's consciousness of how gender was used to construct her as 'other'. It would be possible to include Goffman in this group but it would also be problematic, because although his background was Jewish, he 'was notoriously secret about his personal life, which he assiduously strove to keep completely separate from his professional work. … In Goffman's view, anyone who desired to acquire a detailed understanding of his work did not need to know anything about his life' (Treviño 2003: 2). A rare glimpse of what this stance denied to commentators is provided by Hymes, who recounts how in conversation he was reproached by Goffman with the observation 'You forget that I grew up (with Yiddish) in a town where to speak another language was to be suspect of being homosexual' (1984: 628). This biographical revelation is exceptional, and for the most part Goffman's own 'backstage' was off-limits.

Goffman is unusual among prominent sociologists in respect of how little is known about him as a person, but even where more information is available the relationship between background and ideas is not a simple one to determine. Religious influences have been identified as important in shaping the outlooks of a number of writers, but in diverse ways. The most straightforward of these is Parsons, described by Collins and Makowsky as 'this son of a Calvinist preacher and heir (his very name told us) to a long line of preachers' (1998: 218). The influence was indirect, as Parsons 'did not see himself as a very religious person' (Wearne 1989: 18). What stands out is that the focus of his sociology was on norms and values, and this is why it is notable that 'As an adult, Talcott Parsons spoke frequently about how much he owed to his parents and "to the values they stood for" ' (Camic 1991: xi). Parsons was by no means unique in this respect; rather, his case illustrates 'the long-established link between American sociology and Protestant social reformism' (Rocher 1974: 3), as Parsons himself recognised (Wearne 1989: 17). The association between having a religious family background and particular sociological interests has also been discussed in relation to Weber, but the connection is, as Poggi notes, 'somewhat more complicated' than his famous statement that he was 'religiously unmusical' has led some commentators to believe. Knowledge of the religious and business affiliations of his family helps significantly to locate 'the genesis of *The Protestant Ethic* within Max Weber's biography' (1983: 9, 6, 5). It is possible to see that work as an intellectual engagement with the forces that had shaped him, and the tensions in its argument as an echo of his complex and unresolved relationship with religion. Mills's account of being reared as a Roman Catholic was that in his case 'it never took' (in Mills and Mills 2000: 313), but Tilman has speculated that it may have had an effect nonetheless. He suggests the possibility 'that his Catholic upbringing in a sea of Protestantism made him a "marginal man" ' and thereby drew him to 'the path of the dissenter and intellectual maverick' (1984: 6), critical of conformity in all its guises.

This speculation is no less plausible than those accounts of Marx's life that highlight the influence of his origins as 'a bourgeois Jew from a predominantly Catholic city within a country whose official religion was evangelical Protestantism' (Wheen 2000: 8) on his subsequent development.

Durkheim's case is different again. Unlike Weber, Durkheim was not 'a particularly troubled individual', but Hughes's description of him as 'the rabbi's son turned unbeliever' (Hughes 1974: 288, 284) gives an indication of his personal journey. His experience as a child, of the strength of social solidarity in Jewish communities, was reflected in his sociological writings, although these were not simple celebrations of that solidarity (Lukes 1975: 40). Lemert has pointed out that Durkheim 'would not ... have become a sociologist had he not renounced those traditions', and in making this break he was led 'in adult life to misremember, or misrecognize, his own Jewish past'. In Lemert's view it was only by doing so that Durkheim could square his view of how social forces shape individuals with his own biography, since 'It is perfectly clear that his personal story contradicts his sociology' (1995: 42, 44). The only known example of Durkheim employing humour relates to this tension. LaCapra tells how, 'Passing in front of Notre Dame Cathedral, Durkheim ... remarked "It's from a chair like that, that I ought to be speaking",' thus making a pun that 'played upon the ambiguity of the French word *chaire* ("academic's chair", "church pulpit")' (1985: 29). It also suggests the presence of unresolved issues in his biography. The sociology of religion was an important aspect of his work, from the moment that teaching a course on the subject 'came as a "revelation" to him' (Hughes 1974: 283) down to his last great work, *The Elementary Forms of the Religious Life*, but his interest was purely academic. How Durkheim combined his belief 'that every society *needs* religion' with a personal life in which 'he subscribed to no such beliefs and engaged in no such practices' (Poggi 2000: 1, emphasis in original) therefore remains an enigma.

It is quite consistent to acknowledge that much of the writing about the relationship between sociologists' lives and their ideas is speculative and to hold that some such connections must exist. Oakley's objections to the 'pretence that ... no personal influences in the research process exist' are made on the grounds that 'Whatever research is done, the people who do it have their own personal-historical reasons for engaging in that particular research at that particular time, and they do it in the way that they do it because of the people that they are' (1986a: 209). The point is made particularly directly in her case because her career has included critical examination of the writings of her own father, Titmuss. His influence might be detected in her work that reflects her positive valuation of his 'careful computation of statistics about social groups and life-chances', but her assessment of his work is rigorous and has the potential to find fault where necessary. For example, she describes his analysis of gender inequality as 'a strange mixture of insight and prejudice' (2001: 12, 14–15). Moving on from the certainties of one's childhood by undertaking the often painful reassessment of the beliefs and practices into which one has been socialized is a process that features prominently in many sociologists' biographies, and it is Lemert's view that 'All the great sociologists of the past followed this path of discovery, leaving behind the worlds of their youth' (1997a: 58). Part of the audience for whom a sociologist writes is therefore the sociologist him or herself as they follow the logic of their discipline to make sense of their own lives. As Mills and Mills note of their father, in some of his work 'Mills admitted that he was also writing to himself – using the figure of Tovarich in efforts at self-scrutiny' (2000: xiii). In this mode, Mills acknowledged that 'it's hard to tell the truth about yourself and your ideas' (in Mills and Mills 2000: 255). Oakley has expressed similar sentiments, and identified the cause as the social pressure that exists to conform to other people's expectations: 'the chief obstacle to describing oneself as an individual located in a particular manner in a particular culture is the need *not* to be honest with oneself, to conceal the person one is from oneself and, indeed, from everybody else' (1985: 2–3, emphasis in original). The study on which *From Here to Maternity* was based was amongst other things a project that 'interpreted for me my own first experience of motherhood' (1986b: 4) a decade on from that time. This experience contributed to Oakley's conclusion that it can be 'a most painful and difficult' (1985: 2) process to subject oneself to sociological scrutiny.

It is doubtful if this discomfort would have been endured by the individuals considered in this book if the only benefit to be derived were their own self-enlightenment. Whatever personal agendas they may have had for undertaking their sociological researches, they were also driven by a concern to have an impact on the public debates of their day. Oakley in her transition to motherhood study was seeking to 'actually have an impact on those who formulate policy in maternity care, both in government and in the medical profession' (1986b: 4). Mills made the same point more generally when he identified the task of the sociologist as demonstrating the links between personal troubles and public issues. It was his view that 'As a writer, I have always tried, although in different ways, to do just one thing: to define and dramatize the essential characteristics of our time' (in Mills and Mills 2000: 279). Mills's *White Collar* served this purpose, and was all the more powerful for its autobiographical underpinning. In a similar way Oakley recognises that her personal experiences are far from 'unique', and that by 'writing about something which is recognizable to others' she may be able 'to draw together ... some of the connecting threads between my life and the lives of others' (1985: 2–3). Her story deserves to be put before a wider public because it has the potential to shed light on what she calls 'the quiet revolution that has gone on in many women's heads' (1982a: 280) in recent decades. She draws on personal experience because she believes in 'the existence of some common ground beneath the constantly shifting topsoil on which we mark out our individual postures and directions' (2002: 12). In this context it is pertinent to note Ruggerio's observation that 'beginning on common ground' (1996: 107) is a key part of what needs to be done in order to construct an argument that will engage effectively with others.

If it is accepted that 'sociological writing, like any other type of writing, is concerned with convincing others' (Cuzzort and King 1989: 191), then attention necessarily turns to the methods employed to engage an audience. Reference to personal experience of the phenomena being discussed is one very powerful way of buttressing an argument, and it is Williams's view that 'The most persuasive sociological writing emerges from a personal feeling' (2001: 123). Personal experiences that are shared between sociologists and their audiences can include anxieties about the direction of social change. One prominent theme that has had resonance over the years concerns what would happen if the process of individualisation were to be taken to its extreme conclusion, and this has prompted the use of some compelling imagery. One example of this is Marx's reference to the way in which French peasants 'form an immense mass, the members of which live in the same situation but do not enter into manifold relationships with each other. ... much as potatoes in a sack form a sack of potatoes' (1973b: 238–9). For Marx, this was the very antithesis of class solidarity. Weber likewise looked to rural smallholders for an illustration of 'individualism carried to an extreme' (in Scaff 1989: 51). His later reference to 'a simple heap of sand composed of isolated individuals' (2001b: 112) was made with American society in mind, although it was used to indicate that there were good reasons for considering America more than simply 'a nation of "atomized individuals"' (Gerth and Mills 1970: 57). Durkheim's description of a society composed only of 'a myriad of atoms juxtaposed together' (1984: 173), or 'a dust of individuals' (in Diggins 1996: 22), was also presented as a rival account to be criticised on the grounds that it failed to recognise the modifying effect of civil society. It was noted earlier, however, that Hobbes's 'war of all against all' and Spencer's 'survival of the fittest' were images that exercised Durkheim and Weber, and through them fed into Parsons's concern with 'atomism' (1968: 353) and the social disorder that it entailed, at least as a logical possibility. Hobbes's thinking also engaged Foucault in his discussion of the artificial and unstable foundations of 'individuality' (2003: 94).

The sociological tradition also includes a counterweight to concerns about the over-extension of individualisation, embodied in fears about the over-extension of forces of social control and the imposition of conformity. Weber's views on 'rationalization' and on the 'iron cage', and Mills's remarks on 'banalization' and on the 'cheerful robot' are in this vein, as is Veblen's remark that America had become 'something of a psychiatrical clinic' (in Mills 1953: viii), an observation that preceded Goffman's *Asylums* by almost four decades. Goffman may be located as a theorist of normalisation but he was also a theorist of 'singularization' (1972: 24), and in this respect he was closer to Foucault and the complex attitude that he adopted towards the individual subject that has been termed 'the Foucault Paradox'. As Abercrombie and his colleagues describe it, this paradox is that 'As individuals become more separate and different, they are more recognizably unique. In turn, uniqueness and identity are closely connected and the identification of individuals makes their control that much easier' (Abercrombie *et al.* 1986: 189). Foucault's discussion of the panopticon opened the way for concerns about social control to be given a new twist, by allowing the recognition that 'individualism and govern-mentality are not mutually exclusive' (Turner 2001: 97), and this helps to account for the fact that his writings on the matter have reached audiences far beyond the academy. Foucault might well be considered one of those relatively rare writers whose books 'count in public life', as Gitlin puts it. Gitlin identifies these books as those that have the quality of 'recognizing patterns, offering big interpretations of life, providing names for what, until the volumes appeared, were nothing more than hunches or diffuse sentiments'. Such a book 'crystallizes a fear, a knack, or a hope into a big idea, a sweeping interpretation of reality that strikes a collective nerve in a large general public' (2001: xi). Gitlin's remarks are made in the foreword to the new edition of Riesman's *The Lonely Crowd*, half a century on from the book's first publication. It is a book that stands alongside studies that have had more attention devoted to them in the preceding chapters such as *Capital, Suicide, The Protestant Ethic, The Social System, The Power Elite, The Presentation of Self in Everyday Life, Discipline and Punish,* and *Housewife*. These are books that, in Foucault's phrase, 'look for other angles' (1996: 133), angles that a wide readership have also been persuaded to consider.

The art of sociological argument

The skills required to persuade an audience of the merits of an argument cannot be reduced to a single formula, but it is nevertheless possible to draw a number of conclusions from the works of the writers considered in this book. The first is that it is more productive to work with audiences than to antagonise them. The Soviet Premier Khrushchev famously gained the attention of his United Nations audience by taking off his shoe and banging it on the desk, but he later regretted doing so because 'It got him the attention that he wanted, but it started him off on the wrong foot' (Underhill 2000: 41). Oakley's criticism of sociologists' propensity to be overly didactic is relevant here, since audiences do not necessarily take kindly to being instructed like schoolchildren. Nor is preaching to an audience guaranteed to go down well, if Mills's ventures into this mode of delivery are taken as a guide, and if Goffman's cautionary remarks on what he called 'preachments' (1997: 235) are borne in mind. It is also pertinent to note here Foucault's declaration, 'I don't want to be a prophet and say, "Please sit down, what I have to say is very important" ' (1988a: 9). His preference was for more of a dialogue, and for this to take place some element of common ground needs to be established. Prefacing a statement with the remark, 'As is well known' (Weber 1970c: 308) is one way of conveying to an audience that they are already in possession of useful knowledge that has the potential to be built upon. In a similar way authors may use the word 'we' of themselves and their audience as a means of 'enroling the reader' (Billig 1996: 15) to their point of view, or at least to give it consideration and not to reject it outright.

To seek an audience's attention is not guaranteed to gain it. Marx lamented that many of his writings had been killed 'with silence' (1976: 98), but his suggestion that this response betrayed the fearfulness of his opponents is a more flattering interpretation than that offered by Foucault, that silence reflects 'our failure to produce any such fear at all' (1980: 87). Garland has described *Discipline and Punish* as written in a 'spirit of provocation' (2001: ix), and Foucault is not alone in his preparedness to provoke his audience. There is something shocking about breaking the taboo of examining topics such as exploitation, suicide, domination, madness and sexuality that are not the subject of discussion in polite society. If the sociologist's goal is understood to involve an implicit challenge to commonsense thinking, then what is taken for granted needs to be subjected to a process of 'defamiliarization' (Bauman and May 2001: 10). This can also be understood as Foucault's project of promoting 'the denaturalization of concepts that each era takes to be self-evident' (McNay 1994: 61). This is a potentially upsetting experience, as is the case for example when Oakley encourages her readers to ponder 'the real meaning of the worst swear word in the American lexicon – "motherfucker" ' (1990b: xvii) as a means of reconsidering the politics of reproduction. Marx's description of capital, 'dripping from head to toe, from every pore, with blood and dirt' (1976: 926), provides another illustration of sociologists' preparedness to shock, as does Durkheim's pronouncement that 'there are no religions which are false' (1976: 3). And in the context of American culture's deeply held beliefs about the countryside, Mills's discussion of 'the rural debacle' was shocking in its description of the processes that threatened to 'destroy the traditional character of farming' by removing the opportunities for individual advancement up 'the agricultural ladder' and replacing them with 'a treadmill' (1956: 15, 19, 20). A second conclusion that might be drawn, therefore, is that audiences' presuppositions may be challenged by using shock tactics. Marx made no apologies for refusing 'to depict the capitalist and the landowner in rosy colours' (1976: 92), and Oakley's portrayal of motherhood is 'deliberately black' (1981a: 6) for the same reason, to challenge prevailing myths. If sociologists tend to come across as pessimists, as Lemert suggests they generally do, it is because their propensity to uncover the 'murky' (1997c: 17) character of the world makes audiences uncomfortable.

A third conclusion is that other, more subtle ways of persuading an audience are also available, such as humour. There are shocking passages in Goffman's writings, such as the opening account in *Stigma*, but his work shows that humour and irony can be just as effective in making a point. His account of the interaction in which the doctor's question, 'Have you ever had a history of cardiac arrest in your family?' is met with the patient's response, 'We never had no trouble with the police' (1981a: 55) makes a serious point about the potential that exists for misunderstanding in everyday life. Oakley's account of being employed in market research into women's foundation garments to ask ' "How satisfied are you with your bust?" and "Who sees you in your underwear?" ' (1985: 71) humorously conveys how not to treat interviewees. It is instructive that the criteria according to which research midwives were appointed in Oakley's *Social Support and Motherhood* study included 'last but not least, a sense of humour' (1992: 131); the capacity to see the funny side of things is a useful skill to have when doing and recounting sociological research. A sense of irony might be mentioned in this context since it also features prominently in many sociologists' reports of their work. Goffman is particularly notable in this respect (Treviño 2003: 20–2) although Burns argues that Goffman's writings sometimes overstepped the mark and descended into 'heavy-handed … facetiousness' and 'sardonic comment' (1992: 33, 13). In Weber's hands, irony was devoid of humour, as was perhaps appropriate when discussing 'the death of God' (Diggins 1996: 92) as one of the unintended consequences of the rationalisation process to which Protestantism had contributed.

Perplexing an audience stands as a fourth approach alongside befriending, shocking and amusing them. Literally dozens of paradoxes have been discussed by the writers considered in this book, reflecting the paradoxical nature of the social world. Durkheim can be seen to have reworked Rousseau's 'famous formula about a man being "forced to be free" ' (Parsons 1974: lvii). Marx's claim that 'To save the Russian commune a Russian revolution will be necessary' (in Nicolaievsky and Maenchen-Helfen 1976: 422) was typical of his perspective. Reflecting on statements such as the pronouncement in the *Communist Manifesto* that 'All that is solid melts into air' (Marx and Engels 1969: 111) Berman remarks that 'There is a certain paradoxicality at the heart of Marx's whole enterprise' (1999: 37). Bologh (1990: 301) argues that both Marx and Weber failed to resolve the central paradoxes with which they grappled, leaving a legacy that contemporary feminists have sought to approach from a different angle. In Goffman the reader's attention is directed to the paradox that 'the closely related are obliged to enjoy a greeting encounter' (1997: 255), and to the equally paradoxical observation that 'the patient often gets a doctor's attention when he least needs it' (1968a: 315). It is through the identification of paradoxes that social scientists have often succeeded in engaging the attention of the wider public. In addition to Riesman's *The Lonely Crowd*, mention might be made of other paradoxical titles such as *Fatal Remedies* (Sieber 1981), *The Managed Heart* (Hochschild 1983), *The Solitude of Collectivism* (Kideckel 1993), *The Invention of Tradition* (Hobsbawm and Ranger 1983) and *Pricing the Priceless Child* (Zelizer 1994). Veblen's often-repeated reference to 'the advantages of backwardness' (in Moore 1967: 414) is also in the tradition of presenting readers with a statement that appears self-contradictory and demands further consideration.

Attracting curiosity is only the beginning of the process of engagement, and Lemert has argued that success requires the skill of knowing 'how to get my attention and keep it' (1995: xiv). Mills regarded plain speaking as essential to 'the goal of enabling ordinary people to grasp sociology' (Horowitz 1983: 88), and Marx aspired to make his ideas 'accessible to the ordinary human intelligence' (in Callinicos 1996: 77). The same concern informs Oakley's frustration with 'the "new" language of postmodernism' in which approach 'texts tend to obscurantism' (1992: x). One way of maintaining interest in the development of an argument whilst avoiding opaque jargon is to employ metaphors and analogies, and it was noted in earlier chapters that Goffman famously employed the metaphors of drama and game-playing, while Parsons developed Durkheim's consideration of society as an organism. Durkheim even began *Sociology and Philosophy* with the observation that 'If analogy is not a method of demonstration in the true sense of the word, it is nevertheless a method of illustration and of secondary verification which may be of some use' (1974: 1). Mills's use of metaphors drawn from engineering and geometry may have sensitised him to the way in which 'Marx's texts are full of metaphors from the reproductive cycle and the hospital delivery room. Things are pregnant; there are false alarms; wombs and midwives abound' (1963: 128). In turn, Oakley's interests have led her to consider the way that actual reproduction is typically presented by medical professionals in mechanical terms: 'women are seen as reproductive machines. ... Thus, antenatal care is maintenance- and malfunction-spotting work' (1986a: 75–6). Her suggestion when discussing gender relations that women and men can be thought of as coming from different planets provides a further illustration of a fifth general conclusion, that metaphors and analogies pervade sociological arguments. Indeed, Urry has claimed that 'sociological thinking ... cannot be achieved non-metaphorically' (2000: 21). This is because without them accounts would have difficulty in going beyond descriptions of phenomena that are readily perceivable, as López (2003) has noted.

That metaphors and analogies are so commonly used by sociologists is not surprising because the discipline requires the exercise of imagination in order to look beyond common sense perceptions of the world. In its promotion of thinking differently, Mills's *Sociological Imagination* articulated the very logic of the discipline that is also present in Marx's exhortation to 'doubt everything'. Goffman's pithy comment that 'Universal human nature is not a very human thing' (1967: 45) likewise invites consideration of the potential for diversity that glib references to human nature foreclose, and the same implication follows from Weber's observation that 'all historical experience confirms the truth – that man would not have attained the possible unless time and again he had reached out for the impossible' (1970a: 128). If, as Oakley notes, randomised controlled trials require 'the suspension of belief' (1992: 133), then it ought to be possible for sociologists to expect a hearing when they put forward for further discussion something that 'may sound a fairly way-out idea' (2000: 16). Very often the exercise of imagination is prompted by the formulation of a challenging question. Weber's key problem, according to Lemert, was 'When and why do men obey?' (1995: 103), while the principal question derived from Marx can be formulated bluntly, as Westergaard has: 'Who gets what?' (1995). According to Sombart, 'Marx's greatest genius was his masterly understanding of how to frame questions' (in Blumenberg 1972: 184). Durkheim also stands out because of the questions that he posed, and Parkin's judgement is that 'Durkheim has made his presence felt more by virtue of the kinds of questions he asked than by the answers he gave to them' (1992: 1). The key question that he posed continues to be a matter of concern, as Touraine's recent inquiry *Can We Live Together?* (2000) confirms. A sixth conclusion is therefore that the formulation of an imaginative question is a vital part of the development of a sociological argument.

Recognition of what the central problem is that needs to be addressed may evolve only gradually, and it is a commonplace observation that many great thinkers have had to work away at the identification of their key question over a number of years. In doing so they may be required to shift their focus, and it is for this reason that the literature contains extensive discussion of whether there are two or more Marxes (Gouldner 1980), Durkheims (Giddens 1979: 51; Pearce 1989), Parsonses (Hamilton 1983: 24), Goffmans (Hymes 1984: 621), Foucaults (Baert 1998: 117; Eribon 1993: xi), and Oakleys (Oakley 2000: 21). There is no agreement on whether radical breaks in the development of perspectives outweigh important continuities, but what is clear is the importance of reflexivity on the part of these thinkers. Durkheim has been described as 'Always self-critical' (Alpert 1966: 37), and Alexander's description of Parsons as 'highly self-conscious' (1984: 272) identifies the same characteristic of an individual mindful of how their work falls short of the very high standards they set. Mills's insistence on 'the sociologist's need for systematic reflection' as a means 'to keep your inner world awake' (2000: 196, 197) was similarly a guard against complacency, as was Weber's attitude of 'trained relentlessness in viewing the realities of life, and the ability to face such realities and to measure up to them inwardly' (1970a: 126–7). Foucault presented his 'humble path' (in Callinicos 1999: 280) as having been determined more by setting his own agenda than by following those of others, and Goffman was mindful of how his career had been dedicated to promoting research into the interaction order despite the fact that 'My colleagues have not been overwhelmed by the merits of the case' (1997: 236). These examples illustrate a seventh conclusion, that the capacity for self-criticism is an important resource in arriving at a satisfactory answer to the question posed.

An argument must be clear in one's own mind before it can be confidently presented to others, but this is a crucial next step, and it is one that is complicated by an eighth conclusion, that audiences do not always share sociologists' agendas. This is partly a reflection of Weber's point that rendering something 'more easily understandable' may sacrifice precision in the process: 'The most precise formulation cannot always be reconciled with a form which can readily be popularized' (1978a: 3). Weber regarded it as a particularly difficult challenge for academics 'to present scientific problems in such a manner that an untutored but receptive mind can understand them and ... can come to think about them independently' (1970b: 134). Weber's experiences of being misunderstood were shared by Marx, whose dissatisfaction with certain interpretations of his ideas prompted the exasperated remark 'As for me, I am *not* a Marxist!' (in McLellan 1986: 72, emphasis in original). Oakley's surprise about the partial reception of her work is relevant here, as is her related expectation that her more theoretical writing 'is only going to be appreciated much later' (in Mullan 1987: 207). Sociologists do not have control over how their ideas are received and used, and the selectivity of audiences about what they absorb from sociological works may subvert authors' intentions. In Gitlin's view, 'it is a curious fact about contemporary culture that sociological language has, in many ways, become a normal element in commonplace talk as well as political speech, though often in a degraded form'. It is 'a dreary irony of a spongy culture' that popular journalists regularly treat their subject matter with a crude 'sociological gloss'. Gitlin's regret that 'sociological imagination has been trivialized by success' reflects his belief that such sociology fails to leave the reader 'with a feeling of being challenged beyond one's received wisdom' (2000: 239–40), and serves only to entertain and not to educate.

Gitlin's concerns over the loss that is entailed in the popularisation of sociology run parallel to Ritzer's (1998) analysis of the 'McDonaldization' of the discipline, but the problem identified is not unique to the current period. Sociologists in the past as well as the present have faced the difficulty of relating constructively to their audiences, and it is part of this book's rationale to consider what might be learned from this history. One lesson is that 'Older versions of social science – often conceived as quasi-natural sciences of society – have claimed more than they can deliver' (Bryant 1995: ix) and have left a problematic legacy because of the disillusionment that this was bound to generate. The growing recognition of the problems associated with claims to exclusive scientific expertise led Bauman to posit a shift in the role of intellectuals 'from modern legislators to post-modern interpreters' in which the latter are involved primarily in 'translating statements' (1987: 1, 5) to facilitate communication between different communities. The journey from Marx and Durkheim to Goffman and Foucault might be understood in these terms, given the latter pair's concerns to give voice to powerless groups and their scepticism about the claims of nineteenth-century science with which the former pair identified. Developments in sociology do not fit neatly into this model, however. Oakley's response to postmodernism's 'attack on science' has involved questioning the corrosive implications for knowledge of its underlying philosophy of 'anything goes' (2002: 190–1). In a similar vein, Holmwood has contested the conclusion towards which postmodern thinking points, that sociological judgements are 'malleable in the face of shifts of public opinion'. Holmwood's thesis is that acknowledgement of diverse points of view does not rule out conceiving of sociology as 'a problem-solving activity' that has an important contribution to make in informing public debate, and that only by maintaining this tradition can the discipline achieve 'public relevance' (2000: 47–8). In the light of these debates, the ninth conclusion that can be drawn is that there are dangers in claiming too much for an argument being developed, but there are also dangers in claiming too little.

This is not to argue for a return to a purported golden age of sociological reasoning. It is appropriate to be sceptical of arguments in which, as Gouldner put it, ' "hard" methodologies function as a rhetoric of persuasion'

(1971: 445). Amongst others, Mills (1969: 233) and Oakley (1986a: 209) have questioned the status attached to 'hard' evidence as if it were unproblematic; such conceptions of social science are unsustainable. 'Hard' evidence may be presented as if it speaks for itself, but the reality is that 'Published versions of research ... are forms of reconstructed logic' (Oakley 1992: 18). Put another way, the style in which an argument is put forward matters as well as the content of what is being said. It is now over three decades since Gouldner remarked that 'One of the obvious but invariably neglected aspects of any social theory is the fact that it has a form as well as a content' (1971: 199), but it remains the case that the way in which sociological arguments are framed has had insufficient attention paid to it. Of course, what is being said ultimately matters more than the way those ideas are advanced: style is not a substitute for content. A bad argument cannot be corrected by good presentation. But a good argument is all the better for being well presented, and this is an aspect of social scientific research that matters. This is the tenth and most important conclusion of this book.

Bibliography

Abercrombie, N., Hill, S. and Turner, B. (1986) *Sovereign Individuals of Capitalism*. London: Allen and Unwin.

Abrams, P. (1982) *Historical Sociology*. Shepton Mallet: Open Books.

Adriaansens, H. (1980) *Talcott Parsons and the Conceptual Dilemma*. London: Routledge and Kegan Paul.

Albrow, M. (1970) *Bureaucracy*. London: Macmillan.

—— (1990) *Max Weber's Construction of Social Theory*. Basingstoke: Macmillan.

Alexander, J. (1982) *Theoretical Logic in Sociology, Volume Two: The Antinomies of Classical Thought: Marx and Durkheim*. London: Routledge and Kegan Paul.

—— (1983) *Theoretical Logic in Sociology, Volume Three: The Classical Attempt at Theoretical Synthesis: Max Weber*. London: Routledge and Kegan Paul.

—— (1984) *Theoretical Logic in Sociology, Volume Four: The Modern Reconstruction of Classical Thought: Talcott Parsons*. London: Routledge and Kegan Paul.

Alpert, H. (1966) *Emile Durkheim and his Sociology*. New York: Russell and Russell.

Althusser, L. and Balibar, E. (1975) *Reading Capital*. London: New Left Books.

Anderson, R., Hughes, J. and Sharrock, W. (1985) *The Sociology Game: An Introduction to Sociological Reasoning*. London: Longman.

Andreski, S. (1983) 'Introduction', in S. Andreski (ed.) *Max Weber on Capitalism, Bureaucracy and Religion*. London: George Allen and Unwin.

Antoni, C. (1962) *From History to Sociology: The Transition in German Historical Thinking*. London: Merlin.

Apperley, A. (1997) 'Foucault and the Problem of Method', in M. Lloyd and A. Thacker (eds) *The Impact of Michel Foucault on the Social Sciences and Humanities*. Basingstoke: Macmillan, pp. 10–28.

Applebaum, R. (1988) *Karl Marx*. Newbury Park: Sage.

Aron, R. (1970) *Main Currents in Sociological Thought 2: Durkheim, Pareto, Weber*. Harmondsworth: Penguin.

Atkinson, P. (1990) *The Ethnographic Imagination: Textual Constructions of Reality*. London: Routledge.

Baert, P. (1998) *Social Theory in the Twentieth Century*. Cambridge: Polity Press.

Ball, T. (1991) 'History: Critique and Irony', in T. Carver (ed.) *The Cambridge Companion to Marx*. Cambridge: Cambridge University Press, pp. 124–42.

Barbalet, J. (1983) *Marx's Construction of Social Theory*. London: Routledge and Kegan Paul.

—— (1998) *Emotion, Social Theory and Social Structure: A Macrosociological Approach*. Cambridge: Cambridge University Press.

Barth, L. (1998) 'Michel Foucault', in R. Stones (ed.) *Key Sociological Thinkers*. Basingstoke: Macmillan, pp. 252–65.

Bauman, Z. (1987) *Legislators and Interpreters: On Modernity, Post-modernity and Intellectuals*. Cambridge: Polity.

—— (1992) *Intimations of Postmodernity*. London: Routledge.

Bauman, Z. and May, T. (2001) *Thinking Sociologically*. Oxford: Blackwell.

Beamish, R. (1992) *Marx, Method and the Division of Labour*. Urbana: University of Illinois Press.

Becker, H. (1998) *Tricks of the Trade: How to Think about Your Research While You're Doing It*. Chicago: University of Chicago Press.

—— (2002) 'Professional Sociology: The Case of C. Wright Mills', http://www.soc.ucsb.edu/faculty/hbecker/mills.html, retrieved 13 September, 2002.

Bell, C. and Newby, H. (1971) *Community Studies: An Introduction to the Sociology of the Local Community*. London: George Allen and Unwin.

Bell, D. (1991) *The Winding Passage: Sociological Essays and Journeys*. New Brunswick, NJ: Transaction Books.

Bell, D. and Graubard, S. (1997) 'Preface to the MIT Press Edition', in D. Bell and S. Graubard (eds) *Toward the Year 2000: Work in Progress*. Cambridge, MA: MIT Press, pp. ix–xix.

Bellah, R. (ed.) (1973) *Emile Durkheim on Morality and Society*. Chicago, IL: University of Chicago Press.

Bellah, R., Madsen, R., Sullivan, W., Swidler, A. and Tipton, S. (1996) *Habits of the Heart: Individualism and Commitment in American Life*. Berkeley: University of California Press.

Bendix, R. (1966) *Max Weber: An Intellectual Portrait*. London: Methuen.

Benney, M. (1978) 'The Legacy of Mining', in M. Bulmer (ed.) *Mining and Social Change: County Durham in the Twentieth Century*. London: Croom Helm, pp. 49–58.

Berger, P. and Berger, B. (1976) *Sociology: A Biographical Approach*. Harmondsworth: Penguin.

Berlin, I. (1978) *Karl Marx: His Life and Environment*. Oxford: Oxford University Press.

Berman, M. (1983) *All that is Solid Melts into Air: The Experience of Modernity*. London: Verso.

—— (1999) *Adventures in Marxism*. London: Verso.

Bierstedt, R. (1966) *Emile Durkheim*. London: Wiedenfeld and Nicolson.

Billig, M. (1996) *Arguing and Thinking: A Rhetorical Approach to Social Psychology*. Cambridge: Cambridge University Press, second edition.

Binns, D. (1977) *Beyond the Sociology of Conflict*. London: Macmillan.

Black, M. (1976) 'Some Questions about Parsons' Theories', in M. Black (ed.) *The Social Theories of Talcott Parsons: A Critical Examination*. Carbondale: Southern Illinois University Press, pp. 269–88.

Blumenberg, W. (1972) *Karl Marx*. London: New Left Books.

Bologh, R. (1990) *Love or Greatness: Max Weber and Masculine Thinking – A Feminist Inquiry*. London: Unwin Hyman.

Bonnett, A. (2001) *How To Argue*. Harlow: Prentice Hall.

Boswell, D. (1992) 'Health, the Self and Social Interaction', in R. Bocock and K. Thompson (eds) *Social and Cultural Forms of Modernity*. Cambridge: Polity Press, pp. 169–201.

Bourdieu, P. (1983) 'Erving Goffman, Discoverer of the Infinitely Small', *Theory, Culture and Society* 2 (1), 112–13.

—— (1993) *Sociology in Question*. London: Sage.

Bourricaud, F. (1981) *The Sociology of Talcott Parsons*. Chicago, IL: University of Chicago Press.

Bové, P. (1988) 'Foreword: The Foucault Phenomenon: The Problematics of Style', in G. Deleuze, *Foucault*. Minneapolis: University of Minneapolis Press, pp. vi–xl.

Branaman, A. (1997) 'Goffman's Social Theory', in C. Lemert and A. Branaman (eds) *The Goffman Reader*. Oxford: Blackwell, pp. xlv–lxxxii.

—— (2001) 'Erving Goffman', in A. Elliott and B. Turner (eds) *Profiles in Contemporary Social Theory*. London: Sage, pp. 94–106.

Brown, R. (1987) *Society as Text: Essays on Rhetoric, Reason and Reality*. Chicago, IL: University of Chicago Press.

Brubaker, R. (1984) *The Limits of Rationality: An Essay on the Social and Moral Thought of Max Weber*. London: George Allen and Unwin.

Bryant, C. (1976) *Sociology in Action: A Critique of Selected Conceptions of the Social Role of the Sociologist*. London: George Allen and Unwin.

—— (1983) 'Who now reads Parsons?', *Sociological Review* 31, pp. 383–95.

—— (1995) *Practical Sociology: Post-empiricism and the Reconstruction of Theory and Application*. Cambridge: Polity Press.

Buhle, P. (2002) Obituary of David Riesman, *The Guardian* 13 May, 2002, p. 20.

Burger, T. (1987) *Max Weber's Theory of Concept Formation: History, Laws, and Ideal Types*. Durham, NC: Duke University Press.

Burns, T. (1992) *Erving Goffman*. London: Routledge.

Buxton, W. (1985) *Talcott Parsons and the Capitalist Nation-State: Political Sociology as a Strategic Vocation*. Toronto: University of Toronto Press.

Callinicos, A. (1996) *The Revolutionary Ideas of Marx*. London: Bookmarks, second edition.

—— (1999) *Social Theory: A Historical Introduction*. Cambridge: Polity Press.

Camic, C. (1991) 'Introduction: Talcott Parsons before The Structure of Social Action', in C. Camic (ed.) *Talcott Parsons: The Early Years*. Chicago, IL: University of Chicago Press, pp. ix–lxix.

Campbell, T. (1981) *Seven Theories of Human Society*. Oxford: Oxford University Press.

Carver, T. (1982) *Marx's Social Theory*. Oxford: Oxford University Press.

Carver, T. (1998) *The Postmodern Marx*. Manchester: Manchester University Press.

Chalcraft, D. (2001) 'Introduction', in D. Chalcraft and A. Harrington (eds) *The Protestant Ethic Debate: Max Weber's Replies to his Critics, 1907–1910*. Liverpool: Liverpool University Press, pp. 1–19.

Clarke, S. (1982) *Marx, Marginalism and Modern Sociology: From Adam Smith to Max Weber*. London and Basingstoke: Macmillan.

Cohen, G. (1988) *History, Labour, and Freedom: Themes from Marx*. Oxford: Clarendon Press.

Cohen, J. (2002) *Protestantism and Capitalism: The Mechanisms of Influence*. New York: Aldine de Gruyter.

Cohen, J., Hazelrigg, L. and Pope, W. (1975) 'De-Parsonizing Weber: A Critique of Parsons' Interpretation of Weber's Sociology', *American Sociological Review* 40, pp. 229–41.

Collins, R. (1980) 'Erving Goffman and the Development of Modern Social Theory', in J. Ditton (ed.) *The View From Goffman*. London: Macmillan, pp. 170–209.

—— (1986a) *Max Weber: A Skeleton Key*. London: Sage.

—— (1986b) *Weberian Sociological Theory*. Cambridge: Cambridge University Press.

—— (1988) 'Theoretical Continuities in Goffman's Work', in P. Drew and A. Wootton (eds) *Erving Goffman: Exploring the Interaction Order*. Cambridge: Polity Press, pp. 41–63.

—— (1990) 'The Durkheimian Tradition in Conflict Sociology', in J. Alexander (ed.) *Durkheimian Sociology: Cultural Studies*. Cambridge: Cambridge University Press, pp. 107–28.

—— (1994) *Four Sociological Traditions*. New York: Oxford University Press.

Collins, R. and Makowsky, M. (1998) *The Discovery of Society*. Boston, MA: McGraw-Hill, sixth edition.

Coser, L. (1965) 'The Stranger in the Academy', in L. Coser (ed.) *Georg Simmel*. Englewood Cliffs, NJ: Prentice Hall, pp. 29–39.

Craib, I. (1984) *Modern Social Theory: From Parsons to Habermas*. Brighton: Wheatsheaf.

—— (1997) *Classical Social Theory: An Introduction to the Thought of Marx, Weber, Durkheim and Simmel*. Oxford: Oxford University Press.

Crow, G. (1989) 'The Use of the Concept of "Strategy" in Recent Sociological Literature', *Sociology* 23(1), pp. 1–24.

—— (1997) *Comparative Sociology and Social Theory: Beyond the Three Worlds*. Basingstoke: Macmillan.

—— (1999) 'Sociology and the Discovery of Society's Hidden Dimensions', *Self, Agency and Society* 2(1), pp. 1–22.

Cuzzort, R. and King, E. (1989) *Twentieth-century Social Thought*. Fort Worth: Holt, Rinehart and Winston, fourth edition.

Dahrendorf, R. (1973) *Homo Sociologicus*. London: Routledge and Kegan Paul.

Davidson, A. (2003) 'Introduction', in M. Foucault (ed.) *Society Must be Defended: Lectures at the Collège de France, 1975–76*. London: Penguin, pp. xv–xxiii.

Dean, M. (1994) *Critical and Effective Histories: Foucault's Methods and Historical Sociology*. London: Routledge.

Delanty, G. (1999) *Social Theory in a Changing World: Conceptions of Modernity*. Cambridge: Polity Press.

Deleuze, G. (1988) *Foucault*. Minneapolis: University of Minneapolis Press.

Devereux, E. (1976) 'Parsons' Sociological Theory', in M. Black (ed.) *The Social Theories of Talcott Parsons: A Critical Examination*. Carbondale: Southern Illinois University Press, pp. 1–63.

Diggins, J. (1996) *Max Weber: Politics and the Spirit of Tragedy*. New York: Basic Books.

Ditton, J. (1980) 'Editor's Introduction: A Bibliographic Exegesis of Goffman's Sociology', in J. Ditton (ed.) *The View From Goffman*. London: Macmillan, pp. 1–23.

Domhoff, G. and Ballard, H. (1969) 'C. Wright Mills and His Sociology', in G. Domhoff and H. Ballard (eds) *C. Wright Mills and the Power Elite*. Boston: Beacon Press, p. 1.

Douglas, M. (1996) *Thought Styles: Critical Essays on Good Taste*. London: Sage.

Drew, P. and Wootton, A. (1988) 'Introduction', in P. Drew and A. Wootton (eds) *Erving Goffman: Exploring the Interaction Order*. Cambridge: Polity Press, pp. 1–13.

Dreyfus, H. and Rabinow, P. (1982) *Michel Foucault: Beyond Structuralism and Hermeneutics*. Brighton: Harvester.

Dumont, L. (1977) *From Mandeville to Marx: The Genesis and Triumph of Economic Ideology*. Chicago, IL: University of Chicago Press.

Durkheim, E. (1962) *Socialism*. New York: Collier.

—— (1964a) 'Sociology and its Scientific Field', in K. Wolff (ed.) *Essays on Sociology and Philosophy*. New York: Harper and Row, pp. 354–75.

—— (1964b) *The Division of Labor in Society*. New York: Free Press.

—— (1970) *Suicide*. London: Routledge and Kegan Paul.

—— (1972) *Selected Writings*. Cambridge: Cambridge University Press.

—— (1973) *Moral Education: A Study in the Theory and Application of the Sociology of Education*. New York: Free Press.

—— (1974) *Sociology and Philosophy*. New York: Free Press.

—— (1976) *The Elementary Forms of the Religious Life*. London: George Allen and Unwin.

—— (1982) *The Rules of Sociological Method*. London and Basingstoke: Macmillan.

—— (1983) *Pragmatism and Sociology*. Cambridge: Cambridge University Press.

—— (1984) *The Division of Labour in Society*. Basingstoke: Macmillan.

—— (1992) *Professional Ethics and Civic Morals*. London: Routledge.

Eagleton, T. (1999) *Marx*. New York: Routledge.

Edmondson, R. (1984) *Rhetoric in Sociology*. London: Macmillan.

Elcock, H. (1976) *Political Behaviour*. London: Methuen.

Eldridge, J. (1971) 'Introductory Essay', in J. Eldridge (ed.) *Max Weber: The Interpretation of Social Reality*. London: Michael Joseph, pp. 9–70.

—— (1983) *C. Wright Mills*. London: Tavistock.

Elias, N. (1978) *What is Sociology?* London: Hutchinson.

Elster, J. (1985) *Making Sense of Marx*. Cambridge: Cambridge University Press.

Eribon, D. (1993) *Michel Foucault*. London: Faber and Faber.

Evans, M. (1975) *Karl Marx*. London: George Allen and Unwin.

Fernbach, D. (1973) 'Introduction', in K. Marx, *The Revolutions of 1848*. Harmondsworth: Penguin, pp. 9–61.

Fine, G. (1999) 'Claiming the Text: Parsing the Sardonic Visions of Erving Goffman and Thorstein Veblen', in G. Smith (ed.) *Goffman and Social Organization: Studies in a Sociological Legacy*. London: Routledge, pp. 177–97.

Foote, S. (1986) *The Civil War: A Narrative*. New York: Vintage Books.

Foucault, M. (1971) *Madness and Civilization: A History of Insanity in the Age of Reason*. London: Tavistock.

—— (1972) *The Archaeology of Knowledge*. London: Tavistock.

—— (1974) *The Order of Things: An Archaeology of the Human Sciences*. London: Tavistock.

—— (1975) *The Birth of the Clinic: An Archaeology of Medical Perception*. New York: Vintage Books.

—— (1978a) *The History of Sexuality, Volume 1: An Introduction*. New York: Pantheon.

—— (ed.) (1978b) *I, Pierre Rivière, Having Slaughtered My Mother, My Sister, and My Brother ... A Case of Parricide in the 19th Century*. Harmondsworth: Penguin.

—— (1979) *Discipline and Punish: The Birth of the Prison*. Harmondsworth: Penguin.

—— (1980) *Power/Knowledge: Selected Interviews and Other Writings 1972–1977*. Edited by C. Gordon. Brighton: Harvester.

—— (1982) 'Afterword: The Subject and Power', in H. Dreyfus and P. Rabinow (eds) *Michel Foucault: Beyond Structuralism and Hermeneutics*. Brighton: Harvester, pp. 208–26.

—— (1986a) 'What is Enlightenment?', in P. Rabinow (ed.) *The Foucault Reader*. Harmondsworth: Penguin, pp. 32–50.

—— (1986b) 'Nietzsche, Genealogy, History', in P. Rabinow (ed.) *The Foucault Reader*. Harmondsworth: Penguin, pp. 76–100.

—— (1986c) 'Preface to The History of Sexuality, Volume II', in P. Rabinow (ed.) *The Foucault Reader*. Harmondsworth: Penguin, pp. 333–9.

—— (1988a) 'Truth, Power, Self', in L. Martin, H. Gutman and P. Hutton (eds) *Technologies of the Self: A Seminar with Michel Foucault*. London: Tavistock, pp. 9–15.

—— (1988b) 'The Political Technology of Individuals', in L. Martin, H. Gutman and P. Hutton (eds) *Technologies of the Self: A Seminar with Michel Focault*. London: Tavistock, pp. 145–62.

—— (1990) *Politics, Philosophy, Culture: Interviews and Other Writings 1977–1984*. Edited by L. Kritzman. London: Routledge.

—— (1991) 'Questions of Method', in G. Burchell, C. Gordon and P. Miller (eds) *The Foucault Effect: Studies in Governmentality*. Hemel Hempstead: Harvester Wheatsheaf, pp. 73–86.

Foucault, M. (1992) *The Use of Pleasure: The History of Sexuality: Volume 2*. Harmondsworth: Penguin.
—— (1996) *Foucault Live: Collected Interviews, 1961–84*. Edited by S. Lotringer. New York: Semiotext(e).
—— (1997) *Ethics: Subjectivity and Truth, Volume 1*. Edited by P. Rabinow. Harmondsworth: Penguin.
—— (1999) 'Discourse on the West', in C. Lemert (ed.) *Social Theory: The Multicultural and Classic Readings*. Boulder, CO: Westview, second edition, pp. 415–19.
—— (2003) *Society Must be Defended: Lectures at the Collège de France, 1975–76*. London: Penguin.
Frank, R. (1976) 'Translator's Introduction', in M. Weber, *The Agrarian Sociology of Ancient Civilizations*. London: New Left Books, pp. 7–33.
Freund, J. (1972) *The Sociology of Max Weber*. Harmondsworth: Penguin.
Friedan, B. (1999) 'The Problem That Has No Name', in C. Lemert (ed.) *Social Theory: The Multicultural and Classic Readings*. Boulder, CO: Westview, second edition, pp. 356–9.
Gane, M. (1988) *On Durkheim's Rules of Sociological Method*. London: Routledge.
—— (ed.) (1992) *The Radical Sociology of Durkheim and Mauss*. London: Routledge.
Gans, H. (1962) *The Urban Villagers: Group and Class in the Life of Italian Americans*. New York: Free Press.
—— (1999) *Making Sense of America: Sociological Analyses and Essays*. Lanham, MD: Rowman and Littlefield.
Garland, D. (1990) *Punishment and Modern Society: A Study in Social Theory*. Oxford: Clarendon Press.
—— (2001) *The Culture of Control: Crime and Social Order in Contemporary Society*. Oxford: Oxford University Press.
Geertz, C. (1988) *Works and Lives: The Anthropologist as Author*. Stanford, CA: Stanford University Press.
Gerhardt, U. (1989) *Ideas about Illness: An Intellectual and Political History of Medical Sociology*. Basingstoke: Macmillan.
Gerth, H. H. and Mills, C. W. (1954) *Character and Social Structure: The Psychology of Social Institutions*. London: Routledge and Kegan Paul.
—— (1970) 'Introduction', in H. H. Gerth and C. W. Mills (eds) *From Max Weber: Essays in Sociology*. London: Routledge and Kegan Paul, pp. 3–74.
Giddens, A. (1971a) 'The Suicide Problem in French Sociology', in A. Giddens (ed.) *The Sociology of Suicide*. London: Frank Cass, pp. 36–51.
—— (1971b) *Capitalism and Modern Social Theory: An Analysis of the Writings of Marx, Durkheim and Max Weber*. Cambridge: Cambridge University Press.
—— (1976) 'Introduction', in M. Weber, *The Protestant Ethic and the Spirit of Capitalism*. London: George Allen and Unwin, second edition, pp. 1–12.
—— (1977) *Studies in Social and Political Theory*. London: Hutchinson.
—— (1978) *Durkheim*. Glasgow: Fontana.
—— (1979) *Central Problems in Social Theory: Action, Structure and Contradiction in Social Analysis*. Basingstoke: Macmillan.
—— (1982) *Profiles and Critiques in Social Theory*. London: Macmillan.
—— (1984) *The Constitution of Society: Outline of the Theory of Structuration*. Cambridge: Polity Press.
—— (1987a) 'Weber and Durkheim: Coincidence and Divergence', in W. Mommsen and W. Osterhammel (eds) *Max Weber and His Contemporaries*. London: Unwin Hyman, pp. 182–9.
—— (1987b) *Social Theory and Modern Sociology*. Cambridge: Polity Press.
—— (1996) *In Defence of Sociology: Essays, Interpretations and Rejoinders*. Cambridge: Polity Press.
Gillam, R. (1981) 'White Collar from Start to Finish: C. Wright Mills in Transition' *Theory and Society* 10 (1), pp. 1–30.
Gitlin, T. (2000) 'Afterword', in C. W. Mills, *The Sociological Imagination*. New York: Oxford University Press, pp. 229–42.
—— (2001) 'Foreword', in D. Riesman, *The Lonely Crowd: A Study of the Changing American Character*. New Haven: Yale University Press, pp. xi–xix.
Goffman, E. (1962) 'On Cooling the Mark Out: Some Aspects of Adaptation to Failure', in A. Rose (ed.) *Human Behaviour and Social Processes: An Interactionist Approach*. London: Routledge and Kegan Paul, pp. 482–505.

—— (1963) *Behavior in Public Places: Notes on the Social Organization of Gatherings*. New York: Free Press.

—— (1967) *Interaction Ritual: Essays on Face-to-Face Behavior*. Garden City, NY: Doubleday, Anchor Books.

—— (1968a) *Asylums: Essays on the Social Situation of Mental Patients and Other Inmates*. Harmondsworth: Penguin.

—— (1968b) *Stigma: Notes on the Management of Spoiled Identity*. Harmondsworth: Penguin.

—— (1969) *The Presentation of Self in Everyday Life*. Harmondsworth: Penguin.

—— (1970) *Strategic Interaction*. Oxford: Basil Blackwell.

—— (1971) *Relations in Public: Microstudies of the Public Order*. Harmondsworth: Penguin.

—— (1972) *Encounters*. Harmondsworth: Penguin.

—— (1975) *Frame Analysis: An Essay on the Organization of Experience*. Harmondsworth: Penguin.

—— (1979) *Gender Advertisements*. London: Macmillan.

—— (1981a) *Forms of Talk*. Oxford: Basil Blackwell.

—— (1981b) 'A Reply to Denzin and Keller', *Contemporary Sociology* 10, pp. 60–8.

—— (1987) 'The Arrangement between the Sexes', in M. Deegan and M. Hill (eds) *Women and Symbolic Interaction*. Boston: Allen and Unwin, pp. 51–78.

—— (1997) 'The Interaction Order', in C. Lemert and A. Branaman (eds) *The Goffman Reader*. Oxford: Blackwell, pp. 233–61.

Gouldner, A. (1962) 'Introduction', in E. Durkheim, *Socialism*. New York: Collier, pp. 7–31.

—— (1971) *The Coming Crisis of Western Sociology*. London: Heinemann.

—— (1980) *The Two Marxisms: Contradictions and Anomalies in the Development of Theory*. London and Basingstoke: Macmillan.

Graham, H. (1987) 'Being Poor: Perceptions and Coping Strategies of Lone Mothers', in J. Brannen and G. Wilson (eds) *Give and Take in Families: Studies in Resource Distribution*. London: Allen and Unwin, pp. 56–74.

Granovetter, M. (1973) 'The Strength of Weak Ties', *American Journal of Sociology* 78(6), 1360–80.

Green, B. (1988) *Literary Methods and Sociological Theory: Case Studies of Simmel and Weber*. Chicago, IL: University of Chicago Press.

Green, R. (1973) 'Introduction', in R. Green (ed.) *Protestantism, Capitalism and Social Science: The Weber Thesis Controversy*. Lexington, MA: D. C. Heath and Company, second edition.

Gutting, G. (1994) 'Michel Foucault: A User's Manual', in G. Gutting (ed.) *The Cambridge Companion to Foucault*. Cambridge: Cambridge University Press, pp. 1–27.

Halperin, M. (1997) *Saint Foucault: Towards a Gay Hagiography*. New York: Oxford University Press.

Halsey, A. (2004) *A History of Sociology in Britain: Science, Literature, and Society*. Oxford: Oxford University Press.

Hamilton, P. (1983) *Talcott Parsons*. London: Routledge.

—— (1985) 'Introduction', in P. Hamilton (ed.) *Readings From Talcott Parsons*. London: Tavistock, pp. 7–17.

Harrington, A. (2001) 'Translators' Note', in D. Chalcraft and A. Harrington (eds) *The Protestant Ethic Debate: Max Weber's Replies to his Critics, 1907–1910*. Liverpool University Press, pp. 21–3.

Harris, C. C. (1980) *Fundamental Concepts and the Sociological Enterprise*. London: Croom Helm.

Harvey, D. (1989) *The Condition of Modernity*. Oxford: Basil Blackwell.

Hawthorn, G. (1976) *Enlightenment and Despair: A History of Sociology*. Cambridge: Cambridge University Press.

Hearn, F. (1985) *Reason and Freedom in Sociological Thought*. Boston: Allen and Unwin.

Hennis, W. (2000) *Max Weber's Central Question*. Newbury: Threshold Press, second edition.

Hirschman, A. (1991) *The Rhetoric of Reaction: Perversity, Futility, Jeopardy*. Cambridge, MA: Belknap Press.

Hobbes, T. (1968) *Leviathan*. Harmondsworth: Penguin.

Hobsbawm, E. and Ranger, T. (eds) (1983) *The Invention of Tradition*. Cambridge: Cambridge University Press.

Hochschild, A. (1983) *The Managed Heart: Commercialization of Human Feeling*. Berkeley: University of California Press.

—— (1989) *The Second Shift: Working Parents and the Revolution at Home*. New York: Viking.

Hochschild, A. (2003) *The Commercialization of Intimate Life: Notes from Home and Work*. Berkeley: University of California Press.

Holmwood, J. (1996) *Founding Sociology? Talcott Parsons and the Idea of General Theory*. London: Longman.

—— (2000) 'Sociology and its Audience(s): Changing Perceptions of Sociological Argument', in J. Eldridge, J. MacInnes, S. Scott, C. Warhurst and A. Witz (eds) *For Sociology: Legacies and Prospects*. Durham: Sociology Press, pp. 33–55.

Holton, R. (1998) 'Talcott Parsons', in R. Stones (ed.) *Key Sociological Thinkers*. Basingstoke: Macmillan, pp. 96–107.

Holton, R. and Turner, B. (1988) *Talcott Parsons on Economy and Society*. London: Routledge.

—— (1990) *Max Weber on Economy and Society*. London: Routledge.

Hook, S. (1955) *Marx and the Marxists*. Princeton, NJ: Van Nostrand.

Horowitz, I. (1964) 'An Introduction to *The New Sociology*', in I. Horowitz (ed.) *The New Sociology: Essays in Social Science and Social Theory in Honor of C. Wright Mills*. New York: Oxford University Press, pp. 3–48.

—— (1966) 'Introduction: The Intellectual Genesis of C. Wright Mills', in C. W. Mills, *Sociology and Pragmatism: The Higher Learning in America*. New York: Oxford University Press, pp. 11–31.

—— (1967a) 'An Introduction to C. Wright Mills', in I. Horowitz (ed.) *Power, Politics and People: The Collected Essays of C. Wright Mills*. New York: Oxford University Press, pp. 1–20.

—— (1967b) 'Bibliography of the Writings of C. Wright Mills', in I. Horowitz (ed.) *Power, Politics and People: The Collected Essays of C. Wright Mills*. New York: Oxford University Press, pp. 615–41.

—— (1983) *C. Wright Mills: An American Utopian*. New York: Free Press.

Howe, R. (1978) 'Max Weber's Elective Affinities: Sociology with the Bounds of Pure Reason', *American Journal of Sociology* 84, pp. 366–85.

Hughes, H. (1974) *Consciousness and Society: The Reorientation of European Social Thought 1890–1930*. St Albans: Paladin.

Hughes, J., Martin, P. and Sharrock, W. (1995) *Understanding Classical Sociology: Marx, Weber, Durkheim*. London: Sage.

Hymes, D. (1984) 'On Erving Goffman', *Theory and Society* 13(5), pp. 621–31.

Jenkins, R. (2002) *Foundations of Sociology: Towards a Better Understanding of the Human World*. Basingstoke: Palgrave.

Jessop, B. (1998) 'Karl Marx', in R. Stones (ed.) *Key Sociological Thinkers*. Basingstoke: Macmillan, pp. 21–33.

Johnson, T., Dandeker, C. and Ashworth, C. (1984) *The Structure of Social Theory: Dilemmas and Strategies*. Basingstoke: Macmillan.

Jones, R. (1986) *Emile Durkheim: An Introduction to Four Major Works*. Beverly Hills: Sage.

—— (1997) 'The *Other* Durkheim: History and Theory in the Treatment of Classical Sociological Thought', in C. Camic (ed.) *Reclaiming the Sociological Classics: The State of the Scholarship*. Oxford: Blackwell, pp. 142–72.

—— (1999) *The Development of Durkheim's Social Realism*. Cambridge: Cambridge University Press.

Kalberg, S. (1997) 'Max Weber's Sociology: Research Strategies and Modes of Analysis', in C. Camic (ed.) *Reclaiming the Sociological Classics: The State of the Scholarship*. Oxford: Blackwell, pp. 208–41.

—— (2002) 'Introduction', in M. Weber, *The Protestant Ethic and the Spirit of Capitalism*. Oxford: Blackwell, pp. xi–lxxxi.

Käsler, D. (1988) *Max Weber: An Introduction to his Life and Work*. Cambridge: Polity Press.

Katz, S. (2001) 'Michel Foucault', in A. Elliott and B. Turner (eds) *Profiles in Contemporary Social Theory*. London: Sage, pp. 117–27.

Kemple, T. (1995) *Reading Marx Writing: Melodrama, the Market, and the 'Grundrisse'*. Stanford, CA: Stanford University Press.

Kideckel, D. (1993) *The Solitude of Collectivism: Romanian Villagers to the Revolution and Beyond*. Ithaca: Cornell University Press.

Kitching, G. (1988) *Karl Marx and the Philosophy of Praxis*. London: Routledge.

Kivisto, P. (1998) *Key Ideas in Sociology*. Thousand Oaks, CA: Pine Forge Press.

Kivisto, P. and Pittman, D. (1998) 'Goffman's Dramaturgical Sociology: Personal Sales and Service in a Commodified World', in P. Kivisto (ed.) *Illuminating Social Life*. Thousand Oaks, CA: Pine Forge Press, pp. 235–60.

Kritzman, L. (ed.) (1990) 'Foreword', in M. Foucault *Politics, Philosophy, Culture: Interviews and Other Writings 1977–1984*. London: Routledge, pp. vii–viii.

Korsch, K. (1971) *Three Essays on Marxism*. London: Pluto Press.

LaCapra, D. (1985) *Emile Durkheim: Sociologist and Philosopher*. Chicago, IL: University of Chicago Press.

Lakoff, G. and Johnson, M. (1980) *Metaphors We Live By*. Chicago, IL: University of Chicago Press.

Layder, D. (1994) *Understanding Social Theory*. London: Sage.

Lee, D. and Newby, H. (1983) *The Problem of Sociology*. London: Hutchinson.

Lehmann, J. (1994) *Durkheim and Women*. Lincoln: University of Nebraska Press.

Lemert, C. (1995) *Sociology After the Crisis*. Boulder, CO: Westview.

—— (1997a) *Social Things: An Introduction to the Sociological Life*. Lanham, MD: Rowman and Littlefield.

—— (1997b) 'Goffman', in C. Lemert and A. Branaman (eds) *The Goffman Reader*. Oxford: Blackwell, pp. ix–xliii.

—— (1997c) *Postmodernism is Not What You Think*. Oxford: Blackwell.

—— (ed.) (1999) *Social Theory: The Multicultural and Classic Readings*. Boulder, CO: Westview, second edition.

Lemert, C. and Gillan, G. (1982) *Michel Foucault: Social Theory as Transgression*. New York: Columbia University Press.

Letherby, G. (2003) *Feminist Research in Theory and Practice*. Buckingham: Open University Press.

Liebersohn, H. (1988) *Fate and Utopia in German Sociology, 1870–1923*. Cambridge, MA: The MIT Press.

Lindgren, S. (2000) 'Michel Foucault', in H. Andersen and L. Kaspersen (eds) *Classical and Modern Social Theory*. Oxford: Blackwell, pp. 294–308.

Lockwood, D. (1992) *Solidarity and Schism: 'The Problem of Disorder' in Durkheimian and Marxist Sociology*. Oxford: Clarendon Press.

López, J. (2003) *Society and its Metaphors: Language, Social Theory and Social Structure*. London: Continuum.

Löwith, K. (1982) *Max Weber and Karl Marx*. London: George Allen and Unwin.

Lukács, G. (1980) *The Destruction of Reason*. London: Merlin Press.

Lukes, S. (1975) *Emile Durkheim: His Life and Work: A Historical and Critical Study*. Harmondsworth: Penguin.

McCloskey, D. (1998) *The Rhetoric of Economics*. Wisconsin: University of Wisconsin Press, second edition.

McDonald, L. (1994) *The Women Founders of the Social Sciences*. Ottawa: Carleton University Press.

McLellan, D. (1973) *Karl Marx: His Life and Thought*. London and Basingstoke: Macmillan.

—— (1980) *The Thought of Karl Marx*. London and Basingstoke: Macmillan, second edition.

—— (1986) *Marx*. London: Fontana.

McNay, L. (1994) *Foucault: A Critical Introduction*. New York: Continuum.

Madge, J. (1970) *The Origins of Scientific Sociology*. London: Tavistock.

Mandel, E. (1977) *The Formation of the Economic Thought of Karl Marx*. London: New Left Books.

Manning, P. (1992) *Erving Goffman and Modern Sociology*. Cambridge: Polity Press.

Manuel, F. (1995) *A Requiem for Karl Marx*. Cambridge, MA: Harvard University Press.

Marshall, G. (1980) *Presbyteries and Profits: Calvinism and the Development of Capitalism in Scotland, 1560–1707*. Oxford: Clarendon Press.

—— (1982) *In Search of the Spirit of Capitalism: An Essay on Max Weber's Protestant Ethic Thesis*. London: Hutchinson.

—— (1990) *In Praise of Sociology*. London: Unwin Hyman.

—— (ed.) (1994) *The Concise Oxford Dictionary of Sociology*. Oxford: Oxford University Press.

Marx, G. (ed.) (1972) *Muckraking Sociology: Research as Social Criticism*. New Brunswick, NJ: Transaction Books.

—— (1984) 'Role Models and Role Distance: A Remembrance of Erving Goffman', *Theory and Society* 13(5), pp. 649–62.

Marx, K. (1954) *Capital: Volume One*. London: Lawrence and Wishart.

—— (1959) *Capital: Volume Three*. London: Lawrence and Wishart.

—— (1973a) *Grundrisse*. Harmondsworth: Penguin.

—— (1973b) *Surveys from Exile*. Harmondsworth: Penguin.

Marx, K. (1974) *The First International And After*. Harmondsworth: Penguin.
—— (1975a) *The Poverty of Philosophy*. Moscow: Progress Publishers.
—— (1975b) *Early Writings*. Harmondsworth: Penguin.
—— (1976) *Capital: Volume One*. Harmondsworth: Penguin.
—— (1981) *Capital: Volume Three*. Harmondsworth: Penguin.
Marx, K. and Engels, F. (1968) *Selected Works in One Volume*. London: Lawrence and Wishart.
—— (1969) *Selected Works: Volume One*. Moscow: Progress Publishers.
—— (1970) *Selected Works: Volume Three*. Moscow: Progress Publishers.
—— (1974) *The German Ideology*. London: Lawrence and Wishart.
May, T. (1996) *Situating Social Theory*. Buckingham: Open University Press.
Meek, R. (1973) *Studies in the Labour Theory of Value*. London: Lawrence and Wishart.
Mennell, S. (1974) *Sociological Theory: Uses and Unities*. Sunbury-on-Thames: Nelson.
Menzies, K. (1977) *Talcott Parsons and the Social Image of Man*. London: Routledge and Kegan Paul.
Merquior, J. (1985) *Foucault*. London: Fontana.
Merton, R. (1965) *On the Shoulders of Giants: A Shandean Postscript*. New York: Harcourt Brace Jovanovich.
—— (1976) *Sociological Ambivalence and Other Essays*. New York: Free Press.
Meštrović, S. (1991) *The Coming Fin De Siècle: An Application of Durkheim's Sociology to Modernity and Postmodernism*. London: Routledge.
Mészáros, I. (1987) 'Customs, Tradition, Legality: A Key Problem in the Dialectic of Base and Superstructure', in W. Outhwaite and M. Mulkay (eds) *Social Theory and Social Criticism*. Oxford: Basil Blackwell, pp. 53–82.
Miles, S. (2001) *Social Theory in the Real World*. London: Sage.
Miliband, R. (1969) 'C. Wright Mills', in G. Domhoff and H. Ballard (eds) *C. Wright Mills and The Power Elite*. Boston: Beacon Press, pp. 3–11.
Mills, C. W. (1948) *The New Men of Power: America's Labor Leaders*. New York: Harcourt, Brace & Co.
—— (1953) 'Introduction' in T. Veblen, *The Theory of the Leisure Class: An Economic Study of Institutions*. New York: Mentor, pp. vi–xix.
—— (1956) *White Collar: The American Middle Classes*. New York: Oxford University Press.
—— (1959) *The Power Elite*. New York: Oxford University Press.
—— (1960) *The Causes of World War Three*. New York: Ballantine Books.
—— (1963) *The Marxists*. Harmondsworth: Penguin Books.
—— (1966) *Sociology and Pragmatism: The Higher Learning in America*. New York: Oxford University Press.
—— (1967a) 'The Labor Leaders and the Power Elite', in I. Horowitz (ed.) *Power, Politics and People: The Collected Essays of C. Wright Mills*. New York: Oxford University Press, pp. 97–109
—— (1967b) 'The Problem of Industrial Development', in I. Horowitz (ed.) *Power, Politics and People: The Collected Essays of C. Wright Mills*. New York: Oxford University Press, pp. 150–6.
—— (1967c) 'The Middle Classes in Middle-Sized Cities', in I. Horowitz (ed.) *Power, Politics and People: The Collected Essays of C. Wright Mills*. New York: Oxford University Press, pp. 274–91.
—— (1967d) 'Women: The Darling Little Slaves', in I. Horowitz (ed.) *Power, Politics and People: The Collected Essays of C. Wright Mills*. New York: Oxford University Press, pp. 339–46.
—— (1967e) 'Situated Actions and Vocabularies of Motive', in I. Horowitz (ed.) *Power, Politics and People: The Collected Essays of C. Wright Mills*. New York: Oxford University Press, pp. 439–52.
—— (1967f) 'The Professional Ideology of Social Pathologists', in I. Horowitz (ed.) *Power, Politics and People: The Collected Essays of C. Wright Mills*. New York: Oxford University Press, pp. 525–52.
—— (1969) 'Comment on Criticism', in G. Domhoff and H. Ballard (eds) *C. Wright Mills and The Power Elite*. Boston: Beacon Press, pp. 229–50.
—— (2000) *The Sociological Imagination*. New York: Oxford University Press.
Mills, K. with Mills, P. (eds) (2000) *C. Wright Mills: Letters and Autobiographical Writings*. Berkeley: University of California Press.
Mitchell, G. (1979) *A New Dictionary of Sociology*. London: Routledge and Kegan Paul.
Mitchell, J. and Oakley, A. (1976) 'Introduction', in J. Mitchell and A. Oakley (eds) *The Rights and Wrongs of Women*. Harmondsworth: Penguin, pp. 7–15.
—— (1986) 'Introduction', in J. Mitchell and A. Oakley (eds) *What is Feminism?* Oxford: Basil Blackwell, pp. 1–7.

Mommsen, W. (1994) 'Capitalism and Socialism: Weber's Dialogue with Marx', in *The Polity Reader in Social Theory*. Cambridge: Polity Press, pp. 14–22.

Moore, B. (1962) *Political Power and Social Theory*. New York: Harper and Row.

—— (1967) *Social Origins of Dictatorship and Democracy: Lord and Peasant in the Making of the Modern World*. Harmondsworth: Penguin.

Morgan, D. H. J. (1975) *Social Theory and the Family*. London: Routledge and Kegan Paul.

—— (1992) *Discovering Men*. London: Routledge.

Morrison, K. (1995) *Marx, Durkheim, Weber: Formations of Modern Social Thought*. London: Sage.

Moss, J. (1998) 'Introduction: The Later Foucault', in J. Moss (ed.) *The Later Foucault*. London: Sage, pp. 1–17.

Mullan, B. (1987) *Sociologists on Sociology*. London: Croom Helm.

Nicolaievsky, B. and Maenchen-Helfen, O. (1976) *Karl Marx: Man and Fighter*. London: Penguin.

Nicolaus, M. (1973) 'Foreword', in K. Marx, *Grundrisse*. Harmondsworth: Penguin, pp. 7–63.

Nisbet, R. (1970) *The Sociological Tradition*. London: Heinemann.

—— (1976) 'Introduction' in E. Durkheim, *The Elementary Forms of the Religious Life*. London: George Allen and Unwin, pp. v–xii.

Oakes, G. (1977) 'Introductory Essay' in M. Weber, *Critique of Stammler*. New York: Free Press, pp. 1–56.

Oakley, A. (1972) *Sex, Gender and Society*. London: Maurice Temple Smith.

—— (1974) *The Sociology of Housework*. London: Martin Robertson.

—— (1976a) *Housewife*. Harmondsworth: Penguin.

—— (1976b) 'Wisewoman and Medicine Man: Changes in the Management of Childbirth', in J. Mitchell and A. Oakley (eds) *The Rights and Wrongs of Women*. Harmondsworth: Penguin, pp. 17–58.

—— (1980) *Women Confined: Towards a Sociology of Childbirth*. Oxford: Martin Robertson.

—— (1981a) *From Here to Maternity: Becoming a Mother*. Harmondsworth: Penguin.

—— (1981b) 'Normal Motherhood: An Exercise in Self-Control?', in B. Hutter and G. Williams (eds) *Controlling Women: The Normal and the Deviant*. London: Croom Helm, pp. 79–107.

—— (1982a) *Subject Women*. London: Fontana.

—— (1982b) 'Conventional Families', in R. N. Rapoport, M. Fogarty and R. Rapoport (eds) *Families in Britain*. London: Routledge and Kegan Paul, pp. 123–37.

—— (1984) *The Captured Womb: A History of the Medical Care of Pregnant Women*. Oxford: Basil Blackwell.

—— (1985) *Taking it like a Woman*. London: Flamingo.

—— (1986a) *Telling the Truth about Jerusalem: A Collection of Essays and Poems*. Oxford: Basil Blackwell.

—— (1986b) *From Here to Maternity: Becoming a Mother*. Harmondsworth: Penguin (reprinted with an Introduction).

—— (1986c) 'Feminism, Motherhood and Medicine – Who Cares?', in J. Mitchell and A. Oakley (eds) *What is Feminism?* Oxford: Basil Blackwell, pp. 127–50.

—— (1989) *The Men's Room*. London: Flamingo.

—— (1990a) 'Who's Afraid of the Randomized Controlled Trial? Some Dilemmas of the Scientific Method and "Good" Research Practice', in H. Roberts (ed.) *Women's Health Counts*. London: Routledge, pp. 167–94.

—— (1990b) 'Introduction', in P. Chesler, *Sacred Bond: Motherhood Under Siege*. London: Virago, pp. ix–xvii.

—— (1992) *Social Support and Motherhood: The Natural History of a Research Project*. Oxford: Blackwell.

—— (1993) *Essays on Women, Medicine and Health*. Edinburgh: Edinburgh University Press.

—— (1994) 'On C. Wright Mills's *The Sociological Imagination*', *The Times Higher Educational Supplement* 12 August.

—— (1997a) *Man and Wife: Richard and Kay Titmuss: My Parents' Early Years*. London: Flamingo.

—— (1997b) 'A Brief History of Gender', in A. Oakley and J. Mitchell (eds) *Who's Afraid of Feminism? Seeing through the Backlash*. New York: The New Press, pp. 29–55.

—— (1997c) 'Foreword' in A. Brooks, *Academic Women UK*. Buckingham: Open University Press, pp. x–xii.

—— (1998) 'Gender, Methodology and People's Ways of Knowing: Some Problems with Feminism and the Paradigm Debate in Social Science', *Sociology* 32(4), pp. 707–31.

Oakley, A. (1999a) *Overheads*. London: Flamingo.

—— (1999b) 'A Motley Mirror Image', *The Times Higher* 26 March.

—— (2000) *Experiments in Knowing: Gender and Method in the Social Sciences*. Cambridge: Polity Press.

—— (2001) 'Commentary', in P. Alcock, H. Glennerster, A. Oakley and A. Sinfield (eds) *Welfare and Wellbeing: Richard Titmuss's Contribution to Social Policy*. Bristol: Policy Press, pp. 11–16.

—— (2002) *Gender on Planet Earth*. Cambridge: Polity Press.

—— (2004) 'Social Science and Public Policy: Some Personal Reflections', Marshall Lecture, University of Southampton.

Oakley, A., McPherson, A. and Roberts, H. (1984) *Miscarriage*. Glasgow: Fontana.

Oakley, A. and Mitchell, J. (1997) 'Introduction to the American Edition', in A. Oakley and J. Mitchell (eds) *Who's Afraid of Feminism? Seeing Through the Backlash*. New York: The New Press, pp. xix–xxxv.

Oakley, A. and Oakley, R. (1979) 'Sexism in Official Statistics', in J. Irvine, I. Miles and J. Evans (eds) *Demystifying Social Statistics*. London: Pluto Press, pp. 172–89.

Oakley, A. and Rigby, A. (1998) 'Are Men Good for the Welfare of Women and Children?', in J. Popay, J. Hearn and J. Edwards (eds) *Men, Gender Divisions and Welfare*. London: Routledge. pp. 101–27.

Padover, S. (ed.) (1978) *The Essential Marx: The Non-economic Writings*. New York: Mentor.

Pampel, F. (2000) *Sociological Lives and Ideas: An Introduction to the Classical Theorists*. New York: Worth.

Parkin, F. (1982) *Max Weber*. London: Tavistock.

—— (1992) *Durkheim*. Oxford: Oxford University Press.

Parsons, T. (1951) *The Social System*. London: Routledge and Kegan Paul.

—— (1964) *Essays in Sociological Theory*. New York: Free Press, revised edition.

—— (1966) *Societies: Evolutionary and Comparative Perspectives*. Englewood Cliffs, NJ: Prentice Hall.

—— (1968) *The Structure of Social Action, Volume 1: Marshall, Pareto, Durkheim*. New York: Free Press.

—— (1974) 'The Life and Work of Emile Durkheim', in E. Durkheim, *Sociology and Philosophy*. New York: Free Press, pp. xliii–lxx.

—— (1976) 'The Point of View of the Author', in M. Black (ed.) *The Social Theories of Talcott Parsons: A Critical Examination*. Carbondale: Southern Illinois University Press, pp. 311–63.

—— (1977) *The Evolution of Societies*. Englewood Cliffs, NJ: Prentice Hall.

—— (1991) ' "Capitalism" in Recent German Literature: Sombart and Weber', in C. Camic (ed.) *Talcott Parsons: The Early Essays*. Chicago: University of Chicago Press, pp. 3–37.

—— (1999a) 'The Symbolic Environment of Modern Economies', in B. Turner (ed.) *The Talcott Parsons Reader*. Oxford: Blackwell, pp. 87–97.

—— (1999b) 'Illness and the Role of the Physician: A Sociological Perspective', in B. Turner (ed.) *The Talcott Parsons Reader*. Oxford: Blackwell, pp. 101–8.

—— (1999c) 'The Distribution of Power in American Society', in B. Turner (ed.) *The Talcott Parsons Reader*. Oxford: Blackwell, pp. 220–36.

—— (1999d) 'Youth in the Context of American Society', in B. Turner (ed.) *The Talcott Parsons Reader*. Oxford: Blackwell, pp. 271–91.

—— (1999e) 'Bibliography of Talcott Parsons', in B. Turner (ed.) *The Talcott Parsons Reader*. Oxford: Blackwell, pp. 321–35.

Parsons, T. and Bales, R. (1956) *Family, Socialization and Interaction Process*. London: Routledge and Kegan Paul.

Parsons, T. and Shils, E. (eds) (1951) *Toward a General Theory of Action*. New York: Harper and Row.

Pawson, R. (1989) *A Measure for Measures: A Manifesto for Empirical Sociology*. London: Routledge.

Pearce, F. (1989) *The Radical Durkheim*. London: Unwin Hyman.

Philp, M. (1990) 'Michel Foucault', in Q. Skinner (ed.) *The Return of Grand Theory in the Human Sciences*. Cambridge: Canto, pp. 65–81.

Pickering, W. (1984) *Durkheim's Sociology of Religion: Themes and Theories*. London: Routledge and Kegan Paul.

Plummer, K. (1996) 'Symbolic Interactionism in the Twentieth Century: The Rise of Empirical Social Theory', in B. Turner (ed.) *The Blackwell Companion to Social Theory*. Oxford: Blackwell, pp. 223–51.

Poggi, G. (1983) *Calvinism and the Capitalist Spirit: Max Weber's Protestant Ethic*. London and Basingstoke: Macmillan.

—— (2000) *Durkheim*. Oxford: Oxford University Press.

Poster, M. (1984) *Foucault, Marxism and History: Mode of Production versus Mode of Information*. Cambridge: Polity Press.

Putnam, R. (2000) *Bowling Alone: The Collapse and Revival of American Community*. New York: Simon and Schuster.

Rabinow, P. (1986) 'Introduction', in P. Rabinow (ed.) *The Foucault Reader*. Harmondsworth: Penguin, pp. 3–29.

—— (ed.) (1997) 'Series Preface', in M. Foucault *Ethics: Subjectivity and Truth, Volume 1*. Harmondsworth: Penguin, pp. vii–viii.

Ray, L. (1987) 'The Protestant Ethic Debate', in R. Anderson, J. Hughes and W. Sharrock (eds) *Classic Disputes in Sociology*. London: Allen and Unwin, pp. 97–125.

—— (1999) *Theorizing Classical Sociology*. Buckingham: Open University Press.

Rex, J. (1971) 'Typology and Objectivity: A Comment on Weber's Four Sociological Methods', in A. Sahay (ed.) *Max Weber and Modern Sociology*. London: Routledge and Kegan Paul, pp. 17–36.

—— (1973) *Discovering Sociology: Studies in Sociological Theory and Method*. London: Routledge and Kegan Paul.

Riesman, D. (2001) *The Lonely Crowd: A Study of the Changing American Character*. New Haven: Yale University Press.

Rigney, D. (2001) *The Metaphorical Society: An Invitation to Social Theory*. Lanham, MD: Rowman and Littlefield.

Ringer, F. (2000) *Max Weber's Methodology: The Unification of the Cultural and Social Sciences*. Cambridge, MA: Harvard University Press.

Ritzer, G. (1992) *Classical Sociological Theory*. New York: McGraw-Hill.

—— (1998) *The McDonaldization Thesis: Explorations and Extensions*. London: Sage.

—— (2000) *Sociological Theory*. New York: McGraw Hill, fifth edition.

—— (2001) *Explorations in Social Theory: From Metatheorizing to Rationalization*. London: Sage.

Roberts, H. (1981) 'Women and their Doctors: Power and Powerlessness in the Research Process', in H. Roberts (ed.) *Doing Feminist Research*. London: Routledge and Kegan Paul, pp. 7–29.

Robertson, R. and Turner, B. (1991) 'An Introduction to Talcott Parsons: Theory, Politics and Humanity', in R. Robertson and B. Turner (eds) *Talcott Parsons: Theorist of Modernity*. London: Sage, pp. 1–21.

Rocher, G. (1974) *Talcott Parsons and American Sociology*. London: Nelson.

Rodinson, M. (1977) *Islam and Capitalism*. Harmondsworth: Penguin.

Rosdolsky, R. (1980) *The Making of Marx's 'Capital'*. London: Pluto Press.

Roth, G. (1978) 'Introduction', in M. Weber, *Economy and Society: An Outline of Interpretive Sociology*. Berkeley: University of California Press.

Rubin, L. (1983) *Intimate Strangers*. New York: Harper and Row.

Ruggerio, V. (1996) *A Guide to Sociological Thinking*. Thousand Oaks: Sage.

Runciman, W. G. (1969) *Social Science and Political Theory*. Cambridge: Cambridge University Press, second edition.

—— (1970) *Sociology in its Place and Other Essays*. Cambridge: Cambridge University Press.

—— (1972) *A Critique of Max Weber's Philosophy of Social Science*. Cambridge: Cambridge University Press.

—— (1998) *The Social Animal*. London: HarperCollins.

Savage, S. (1981) *The Theories of Talcott Parsons: The Social Relations of Action*. London: Macmillan.

Sawicki, J. (1991) *Disciplining Foucault: Feminism, Power and the Body*. New York: Routledge.

Sayer, D. (1979) *Marx's Method: Ideology, Science and Critique in 'Capital'*. Hassocks: Harvester.

Scaff, L. (1989) *Fleeing the Iron Cage: Culture, Politics and Modernity in the Thought of Max Weber*. Berkeley: University of California Press.

Schluchter, W. (1979) 'The Paradox of Rationalization: On the Relation of Ethics and the World', in G. Roth and W. Schluchter (eds) *Max Weber's Vision of History: Ethics and Methods*. Berkeley: University of California Press, pp. 11–64.

Seidman, S. (1998) *Contested Knowledge: Social Theory in the Postmodern Era*. Oxford: Blackwell, second edition.

Sennett, R. (1970) *The Uses of Disorder: Personal Identity and City Life*. Toronto: Random House.

Sennett, R. (2003) *Respect: The Formation of Character in a World of Inequality.* London: Penguin.

Shanin, T. (1984) *Late Marx and the Russian Road: Marx and 'The Peripheries of Capitalism'.* London: Routledge and Kegan Paul.

Sheridan, A. (1980) *Michel Foucault: The Will to Truth.* London: Tavistock.

Sica, A. (1988) *Weber, Irrationality, and Social Order.* Berkeley: University of California Press.

Sieber, S. (1981) *Fatal Remedies.* New York: Plenum Press.

Simpson, G. (1970) 'Editor's Preface', in E. Durkheim, *Suicide.* London: Routledge and Kegan Paul, pp. 9–12.

Skocpol, T. (1988) 'The Uppity Generation and the Revitalization of Macroscopic Sociology: Reflections at Mid-Career by a Woman from the Sixties', *Theory and Society* 17, pp. 627–43.

Smart, B. (1988) *Michel Foucault.* London: Routledge.

—— (1992) *Modern Conditions, Postmodern Controversies.* London: Routledge.

Smith, A. (1974) *The Wealth of Nations.* Harmondsworth: Penguin.

Smith, C. (1979) *A Critique of Sociological Reasoning: An Essay in Philosophical Sociology.* Oxford: Basil Blackwell.

Smith, G. (1999) 'Introduction: Interpreting Goffman's Sociological Legacy', in G. Smith (ed.) *Goffman and Social Organization: Studies in a Sociological Legacy.* London: Routledge, pp. 1–18.

Spencer, H. (1969) *The Man Versus the State.* Hamondsworth: Penguin.

Spender, D. (1985) *For the Record: The Making and Meaning of Feminist Knowledge.* London: The Women's Press.

Stedman Jones, S. (2001) *Durkheim Reconsidered.* Cambridge: Polity Press.

Stones, R. (1996) *Sociological Reasoning: Towards a Past-modern Sociology.* Basingstoke: Macmillan.

Sydie, R. (1987) *Natural Women, Cultured Men.* Milton Keynes: Open University Press.

Sztompka, P. (1986) *Robert K. Merton: An Intellectual Profile.* Basingstoke: Macmillan.

Tannen, D. (1998) *The Argument Culture: Changing the Way We Argue and Debate.* London: Virago.

Taylor, A. (1967) 'Introduction', in K. Marx and F. Engels, *The Communist Manifesto.* Harmondsworth: Penguin, pp. 7–47.

Taylor, S. (1982) *Durkheim and the Study of Suicide.* London and Basingstoke: Macmillan.

Therborn, G. (1976) *Science, Class and Society: On the Formation of Sociology and Historical Materialism.* London: New Left Books.

—— (1996) 'Critical Theory and the Legacy of Twentieth-Century Marxism', in B. Turner (ed.) *The Blackwell Companion to Social Theory.* Oxford: Blackwell, pp. 53–82.

Thompson, K. (1982) *Emile Durkheim.* London: Tavistock.

Tilman, R. (1984) *C. Wright Mills: A Native Radical and His American Intellectual Roots.* University Park: Pennsylvania State University Press.

Touraine, A. (2000) *Can We Live Together? Equality and Difference.* Cambridge: Polity Press.

Treviño, A. (2001) 'Introduction: The Theory and Legacy of Talcott Parsons', in A. Treviño (ed.) *Talcott Parsons Today: His Theory and Legacy in Contemporary Sociology.* Lanham, MD: Rowman and Littlefield, pp. xv–lviii.

—— (2003) 'Introduction: Erving Goffman and the Interaction Order', in A. Treviño (ed.) *Goffman's Legacy.* Lanham, MD: Rowman and Littlefield, pp. 1–49.

Tribe, K. (1988) 'Translator's Introduction', in W. Hennis, *Max Weber: Essays in Reconstruction.* London: Allen and Unwin, pp. 1–17.

Tribe, K. (1989) 'Introduction', in K. Tribe (ed.) *Reading Weber.* London: Routledge, pp. 1–14.

Turner, B. (1974) *Weber and Islam: A Critical Study.* London: Routledge and Kegan Paul.

—— (1981) *For Weber: Essays on the Sociology of Fate.* London: Routledge and Kegan Paul.

—— (1999a) *Classical Sociology.* London: Sage.

—— (1999b) 'Introduction: The Contribution of Talcott Parsons to the Study of Modernity', in B. Turner (ed.) *The Talcott Parsons Reader.* Oxford: Blackwell, pp. 1–20.

—— (2001) 'Social Systems and Complexity Theory', in A. Treviño (ed.) *Talcott Parsons Today: His Theory and Legacy in Contemporary Sociology.* Lanham, MD: Rowman and Littlefield, pp. 85–99.

Underhill, R. (2000) *Khrushchev's Shoe and Other Ways to Captivate Audiences from One to One Thousand.* Cambridge, MA: Perseus.

Urry, J. (2000) *Sociology Beyond Societies: Mobilities for the Twenty-First Century.* London: Routledge.

Wakefield, D. (2000) 'Introduction', in K. Mills with P. Mills (eds) *C. Wright Mills: Letters and Autobiographical Writings.* Berkeley: University of California Press, pp. 1–18.

Wallace, R. and Wolf, A. (1995) *Contemporary Sociological Theory: Continuing the Classical Tradition.* Englewood Cliffs, NJ: Prentice Hall.

Walton, P. and Gamble, A. (1976) *From Alienation to Surplus Value.* London: Sheed and Ward.

Waters, M. (1994) *Modern Sociological Theory.* London: Sage.

Watson, R. (1999) 'Reading Goffman on Interaction', in G. Smith (ed.) *Goffman and Social Organization: Studies in a Sociological Legacy.* London: Routledge, pp. 138–55.

Watts Miller, W. (1996) *Durkheim, Morals and Modernity.* Montreal: McGill-Queen's University Press.

Wearne, B. (1989) *The Theory and Scholarship of Talcott Parsons to 1951: A Critical Commentary.* Cambridge: Cambridge University Press.

Weber, Marianne (1988) *Max Weber: A Biography.* New Brunswick: Transaction Books.

Weber, Max (1949) *The Methodology of the Social Sciences.* New York: Free Press.

—— (1952) *Ancient Judaism.* Glencoe, IL: The Free Press.

—— (1964) *The Theory of Social and Economic Organization.* New York: The Free Press.

—— (1970a) 'Politics as a Vocation', in H. H. Gerth and C. W. Mills (eds) *From Max Weber: Essays in Sociology.* London: Routledge and Kegan Paul, pp. 77–128.

—— (1970b) 'Science as a Vocation', in H. H. Gerth and C. W. Mills (eds) *From Max Weber: Essays in Sociology.* London: Routledge and Kegan Paul, pp. 129–56.

—— (1970c) 'The Protestant Sects and the Spirit of Capitalism', in H. H. Gerth and C. W. Mills (eds) *From Max Weber: Essays in Sociology.* London: Routledge and Kegan Paul, pp. 302–22.

—— (1970d) 'Capitalism and Rural Society in Germany', in H. H. Gerth and C. W. Mills (eds) *From Max Weber: Essays in Sociology.* London: Routledge and Kegan Paul, pp. 363–85.

—— (1971a) 'A Research Strategy for the Study of Occupational Careers and Mobility Patterns', in J. Eldridge (ed.) *Max Weber: The Interpretation of Social Reality.* London: Michael Joseph, pp. 103–55.

—— (1971b) 'Socialism', in J. Eldridge (ed.) *Max Weber: The Interpretation of Social Reality.* London: Michael Joseph, pp. 191–219.

—— (1976a) *The Protestant Ethic and the Spirit of Capitalism.* London: George Allen and Unwin, second edition.

—— (1976b) *The Agrarian Sociology of Ancient Civilizations.* London: New Left Books.

—— (1978a) *Economy and Society: An Outline of Interpretive Sociology.* Berkeley: University of California Press.

—— (1978b) 'Anticritical Last Word on The Spirit of Capitalism', *American Journal of Sociology* 83 (5), pp. 1105–31.

—— (1978c) 'The Prospects for Liberal Democracy in Tsarist Russia', in W. G. Runciman (ed.) *Weber: Selections in Translation.* Cambridge: Cambridge University Press, pp. 269–84.

—— (1981) *General Economic History.* New Brunswick: Transaction Books.

—— (1989) 'Developmental Tendencies in the Situation of East Elbian Rural Labourers', in K. Tribe (ed.) *Reading Weber.* London: Routledge, pp. 158–87.

—— (2001a) 'Weber's First Reply to Rachfahl, 1910', in D. Chalcraft and A. Harrington (eds) *The Protestant Ethic Debate: Max Weber's Replies to his Critics, 1907–1910.* Liverpool: Liverpool University Press, pp. 61–85.

—— (2001b) 'Weber's Second Reply to Rachfahl, 1910', in D. Chalcraft and A. Harrington (eds) *The Protestant Ethic Debate: Max Weber's Replies to his Critics, 1907–1910.* Liverpool: Liverpool University Press, pp. 93–132.

—— (2002) *The Protestant Ethic and the Spirit of Capitalism.* Oxford: Blackwell.

—— (2003) *The History of Commercial Partnerships in the Middle Ages.* Lanham, MD: Rowman and Littlefield.

Weeks, J. (2000) *Making Sexual History.* Cambridge: Polity Press.

Weiss, H. (1973) 'Karl Marx's "Enquête Ouvrière"', in T. Bottomore (ed.) *Karl Marx.* Oxford: Basil Blackwell, pp. 172–84.

Westergaard, J. (1995) *Who Gets What? The Hardening of Class Inequality in the Late Twentieth Century.* Cambridge: Polity Press.

Wheen, F. (2000) *Karl Marx.* London: Fourth Estate.

White, H. (1979) 'Michel Foucault', in J. Sturrock (ed.) *Structuralism and Since: From Lévi-Strauss to Derrida.* Oxford: Oxford University Press, pp. 81–115.

Williams, G. (2001) 'Theorizing Disability', in G. Albrecht, K. Seelman and M. Bury (eds) *Handbook of Disability Studies*. London: Sage, pp. 123–44.

Williams, Raymond. (1977) *Marxism and Literature*. Oxford: Oxford University Press.

Williams, Robin (1988) 'Understanding Goffman's Methods', in P. Drew and A. Wootton (eds) *Erving Goffman: Exploring the Interaction Order*. Cambridge: Polity Press, pp. 64–88.

—— (1998) 'Erving Goffman', in R. Stones (ed.) *Key Sociological Thinkers*. Basingstoke: Macmillan, pp. 151–62.

Winkin, Y. (1999) 'Erving Goffman: What is a Life? The Uneasy Making of an Intellectual Biography', in G. Smith (ed.) *Goffman and Social Organization: Studies in a Sociological Legacy*. London: Routledge, pp. 19–41.

Woodiwiss, A. (2001) *The Visual in Social Theory*. London: Athlone.

Worsley, P. (1982) *Marx and Marxism*. London: Tavistock.

—— (1997) *Knowledges: What Different Peoples Make of the World*. London: Profile.

Wrong, D. (1970) 'Introduction', in D. Wrong (ed.) *Max Weber*. Englewood Cliffs, NJ: Prentice Hall, pp. 1–76.

—— (1995) *The Problem of Order: What Unites and Divides Society*. Cambridge, MA: Harvard University Press.

—— (1999) *The Oversocialized Conception of Man*. New Brunswick: Transaction Books.

Zeitlin, I. (1987) *Ideology and the Development of Sociological Theory*. Englewood Cliffs, NJ: Prentice Hall, third edition.

Zelizer, V. (1994) *Pricing the Priceless Child: The Changing Social Value of Children*. Princeton: Princeton University Press.

Index

Printed and bound by CPI Group (UK) Ltd, Croydon, CR0 4YY